UNDER

THE

COVER

PRINCETON STUDIES IN
CULTURAL SOCIOLOGY

Paul J. DiMaggio, Michèle Lamont,
Robert J. Wuthnow, and Viviana A. Zelizer,
Series Editors

A list of titles in this series appears at the back of the book.

UNDER THE COVER

THE CREATION, PRODUCTION, AND RECEPTION OF A NOVEL

CLAYTON CHILDRESS

PRINCETON UNIVERSITY PRESS
PRINCETON AND OXFORD

Copyright © 2017 by Princeton University Press

Published by Princeton University Press,
41 William Street, Princeton, New Jersey 08540
In the United Kingdom: Princeton University Press,
6 Oxford Street, Woodstock, Oxfordshire OX20 1TR
press.princeton.edu

All Rights Reserved

ISBN 978-0-691-16038-2

Library of Congress Control Number: 2016960240

British Library Cataloging-in-Publication Data is available

This book has been composed in Adobe Text Pro and Gotham

Printed on acid-free paper. ∞

Printed in the United States of America

10 9 8 7 6 5 4 3 2 1

CONTENTS

PART V: THE FIELD OF RECEPTION 183

PART VI: CONNECTING THE CIRCUIT 223

UNDER
THE
COVER

INTRODUCTION

THE ESTRANGEMENT OF CREATION,

PRODUCTION, AND RECEPTION

A NOVEL MUST BE MANY THINGS

Of the thousands of novels that were published in the United States at around the same time, *Jarrettsville* was one of the very few that ended up on the front tables of bookstores around the country, although the novel's publisher, Counterpoint Press, eventually regretted that. Of the thousands of novels released around the same time, *Jarrettsville* was also one of the very few that was reviewed in the *New York Times*, although perhaps Counterpoint eventually regretted that too. Yet *Jarrettsville* sold reasonably well. *Jarrettsville* was, in the words of Counterpoint's CEO Charlie Winton, "a typical publishing story." According to Winton, a typical publishing story ends like this: "Well, that was good, sort of."

For *Jarrettsville*'s author, Cornelia Nixon, the story that would become "good, sort of" to her publisher had first been a family secret. The gist of the once-secret story revealed in Nixon's novel was that following the Civil War, just south of the Mason-Dixon line in Jarrettsville, Maryland, one of Nixon's ancestors, Martha Jane Cairnes, shot and killed her newborn baby's father, Nicholas McComas, in front of about fifty eyewitnesses during a parade celebrating the Confederate surrender. Despite all those witnesses, and even her own admission of guilt, a jury of her peers found Cairnes innocent on the ad hoc grounds of "justifiable homicide." The story had been front-page news in the *New York Times* before it was lost to history.

As a novelist, Cornelia Nixon took this family story and transformed it into a work of historical fiction. Or maybe *Jarrettsville* was better described as a work of popular fiction, or literary fiction, or something in between; while writing the novel Nixon was hoping it might garner a wider audience of readers to match all of her literary awards. Or, perhaps Nixon had transformed her family story into somewhat of a romance novel or, for her publisher, maybe just a bit too much of a romance novel. For Winton, Nixon's novel was reminiscent of *Cold Mountain*, an investment in a second chance at catching lightning in a bottle. For Adam Krefman, *Jarrettsville*'s editor at Counterpoint, the novel was an intimate examination of a one-time second-ary character's failings, his inability to do the right thing, and the mistakes made by young men that young men like Krefman might understand. For Counterpoint's publicity staff, and for the field reps at Counterpoint's dis-tributor, *Jarrettsville* was a work of literary historical fiction. It was "literary" because both Nixon and Counterpoint were "literary," and it was historical fiction not only because the story was historical and a work of fiction, but also because "historical fiction" existed as a market category. Importantly for Counterpoint, *Jarrettsville* was not just historical fiction, but it was *Civil War* historical fiction, a profitable and perhaps even dependable market category. That none of the novel actually took place during the Civil War was treated by all involved as mostly incidental. If "postbellum fiction" had existed as a recognizable market category, perhaps *Jarrettsville* would have been that, but it didn't, so Civil War fiction it became.

For reviewers, *Jarrettsville* was about the inescapability of racism in the United States, or the lingering tensions of the Civil War, or not really either of those things as it was instead a timeless morality tale about the charac-ters. For one reviewer, *Jarrettsville* was an exquisite story about social con-ventions, emotional connections, and the human experience, reminiscent of Tolstoy and worth reading for the impressive quality of the writing alone. For a different reviewer, *Jarrettsville* was a failed effort rife with historical inaccuracies, with writing so bad it was "timeless." For a book group of women in Nashville, Tennessee, *Jarrettsville* was compared to what they jok-ingly referred to as "the sacred text," *Gone with the Wind*. For a book group of men in Massachusetts, the prose was too flowery, but the plot offered an opportunity to discuss if a woman can rape a man. For a group of teachers in Southern California, *Jarrettsville* was an entry point into its readers' own stories about racism in America. For a group of lawyers and their friends in Northern California, it was about whether juries can break from a judge's guidelines in meting out convictions and acquittals. "Is 'justifiable homicide' something that a jury can use? Doesn't that seem crazy?" a poet asked. "It's rare, but juries can do whatever they want," a lawyer replied.

For readers in present-day Jarrettsville, Maryland, the story was about much more than long-dead people from a bygone time. The story was also about them. Over the past hundred thirty years, had Jarrettsville changed, or was it still like *Jarrettsville*? Some things had remained the same. In the new Jarrettsville branch of the Harford County Library, which sits across the street from a rolling field of sunflowers which is both idyllically pastoral and an investment in bird feed as a cash crop, the first question of the morning book club was a difficult one that set the terms of the discussion: were its members, as residents of Jarrettsville and readers of *Jarrettsville*, Northerners or Southerners?

Although *Jarrettsville* would go on to be many different things for different people, for Cornelia Nixon, at first at least, it was just a family story. For a story to become a novel—for it to be written by an author, make it through a literary agency, get into a publishing house and out the other end, be promoted by publicity staff, be hand-sold in bookstores, be evaluated by reviewers and ultimately connected with by readers—it must be multiple. To ultimately be a novel, *Jarrettsville* had to be many things.

Jarrettsville was a personal story, a work of fiction, a work of Civil War historical fiction, a salable commodity, and a chance to reboot a career. At the same time it was an opportunity to reactivate embedded social ties within an industry around a new product, a text that had to be read before a meeting, a leisure activity, and a break from life that was "perfect cross-country flight" length. It was a story that was really about a relationship between a mother and a daughter, and a story that was, according to two women on opposite sides of the country who had never met and who were both ultimately dissuaded from this interpretation, really about the US occupation of Iraq. *Jarrettsville* was also contract work for a moonlighting copy editor, a chance to flex a different muscle for the cover designer of travel books, and the day job of an editor-in-chief. For a novel to be a novel it must pass through the hands of many people who have many different orientations to novels and who occupy different locations and milieus. In order for it to continue passing through those hands and still be meaningful and worthy of passing on, *Jarrettsville* had to change too. This book is a collection of all of the stories of what *Jarrettsville* was, and how it came to be all of those things at once.

This book is also an academic work of sociology, and hopefully one with some of its more inscrutable edges smoothed off. If you are not a sociologist (amateur, budding, or full-blown), the next three sections of this introduction (before the final one) are about those more inscrutable edges. If you just want the story of how a novel was created, produced, and consumed, feel free to skip them. All you need to know is that they describe how sociologists came to an arrangement about how to study things like *Jarrettsville*, and how this book offers a different and more integrative path. If you don't care about that sociological theorizing, this book still has a narrative arc built into it, complete with a clearly defined beginning, middle, and end. For sociologists this three-act structure is a story about three interdependent fields, whereas for non-sociologists it's just a three-act structure, a pretty good way to tell a story.

THE SOCIOLOGICAL STUDY OF THINGS THAT ARE MANY THINGS

Novels travel, through hands and across place and time, and in and out of different fields occupied by people with different orientations, experiences, needs, constraints, expectations, and preferences. Yet in making sense of cultural objects such as *Jarrettsville*, subjects of analysis have been cordoned off into discrete terrains. While some focus on the value of cultural objects, others study their values. While some study the objects themselves, others consciously avoid the object, and instead focus on either the industries from which they emerge or the communities of consumers into which they pass. When studying cultural objects such as novels, equations have been simplified through the construction of disciplinary-dependent binaries: when talking novels, are we talking about art or commerce, production or reception, creativity or constraint, the making of meaning or the extraction of value?

Because different elements of cultural objects have been split apart across disciplines and subfields, it is not just harder to make sense of their multiplicity, but it is also harder to make sense of them as wholes. Once you have entirely bracketed out the twists and turns of a novel's creation, it's hard, if not impossible, to fully understand what an editor or marketing rep are doing as they balance the text they're working on with the context they're working under. For cultural reception, a novel can be treated as being of infinitely variable meanings only if all the years of work by an author and publisher to make it meaningful at all have also been bracketed out as an "unobservable" prehistory to reader engagement. If creation, production, and reception all matter, what is lost by independently studying these processes and the transitions between them is actually *most* things.

As a result of this arrangement, to make sense of a novel by describing only its authoring can be like trying to describe an elephant by describing only its ear. So too can describing a novel by describing only its production be like describing an elephant by describing only its trunk. Maybe the reception of a novel in the metaphor is an elephant's legs: another important component in the description of an elephant, but still not the elephant.[1] There are no shortages of things to learn and know when specializing in ears, trunks, or legs—and thankfully for us, there are cardiologists, neurologists, and oncologists who specialize in this way—but if the goal is to *really* understand an elephant, descriptions of its individual body parts must be brought back together in order to describe the whole. Following the creation, production, and reception of a novel from start to finish is how this book goes about doing that.

THE ESTRANGEMENT OF PRODUCTION
FROM RECEPTION IN SOCIOLOGY

From the early twentieth century through the beginning of the 1970s, the sociological analysis of cultural objects took one of two competing paths, which interestingly shared a core assumption. The products of mediated culture, whether books, songs, or fashion, were thought to be expressive symbols that changed in lockstep with evolutions in society. For example, in 1919 the anthropologist Alfred Kroeber argued that the hemlines of women's dresses were prescribed through "civilizational determinism"; they were a window into macro-level cultural values and belief systems.[2] In turn, by the mid-1920s the economist George Taylor argued that instead the hemlines of dresses go up with rises and go down with declines in the stock market.[3] For Taylor, hemlines were determined by macro-level economic, not cultural, shifts. While these "nothing-but" arguments quibbled on the direction of the association between culture and the economy, they both assumed that hemline lengths in women's fashion were reflections of outsized societal forces.[4] Such was also the case with the sociological understanding of cultural objects as reflective of either a more abstract Parsonian values system, or a less abstract capitalist system within a Marxist framework.[5] In both accounts, the production and reception of culture were conjoined and determined by outside forces.[6]

In reaction to both of these macro-level functionalist theories of culture, starting in the 1970s, the sociological study of production and reception split. Scholars of production, like scholars of reception, scaled down from grand narratives into thinking of culture and structure as "elements in an ever changing patchwork."[7] Like all patchworks, the details of one piece may tell you very little about the details of another. Such was also the case with production and reception, it seemed. Production-oriented scholars noted that changes in popular culture are generally asynchronous with bigger transformations in society; hemlines change because of what's happening in the fashion industry, not because of the stock market or broader shifts in values.[8] For reception-oriented scholars, how people actually made sense of things like hemlines and what they did with them proved to be much more interesting than the theories we had saddled onto them. For both production and

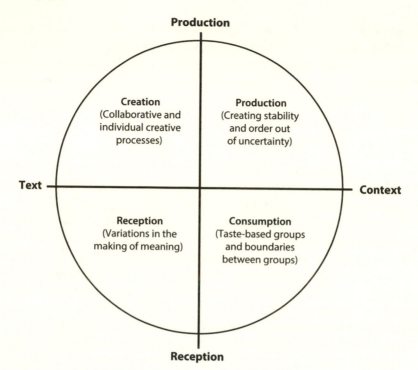

FIGURE 1.1: The Friendly Divvying Up of Material Culture.

reception scholars, once they pried open the black box of assumed values or ideological intentions, it turned out there were real people inside, working within systems of conventions and constraints in the case of production, or to foster identities and senses of meaning in the case of reception.[9] Yet over time, as this split between the studies of production and reception widened, rather than having grouped into competing teams, scholars of each area had basically resigned themselves to playing entirely different sports (see Figure 1.1).[10]

Production-oriented scholars focused on the specific *contexts* of production, investigating how order and stability were created in the construction of one-off cultural goods for which audience demand was unpredictable.[11] The culture that was produced was, in effect, conditioned on the circumstances in the industries in which it was created.[12] As cultural objects were the "outcomes" of industry conditions, their meanings became dependent variables, which was part of a self-conscious research position to move away from prior models. As Richard Peterson argued, "If production studies run the risk of eliminating 'culture' from the sociology of culture, researchers who focus on the content of cultural products run the risk of . . . taking the 'sociology' out."[13] As such, as noted by Wendy Griswold, for production scholars meaning was thrown "overboard in some sort of disciplinary triage."[14]

Not so, however, for scholars of reception, who empirically doubled-down on the study of cultural objects and their meanings by focusing on an underlying instability of meaning as based on who was doing the reception, and what they were doing with that reception.[15] While the focus remained on texts, here too cultural objects became the dependent variable in a quite different, if ultimately somewhat similar, denuding of objects' possible ability to do things.[16] Most importantly for both parties, however, was that if the contents of texts were wholly based on the conditions of their production and the meanings of that content were wholly based on the specifics of their reception, very little was to be lost by studying these processes independently from one another.

With the split of production and reception, from one path two diverged, and at least in the core of mainstream sociology, the path to reception was the road less traveled. As Paul DiMaggio had noted by 1987: "The divorce of consumption and production studies has led to an estrangement . . . and a marginalization of the former, that a more integrative position can help bridge."[17] In 1993, Wendy Griswold echoed DiMaggio's call for integration in an *Annual Review* piece, and with little changed by 2000, Richard Peterson took his turn, suggesting to production perspective adherents that "it may prove useful to focus on . . . a reception process in which people actively select and reinterpret symbols to produce a culture for themselves."[18] By 2015, almost three decades after DiMaggio's call to action, in yet another *Annual Review* piece the consumption scholar Alan Warde again noted the problem, writing that "to separate out consumption [from production] for specialized attention was very valuable . . . but other ways to reconnect with production . . . are needed."[19]

Somehow also lost in this split was "that forgotten soul, the author," who for both production- and reception-focused scholars seemed to mostly provide the raw materials so that the "real" work could be done.[20] As a result, what could be gained by moving "upstream" from production and reception and into "the mental and material workshop of the creative artist" has also been a question that has mostly gone unanswered in this arrangement.[21] Although for nearly forty years both production- and reception-oriented scholars have repeatedly and consistently noted problems with these estrangements, over time reconnection has become harder rather than easier, as production and reception have become increasingly dissimilar research programs, with their own ritualistic citations, underlying assumptions, and research traditions.

In the story of this divorce, as it was for the increasing invisibility of cultural creators, there was, however, a notable exception. While scholars such as Pierre Bourdieu took up topics of production and consumption in separate studies, Griswold integrated empirical research across creation, production, and reception.[22] First in a study of the revivals of revenge tragedies and city comedies in London and then later in a study of the Nigerian "fiction complex," rather than specializing in the ears, trunks, or legs of elephants, Griswold empirically investigated them as wholes.[23] Her notion of a "complex" of creation, production, and reception serves as an important intervention in the split of production from reception, as the goal of the "complex" is to treat these things not as an overly integrated "system" (as was the case for the pre-1970s dominant frameworks) nor as separate "worlds" divorced from each other (as is the case, in consequence if not design, for the post-1970s dominant frameworks). For Griswold, and in this book, the relationships between creation, production, and reception fall somewhere in between.

Yet this book both builds off of and differs from Griswold's work in three important ways. First, rather than taking a bird's-eye view on the relationship between creation, production, and reception of a nation's literature, the empirical work of this book is anchored down in the dirt; it builds its arguments up from a worm's-eye view of the creation, production, and reception of a single novel. Second, while Griswold's goal is to clarify that creation, production, and reception are neither worlds apart nor a single integrated system, this book delves into the nuts and bolts of both *how* they are linked and the *ways through which* cultural objects are pitched and translated across them. Last, although it is the perspective here that creation, production, and reception are in fact a "complex" made up of three adjoining subsystems, what are those subsystems, and how are they similar or different from one another? What happens when you have three interdependent fields that each contain their own novel cultures?

THREE INTERDEPENDENT FIELDS

Field theory is a tree from which several limbs have sprouted.[24] Fields, regardless of which variation in sociology one is using, are social arenas of focused attention and habituated action.[25] Put most simply, fields are made up of people who orient their attention toward each other, and toward similar stakes and issues that are specific to the field they are in. Until quite recently, field theory has almost exclusively been concerned with the relationships *within* fields. This has begun to change with a recent interest in the relationship *between* fields, as well as how inter-field relations affect intra-field activities and practices.[26] This book empirically addresses these recent theoretical advancements and the questions they engender head-on. It also takes up two more recent developments in field theory. First, until quite recently the underlying premise of field theory has presupposed that actors within fields are mostly operating on autopilot; preprogrammed through their positions and habitus, they follow their scripts.[27] Yet, as this book shows, down in the dirt, rather than action in any given situation always being automatic, to participate in a field regularly requires deliberation: people have to figure out if the rules apply to a situation, and if they do, *which* of the rules are the ones that apply, and *how* they do apply or not.[28] Second, the structural relations of field theory have at times been pitted against the interpersonal relations of different approaches.[29] As a result, field theory can sometimes present as a deeply relational world that seems unencumbered by interpersonal relationships. As this book shows, while structural relations surely matter, so do relationships, as meanings are made in substantive interactions, and it is through the circuits of those interactions that novels are pitched across fields. As a practical matter, writers, publishers, and readers aren't living in different worlds, but they are certainly spending the vast majority of their time in different fields. How cultural objects like novels actually get from there to here requires a different conceptualization of the relationships within fields, and between fields (see Figure 1.2).

With each field come different orientations, issues at stake, hierarchies of values, and returns on symbolic investments that don't apply or even make sense in companion fields. Put another way, most authors in the field of creation no more understand the "rules of the game" in the field of production than do readers in the field of reception, just as a publisher does not know, or need to know, the "rules of the game" as authors and readers write or read together.[30] While a lover of novels may be able to draw out her mental map of the field of reception—what are "good" and "bad" novels, which people consume which type and where they are positioned—the processes and social arrangements between authors (in the field of creation) or publishers (in the field of production) resulting in her most and least favorite novels appear as far-off mountains, visible, but with details obscured by distance and haze. An avid reader surely knows that the fields of creation and production exist, but even she would have considerable trouble creating mental maps of them, if she ever considered doing so in the first place.

A field in focus surrounded by blurry fields is also experienced by a publishing professional who can elaborately map out subtle distinctions and

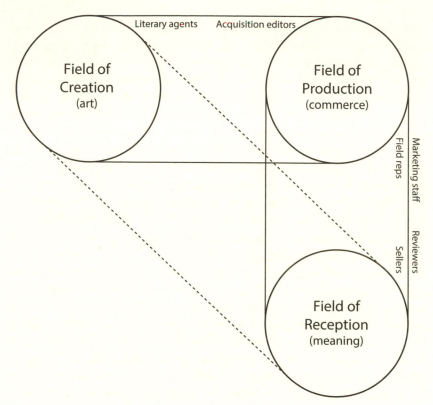

FIGURE 1.2: Three Interdependent Fields of Creation, Production, and Reception.

hierarchies between different presses, wax poetic about the multifaceted dangers of Amazon to some categories of books and not others, and passingly discuss the different field-configuring effects of BookExpo America and the Frankfurt Book Fair. But this publishing professional may actually know very little about the creative processes of authors, or the meanings made of their books by readers, beyond sales figures. By way of example of the different issues at stake across the fields of creation, production, and reception, describing a book as "similar to *Harry Potter*" in the field of reception is an entirely different statement from describing a book as "similar to *Harry Potter*" in the other two. Whereas in the field of reception by this statement a reader would likely mean in plot or style (e.g., "if you like Harry Potter, you'll like this too"), in the field of production nobody would ever compare a book to *Harry Potter* unless they meant sales, and in the field of creation the statement could mean any number of things: a decently written book with inconceivable levels of success, or just another author writing schlock to try to ride the wave of *Harry Potter*.

While the creation, production, and reception of novels mostly happen in three different fields, novels travel across them, which makes them interdependent. The field of production cannot exist without those in the field of creation generating the objects that they'll go on to produce and distribute, or without readers in the field of reception who will vote for their offerings with their eyes, mouths, and wallets. It is a similar story for the field of reception, which to meaningfully exist requires cultural creation and production; where the things came from and how they got there—the "real" stories to those who made and produced them—might not be interesting or observable to most readers, but they had to happen for people to have reading experiences at all.

If creation, production, and reception exist in three distinct yet interdependent fields, we would expect different values and issues to be at stake in each of them.[31] These values are most typically expressed through the language of art in the field of creation, the language of commerce in the field of production, and the language of meaning in the field of reception. While all three languages can be deployed across all three fields, each has its own home turf in which it is the dominant language through which talk of novels is expressed. In the transition across fields, as objects are "pitched" from one field into another, their values must be translated so that they can make sense in ways that are familiar rather than foreign to their new hosts. These translations can result in the blending of languages and values by those who keep each foot planted in a different field, as they are tasked with shepherding objects across them. Literary agents and acquisition editors blend language from the fields of creation and production as they shepherd texts across them, just as field reps, bookstore buyers, and reviewers blend language from the fields of production and reception as they shepherd texts across that divide. Likewise, as the three fields operate both independently and interdependently, changes in one field can necessitate changes in others—or not, depending on how or if those changes affect "business as usual" in their companion fields.

This book makes the case for reconnecting creation, production, and reception as a dynamic and interlocking system by focusing both on the *internal* order of each field, and on what happens at boundary-spanning points of overlap as cultural objects pass *between* fields. It goes under the cover of a book, and under the covers of fields, to tell the full story of a novel named *Jarrettsville*.

HOW TO TELL A TYPICAL PUBLISHING STORY

To tell a "typical publishing story," as Counterpoint's CEO Charlie Winton described *Jarrettsville*, requires finding an author who is willing to let an outsider into her creative process. It means interviewing her many times over, and poring over the notes, drafts, emails, and communications she generated while writing. It means sitting side by side with her for enough time to apprehend her aspirations and her fears, her decisions and why she made them, what she has been proud of, and what she regrets. It also means tracing out to the silent partners in her creative process: the novelists, friends, and allies who sent her novel into directions she could not have arrived to on her own. To tell a typical publishing story also means to know why publishers that rejected the novel did reject it, and why the publisher that published it did so too.

To know this means that the next step is to then embed oneself inside the publishing house that published the book, to work and watch, and then ask questions, as a whole new set of people collaborate to make culture. It means getting to know the editor: what attracted him to the story, and what about it concerned him? What were his solutions to alleviate these concerns, and why were they solutions? To tell a typical publishing story also means to learn why the publisher made its decisions: why one cover was selected from five options, or why discussion over how to describe the novel on its back cover became contentious. To tell a publishing story means getting inside these processes.[32] Yet like the novel itself, the study of the novel again has to travel, over to its marketing and distribution, and into why it can be a mistake to talk about the plot of a novel "too much" when pitching it to a review outlet, and why it's important for publishers to possess good reputations despite the fact that their names usually signal very little to readers.

To have done this is to watch a book being *born*, without yet knowing how, where, or even if it will *live*.[33] To follow a book into its life means to then follow it over into the field of reception. It means asking questions of readers of the novel across the country, and sitting and listening in order to make sense of how *they* make sense of the novel. Did they like it? What for them was it about? What, if anything, did it mean to them? And again, after the book has long since been released, what, in retrospect, does it then mean to its author, her agent, or its publisher?

To get to this point is to tell a full publishing story: it is to follow a novel all the way from start to finish.[34] But even after this has been done, what makes the publishing story a *typical* publishing story? Was the publishing story typical throughout the process, just sometimes typical, or really not typical at all? To answer this question means retracing your steps back to the beginning of the circuit in order to find out from *other* authors who write different novels what for them is a typical authoring story. In turn, how do agents or editors make decisions for books that *aren't Jarrettsville*, and so on, for everyone else whose hands touch novels? To tell a typical publishing story one has to know what is typical and what isn't, so in addition to following *Jarrettsville* from its creation through its reception, that is what I did. As a result, while in some ways this is a book about the creation, production, and reception of a novel, in other ways, it's a book that uses that novel as a keyhole to peer into the relations within and between the fields through which it passed. From both of these perspectives, to fully understand how Cornelia Nixon's family story became a book called *Jarrettsville* requires many more stories, told in an entirely separate book—this one.

PART I

THE FIELD OF CREATION

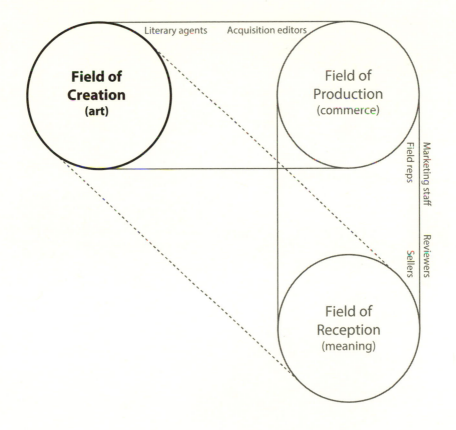

Literary agents   Acquisition editors

Field of Creation
(art)

Field of Production
(commerce)

Field of Reception
(meaning)

Marketing staff

Field reps

Reviewers

Sellers

THE STRUCTURE OF CREATIVITY

OR, WHY *JARRETTSVILLE* ALMOST WASN'T

CALLED *JARRETTSVILLE*

ON LONELINESS

Were you to come across Cornelia Nixon at the Starbucks on the corner of Oxford and Center streets in Berkeley, California, she would be writing on her laptop with her headphones on. Sitting upstairs and looking out at the UC Berkeley campus where she had written a dissertation on D. H. Lawrence and earned her PhD in English literature two decades earlier, between 1998 and 2004 Nixon was working on a novel titled *Martha's Version*. The title was a literal one; *Martha's Version* was the story of *Jarrettsville* told entirely from Martha's first-person perspective.

At first blush, Nixon's life as a novelist seems like a lonely one. If her first three novels are any indication, it takes about a decade for her to write a novel; a decade of sitting alone in Starbucks with her headphones on. Yet Nixon didn't use her headphones to block out the world around her so that she could write, as instead her headphones, and the music she played through them, were a tool to bring the world into her writing process: music was for Nixon a way to inspire and capture feelings. Even with music, however, the act of writing is lonely, or can feel lonely, depending on the writer. As Ernest Hemingway remarked in favor of loneliness in his acceptance speech for the Nobel Prize in literature in 1954, "Writing, at its best, is a lonely life . . . for [an author] does his work alone, and if he is a good enough writer he must face eternity, or the lack of it, each day."[1] For many authors, loneliness, or at least recounting stories of loneliness, is as much about their *identities* as novelists as it is about the creative acts of writing novels. How do we make sense of novelists' loneliness when for many writers, such as Hemingway, the "lonely life" of the novelist is also a romantic ideal of what it means to be a writer?

That novelists may have a possessive investment in the narration of their loneliness can cause problems in the study of their creative processes. Some novelists, when you ask them about the social processes of their literary creations, can become reluctant respondents who don't quite want to answer the questions you're asking.[2] They can bristle at these lines of questions, as through the lens of the field of creation they can seem to suggest that a novelist is more of a reporter than an artist. As Hannah, a writer of several well-received works of literary fiction, described her frustration with this line of questioning during book tours: "The book tour . . . [is] the same questions over, and over again, 'He felt so real, he must be a real person in your life, right? What does he think about the book?' or 'Tell me about your time in New Hampshire, your description of the scenery was beautiful.' I mean, just let it be what it is!"

Other novelists, like Cornelia Nixon, simply struggle in answering these types of questions because they require a new way of thinking. On a sunny Wednesday afternoon, while sitting with Nixon upstairs at Starbucks and after asking a series of questions about loneliness and the social underpinnings of her writing, I apologized for having taken up so much of her time. "Oh, no," she responded, "you know, oddly enough, this is really interesting for me. It's got me thinking about the book in a way I never think about it." For many novelists, as for Hannah Thompson and Cornelia Nixon, writing alone is not just something that they *do*, but is instead part of who they *are*. While crafting stories most novelists are poorly paid or not paid at all, but they are still writers. As income from writing is unpredictable and irregular, the romantic image of toiling away and facing eternity or the lack of it each day is not an insignificant part of a novelist's social status among other novelists and some readers.

The loneliness of writing when things aren't working is a topic that is frequently discussed between authors. In the social assemblages of the field of creation—in writing groups, in MFA programs, or in pairs over cups of coffee—a novelist cannot always appear to write easily, lest her artistry be viewed with suspicion by other novelists. Instead, the glorious moments of being struck by the muse and writing at a torrid pace must be contrasted with stories of agony and struggle. In this way, writers block, feeling despondent, and forcing oneself to sit down and write each day are not signs of one's failure as a novelist, but, between novelists, are instead ways to brag about sacrifices made for one's art. To be a novelist one must work, and work cannot be easy, lest a novelist not have labored for her genius. While those in the fields of production and reception don't much think or care about if a novelist found her work on any particular novel to be easy or hard, in the field of creation effort is itself an important and meaning-laden signal of group membership, worth, and expertise. Through this logic, for outsiders to ask about the insertion of real people or experiences into one's fiction is to unintentionally imply that the writing was "easy," whereas creation from whole cloth would be "hard." Some novelists don't like the question because as artists they are *supposed* to write from their own experiences, just as their works are *supposed* to be representations of themselves.[3] To be "lonely" then, even when fictionalizing one's understandings of the world, is to embody what is "hard" about writing.

In reality, how alone are authors when writing alone, and more pointedly, what else do they talk about when they congregate to discuss their loneliness? In fact, if Cornelia Nixon had really been all alone when writing, *Martha's Version* would never have existed, nor would it have ever become *Jarrettsville*. To understand how *Jarrettsville* came to be, and how even its name was eventually derived, requires getting under the cover of the field of creation to trace the social life of artistic creation within it.

THE TIP OF THE ICEBERG

How collaborative are creative endeavors? For most media it is not hard to visualize the collective work that goes into their production.[4] Despite the quality of films being attributed to their directors, they are easily recognized as collaborative creations: writers, actors, producers, editors, and many others contribute their voices and artistic visions to a film.[5] This is also the case for music, for which one person (or a team of people) may compose the lyrics while a different person (or team of people) composes the melody and a wholly different person (or team of people) sings and performs.[6] Yet when thinking about writing, the image of a lonely author remains common; when we visualize a novelist we see a "writer who writes alone."[7]

Part of the perceived loneliness of authoring is due to the physical separation between the fields of creation and production for writing. For movies these fields meet in the same physical space: on set are the actors, the makeup artists, the money people, and the script supervisors. For novelists, however, collaborative creation is less easily observable, as rather than being done on sound stages or in public performances (as is the case for stage plays, concerts, and dance), it's done behind the closed doors of homes or over personal calls and emails. Novelists, perhaps because they create in less easily observable places, are thought of as isolated and lonely geniuses; they're like inventors tinkering away in their garages, struggling to interact with the outside world about their ideas, which are too deeply embedded inside their heads to make much sense until they are completed.[8] For novelists, like inventors, however, this characterization mistakes the unobservability of what is happening behind closed doors for a lack of collaboration behind those doors. As one of Thomas Edison's assistants once observed, "[Thomas] Edison is in reality a collective noun and means the work of many [people]."[9] Such is also true for writers. Like Edison's assistant, an editor described what happens behind closed doors in the creative process for Donald, a famous and celebrated poet: "Sometimes Donald doesn't write 'Donald' lines, so Cherri [his spouse], or Cynthia [his typist] or myself rewrite things to make them more 'Donald'-like or truer to 'his' voice."

When investigating the loneliness of the writer who writes alone, we must also differentiate between the physical *act* of writing creatively, and the more general *practice* of writing creatively. The act of writing creatively, that is, typing or writing words onto a page, may very well be done alone, and often is. Yet at the same time the practice of writing creatively—conceiving ideas or solutions to problems, planning for and reflecting on acts of writing, searching for inspirations, receiving the social support required for writing "in isolation"—is almost always deeply social. With regard to the *practice* of writing, there is an abundance of good archaeological evidence to this effect that goes regularly unacknowledged in the story of the writer who writes alone. A personal record keeping of the collaborative foundations on which creative writing is based can be found in the oft-skipped text that precedes or closes almost all book-length works: the acknowledgments page, which documents the social practice of authoring. In the acknowledgments for *Jarrettsville*, Cornelia Nixon thanks thirty-four individuals and four institutions, an acknowledgment for about every eight or nine pages of text. Yet Nixon believes that an acknowledgments page "will always be inadequate"; flipping through that of *Jarrettsville*, she remarked, "Gosh, so many names that should have been in here. It's really just the tip of the iceberg."

Rather than, as Neil Gross writes, "downplay[ing] the mundane social processes involved in knowledge making in favor of discourse of creative genius," the everyday lives of novelists must be focused on.[10] For *Jarrettsville*, the social underpinnings of Nixon's creative writing occurred in three ways, organized here from the least to the most overtly social. From Nixon's family and personal life, she imported the raw materials for *Jarrettsville*. From her educational experiences she developed a sense of style, prose, and command of the research process that turned *Jarrettsville* from a collection of raw materials into the novel that it became. Last, through the face-to-face creative exchange of assembled novelists creating together, what for Nixon was the ultimate meaning of *Jarrettsville* was collaboratively defined and then refined.

CREATIVITY AS SOCIAL COLLAGE

FROM FAMILY AND PERSONAL LIFE: THE RAW MATERIALS

Cornelia Nixon was sixteen years old on a cross-country flight when her mother first shared with her the family story that would become *Jarretts-ville*. Yet Nixon waited almost twenty years into her career as a published novelist to tell the story. She did not wait because she thought it inferior to other stories she wanted to tell. Instead the opposite was true: ever since her mother shared the story with her, Nixon knew that she would write it, and throughout her career thought of the story as her "ace in the hole." She had waited to tell it for personal reasons. From a career perspective, it may have been a mistake for Nixon to wait so long to tell the story of *Jarretts-ville*—it was a good one—but from a relational perspective, waiting to tell the story, which embarrassed her mother, was her only choice.

There was a chance that Nixon would have never heard the family story, as it had for at least two generations been a family secret. The story was front-page news in the *New York Times* in 1869, but had been suppressed within the family until Nixon's uncle George rediscovered it during World War II in an American history book while stationed in Denver with the Air Force. Having grown up in Jarrettsville, Maryland, George knew the story had to be about his family, and he later came across it again in a *Ripley's Be-lieve It or Not* and shared it with his sister, Nixon's mother. She, in turn, told her teenaged daughter, explaining that her reason for doing so was because Nixon wanted to be a writer. If Nixon's mother hadn't known of and supported her early aspirations, *Jarrettsville* may not have ever been written.

The true events that were fictionalized in *Jarrettsville* are as follows. Nixon's direct ancestors, the Cairneses, lived in Jarrettsville, Maryland. After the Civil War, Martha Jane Cairnes became romantically involved with a slightly older former Union militiaman, Nicholas McComas, also from the area. Martha Cairnes's brother was a member of one of two Southern militias in the county, the Rifles and the Dragoons; John Wilkes Booth was a member of the Rifles. Cairnes became pregnant, and McComas left Jarrettsville, for reasons that are historically unknown. McComas returned to march in a parade celebrating the fourth anniversary of the Confederate surrender at Appomattox. At the parade, Cairnes, four months after giving birth, shot him four times at close range, twice while he was standing and twice after he had fallen, saying, according to the *New York Times*, "Gentleman, you all know what it's done for." Cairnes was charged with murder, and at her trial it was suggested that she might have been carrying a child conceived not with McComas but with a married man, or even more scandalously then, a freedman. Despite the presence of around fifty eyewitnesses to Cairnes's murder of McComas, the jury, stacked with Southern sympathizers, found Cairnes innocent on the ad hoc grounds of "justifiable homicide." All of this was a source of shame for the Cairneses, who were the descendants of what had been a landed and important family in the small town of Jarrettsville.

Just as Nixon's mother had gifted her the story because she knew Nixon wanted to be a novelist, Nixon gifted her mother the reprieve from authoring it until she had passed away. Even after her mother's passing, while writing *Jarrettsville* Nixon agonized over her portrayal of Richard Cairnes, Martha Jane Cairnes's brother, who was a clear antagonist, if not an outright villain in the story. In Nixon's fictionalization, the Cairneses own three slaves: Creolia and her two children, Tim and Sophie. In *Jarrettsville*, when Martha opines that the climate in Maryland has caused each generation of Creolia's family to have lighter skin (a theory at the time), Nixon indirectly suggests that Creolia and her children are the products of rape at the hands of generations of Cairnes family patriarchs.

To explain the true event of McComas leaving Jarrettsville after conceiving a child with Cairnes, Nixon conceived a new story: Richard has raped and impregnated Sophie, and Tim has been beaten. McComas, as a result of these events and as the son of a minister involved in the abolition movement, helps the freed Tim and Sophie escape Richard and offers them shelter on his land. Richard, in retribution, publicly accuses Nick of raping and impregnating Sophie and thereby defiling his "property." Under a loose interpretation of the Black Codes in Maryland, Richard then publicly bullwhips McComas to near death, at which point McComas retreats to the safer expanse of Amish country in southern Pennsylvania. All told, the major Cairnes characters do not come off as sympathetic in *Jarrettsville*, and the most sympathetic of the bunch, Martha, is still a murderer. Richard is, nonetheless, the worst of the Cairneses. According to both historical record and family lore Richard Cairnes was not someone most would recall fondly. But as a family member holding a long-kept family secret, Nixon very often worried about portraying him unfairly.

Her family's influence on *Jarrettsville* did not, however, simply constrain Nixon's storytelling. Instead, fingerprints of her family and their experiences are scattered throughout the text. In the story of *Jarrettsville* Martha Jane Cairnes is a liberated woman in an unliberated place and time, and Martha's mother Mary is a traditionalist who bristles at Martha's boundary pushing. According to Nixon, at some points throughout the story Martha and her relationship with her mother Mary is based on Nixon's own relationship with her mother, and at other points Martha is Nixon's mother and Martha's mother is Nixon's grandmother. For instance, in one scene in *Jarrettsville* Martha is on the family farm wearing a dress and outshooting her brothers in target practice. It's a familiar image to those close to Nixon, as it is a written reproduction of a real photograph of her own mother as a young woman on the family farm in Jarrettsville that Nixon keeps on her mantel.

The Nicholas McComas of *Jarrettsville* also came from Nixon's life. The furtive letters written between Martha and Nick were inspired by emails Nixon had sent back and forth with a romantic partner: "Nick's looks, and how he acts, and how he corresponds with her is based on someone. But he also just became somebody else, too. He's a much nicer and deeper person than the guy that I based him on. I guess because he's partly me, you know? All of them are partly me." Nick, who would eventually become one of Nixon's favorite characters, was more than a simple reproduction of Nixon blended with a man she once knew. Instead, the people and experiences in Nixon's life were the raw materials from which she whittled and created something new. Nixon's love for the character of Nick was retrospective, and came about through her own reflection on the difficulty she had with capturing who he was. Back when *Jarrettsville* had been *Martha's Version*, Nicholas McComas was a cipher, and his decisions were never explained because they were not known from Martha's perspective. Nixon recalled sidestepping McComas's motivations in *Martha's Version* due to her own experiential limitations: "Sometimes men do things. I don't know why. I didn't explain why Nick up and left because Martha didn't know why, and I don't really know why men do some of the things they do." Put another way, Nixon did not feel she had the raw materials from which to construct a first-person narrative of McComas's motivations, so she stuck with the things she did know, and those she could successfully breathe life into, such as Martha's inner thoughts and the story's geographic landscape.

Unlike the black box that was initially McComas's thoughts and motivations, the topography of Harford County was familiar to Nixon. The sense of place in *Jarrettsville* comes from Nixon's childhood summers spent on the large Cairnes family farm in Jarrettsville, Maryland. In capturing the details of the locale, Nixon remarked, "The landscape and the ground and the dirt and the cows, you know, they're all part of me." With a sense for the setting, Nixon was able to blend the people and places. This was especially true for the interactions Nixon wrote between Martha and her friend Tim, the freedman and suspected father of Martha's child. In one scene Martha and Tim climb adjoining trees and speak to one another across their branches, a scene plucked from Nixon's own life.

The descriptions of the "craggy and mountainous Pennsylvania hills" into which Nicholas McComas retreated after being beaten by Richard Cairnes came from a quarter century of holiday visits to that region with her ex-husband, the poet Dean Young. His family lived in Lancaster County, and the geography, the people, and even an old parlor saloon on the outskirts of Lancaster were folded into *Jarrettsville* to better describe what Nick was doing and where he was after he had left. There is no historical record of where exactly McComas went when he left Jarrettsville, but the nearby Pennsylvania hills were plausible—a place he reasonably could have gone and experienced peace—and just as importantly for Nixon, they were known to her. While she couldn't initially get into Nick's head, she at least could write from experience about where he might be. Yet raw materials like these, while necessary, are not the only tools required in creating a novel. In addition to knowing and living, Nixon also had to have learned the *art*, or perhaps better the *conventions*, of novel writing, and the skills required to successfully enact those conventions. For this she had a formal and informal education.

FROM EDUCATION: STYLE, PROSE, AND THE RESEARCH PROCESS

Like Nixon's familial relationships and experiences, her education and literary influences cannot be divorced from the text that *Jarrettsville* became. While Nixon knew from childhood that she wanted to be a writer, she credits a middle school teacher, Mr. Schwartz, with providing her first nonfamilial encouragement. Nixon remembers feeling "small and ugly" at the time, and it was Schwartz who gave her confidence about her ability as a writer. Nixon remembers Schwartz telling her, " 'You must go to college, you have to start reading more books, just forget about all the dances and boys and stuff like that,' he said, 'you have talent and I want you to do this.' "

In high school Nixon discovered Albert Camus, around whom her writing life orbited for a while. With some embarrassment she remembers being a teenager and writing poems to Camus in French to express her admiration. Camus's influence on *Jarrettsville*, and all of Nixon's fiction, is inescapable for her: "Once you've taken something on that way, it becomes part of your way of thinking." From Camus she had taken on that life, as it is written in a novel, "is not sweet and nice and automatically meaningful; it's uncomfortable." From Camus, like Hemingway, she learned to write with "a clear realistic vision. . . . I want my senses to be euphonious but not overtly so. I distrust a writer whose senses sound like the organist playing in the background. They're trying to hype the emotion with the senses. I don't go there."

For her undergraduate degree Nixon decided to attend UC Irvine because at the time it was the only University of California campus that had a creative writing emphasis within its English major. While there, the Blake and Yeats scholar Hazard Adams became her mentor, and she began experimenting with imitating nineteenth-century English Romantic prose stylists. She found this easier having grown up with the Bible and in the Presbyterian church:

> You get this kind of rhyme scheme in your head from singing the Presbyterian hymnal. It's very easy for me to reproduce that in my own prose if I'm allowing myself. If I'm writing a story that it wouldn't be appropriate for I have to really watch out for it. Because I'll come up— the word I decide I want to end a sentence with will just turn out to be a perfect rhyme with a word about eight syllables before—or eight words before. And that's partly from reading the Bible, but it came from writing for Hazard Adams. . . . [I had to] shed those expectations.

Nixon would later take a graduate course at UC Berkeley with Ralph Rader, who taught her the narrative structure of a novel, and made her think differently about creative writing. Through Rader, unlike the Romantic poets, Nixon "realized I shouldn't be worried about expressing my puny self, I should be worried about the reader's brain and what the reader is going to get out of this." Perhaps her biggest influence, however, was still another Romantic writer, D. H. Lawrence. As Nixon recalls her first exposure to Lawrence, "He was writing about sex and emotion in ways that nobody else had. He was open about it. And it was incredible." Yet as a PhD student in English at Berkeley, Nixon turned away from Lawrence, due to, as she argued in her first and only book of literary criticism, the antifeminist strains in his work.

Despite this intellectual turn away from Lawrence, Nixon still felt his influence on her own creative writing. In the first draft of *Jarrettsville* (i.e., *Martha's Version*), D. H. Lawrence "was right there. He was all over me." Part of Lawrence's impact was reflected in Nixon's decision to write *Martha's Version* in a nineteenth-century Romanticist style to match the time period of the story. This decision could lead modern readers to interpret her work as florid and overly emotional either because they did not appreciate or recognize the antiquated writing style as an artistic choice. Would readers view it as a virtuoso performance of matching style to setting or as a failed and anachronistic pastiche of the Romanticist tradition? Or maybe they would read right past the intent and conclude that Nixon was not a good writer according to modern sensibilities. In revision, due to these concerns, Nixon decided to eliminate these stylistic elements and to, as she phrased it, "keep D. H. Lawrence out of there most of the time."

Yet Nixon did decide to "leave Lawrence a scene," Martha and Nick's last sexual encounter, instigated by Martha in a sleigh and ostensibly when their child was conceived. Figuring that Lawrence had "gotten there [i.e., to the scene] first," she wrote the scene in his style and echoed a sentence from *Women in Love*. According to Nixon, "that was definitely Lawrence. I felt him crowding in and taking over the writing." Although Nixon had done this as an embedded dedication and authorial Easter egg for others in the field of creation, as discussed in chapter 9, leaving this scene to Lawrence would have major consequences for *Jarrettsville* as it transitioned from the field of production into the field of reception. For the most part, however, while writing the story Nixon was fighting with her background as a Lawrence scholar. She tried keeping him at bay, and when she noticed his authorial voice crowding in, to his influence she would metaphorically shout out, "Wait, wait, give me my hand back!"

Nixon was happier to intermingle other literary influences from her training with her own storytelling. *Romeo and Juliet*, for instance, she was willing to "let in": "The Montagues and Capulets [are an inspiration], for sure. It was justified. They lived together, they are sworn enemies; they had been at war. There's a semi-truce, and circumstances separate them, but also misunderstandings that they could have cleared up, but they're young and impulsive. That's all quite clearly there [in *Jarrettsville*]." Nixon was also influenced by *Middlemarch* by George Eliot, and the Pulitzer Prize–winning *The Killer Angels*, a historical novel by Michael Shaara, for whom a Civil War fiction award would later be named.

In addition to learning style and prose through her formal and informal schooling, as a PhD student in English at Berkeley she also learned the archival research process, which dramatically influenced her writing of *Jarrettsville*. Although Nixon knew the topographical landscape of the setting and had obtained news reports depicting the trial—the court records had been lost to a fire long ago—it took years of archival work for her to feel that she understood the people and the period. Nixon relied on both primary and secondary sources to capture what was happening at the place and time, blending things that happened to her characters with things that *could have* happened, a menagerie of specific events and general realities of post–Civil War life in Harford County and the surrounding areas that could be imprinted onto her characters to bring them to life.

For instance, while there is no record of Richard Cairnes having beaten Nicholas McComas under the false pretense of McComas impregnating a freedwoman from Richard's farm, from Barbara Jeane Field's history of Maryland in the nineteenth century, *Slavery and Freedom on the Middle Ground*, Nixon knew that a similar event had happened in the area following the Civil War, making the story "safe" for imprinting onto Richard and Nick in a work of fiction. The motivation for that beating, Richard's sexual assault of Sophie and Nick's providing a safe harbor for her and her family, came from a similar blend of fact and fiction, as there is no record of their historical existence. To include them was "safe" for fiction, however, as it was very likely that prior to the Civil War the Cairnes family farm housed several slaves. That they may have stayed on the farm after the Civil War was accurate too; the "Creolia" of *Jarrettsville* was inspired by a real-life Creolia who worked and lived on the Cairnes farm several generations later when Nixon was a child. From a passing mention of a rumor that the father of Martha's child may have been a freedman, which Nixon found on a microform record of the *Aegis* (née the *Southern Aegis*), the newspaper of record for Harford County since 1856, "Tim," Creolia's son, was born.

In many cases for Nixon, her research, which provided the scaffolding for her creative inventions, would ultimately necessitate more research. In one example of this iterative process, if Sophie, Tim, and Creolia were to be major characters in the story, Nixon then had to go back to research how they would speak. Nixon learned that in Maryland during Tim's upbringing it was illegal to teach African Americans to read or write. As a result, *how* African American freedmen actually spoke in Maryland at the time is essentially unknown. The written record was likely inaccurate, Nixon figured, as abolitionists writing the stories of Mid-Atlantic slaves and freedmen were likely either converting the local African American dialect into more standardized English to make them more "presentable" to a white audience, or at other times exaggerating the differences in dialect to appeal to abolition-minded whites whose desire to "help" would be spurred by portraying the words and thoughts of African American slaves as simple and childlike. At the same time, supporters of slavery recounting the voices of the enslaved and recently freed may have been perverting their dialect for dehumanizing purposes, whereas in popular culture at the time these perversions were performed for white audiences with comedic effect. For this question Nixon had to first be aware of the historical record to reconcile the lack of answers it provided. She ultimately decided to split the difference.

Nixon concluded that because education was illegal for slaves and former slaves in Maryland, it would be inaccurate for them to speak like Frederick Douglass, although they probably also had the ability to speak formal English, or at least as much as the nonlanded or indentured white residents of the region. Her solution was to take some of the slang that was common to the era, soften the edges from deep Southern dialects (this was Maryland, after all), and include a scene of Tim code-switching while speaking with Martha to signal the complications of life for a recently freed slave. Much as was the case with the Romanticist style Nixon had toyed with, however, the efficacy of this solution was dependent on her successfully balancing these different considerations and accurately conveying the subtleties to the reader. It was not an option to render Tim, Creolia, and Sophie entirely voiceless, she figured, but without a historical record, how exactly those voices might have sounded was not entirely clear either. Like the decision to echo Lawrence's *Women in Love* in a scene, this decision too would have consequences for *Jarrettsville*'s future field transitions.

In other cases, the historical record would prove more reliable. Going through old records Nixon pieced together the genealogy of all the characters and their families: who was living where, how old siblings and children would be when the story was taking place, the backgrounds of the jurors for the trial and where their sympathies likely lay, and so on. Richard Cairnes's confirmed membership in a Southern-sympathizing militia made it clear where his sympathies lay. The real-life Nicholas McComas was in a Union militia, whereas his brother was in the Union Army and his father was a minister; thus, where the McComas family's sympathies lay was also clear. There were church records from the period to lean on, and diaries, such as that of Madge Preston, from which small details like sheep grazing the local fields would be transplanted into the story. From the Harford County Antiquarian Society, Nixon learned that Rebel militias had burned a railroad bridge to stop the movement of Union troops, which Nixon used to set the scene and establish the context toward the beginning of *Jarrettsville*. From a month spent at the American Antiquarian Society in Worcester, Massachusetts, Nixon learned what types of goods people were consuming, what they cost, and what people were thinking about. She also learned phrasing and the etymology of various words to try to avoid anachronisms: "I was worried about the phrase 'all right.' I was wondering if it was [from the] twentieth century. I wouldn't use 'okay,' I know that's [from the] twentieth century, but then [in] the *Baltimore Sun* coverage of the trial somebody says, 'Do you think the jury is all right?'"

Although historical records, the types of consumer goods available, and etymology helped Nixon capture some elements of the time and place, accurately identifying these things lengthened the research process. Rather than merely trying to sprinkle historically accurate details into the text, Nixon found that she wanted to know "everything," not just for the sake of historic detail, but to "have a feeling" while writing. Having a feeling encapsulated everything from the church attendance records of periphery characters to where a freedman might build a cabin, what supplies would be used, and how it would be constructed. To have a "feeling" for how the characters lived, Nixon felt she needed answers to those types of questions too: "How *do you* churn butter? Stuff like that. These details you just—I mean I could have written an article about the time without knowing how people lived— but to write a novel you've got to know."

From learning how to churn butter, Nixon could create subtle distinctions between characters, such as Creolia's success (as the former Cairnes's family slave) and Martha's failure at churning butter after a freed Creolia leaves the farm. As a result of a need to know, Nixon's creative process while writing was a dialectical one in which she had to both "have a feeling" and then go back to make sure the feelings she had were historically accurate: "I would very often imagine something fully and use my senses to enter it and live there, to feel like I was there. And later I would go back and say, 'huh, you know, I'm wondering about this detail here.' And then the scholar would kick back in and I'd go try to figure out if my feeling was possible."

As the dialectical process progressed, Nixon would move beyond researching the mundane details of life. In this stage, she relied on fine art and literature from the period to better imagine her characters. For instance, while from nuts-and-bolts research Nixon knew that Richard Cairnes was a Southern sympathizer, had a reputation for being a hothead, and also had red hair, to build onto this historical scaffolding and really have a "feeling" for him she leaned on the 1866 Winslow Homer painting *Prisoners from the Front*. The man standing front and center in the painting is the image Nixon kept in mind when writing Richard, and his defiant pose fit the hothead history Nixon knew of the real Richard Cairnes. The character, now visually represented, could be melded with her more general historical research about the intersecting complexities of masculinity, violence, and Southern honor that could animate his temperament.

For Martha, Nixon relied on a range of visual inspirations to "get inside" her head and actions. For Martha's rebellious spirit and "tomboy" qualities, Nixon leaned on the photo of her own mother, in a dress and shooting a rifle, that was placed on her mantel. The picture was a part but not all of Martha. From James McNeill Whistler's 1862 *Symphony in White, No. 1*, Nixon had another feeling for Martha that could be coupled with historical knowledge of the role that white women were assumed to play in that setting: "childlike, easily manipulated, and with sexual feelings that needed to be controlled and protected," as Nixon summarized it. This too was a part of

FIGURE 2.1: Martha, Martha, Martha. Photos courtesy of Cornelia Nixon.

Martha. Last, and most important, from her "family historian" aunt and uncle, Nixon had a picture of the real Martha Jane Cairnes, seemingly wracked with sadness, a third side to the new complex character, which completed the trifecta of visualized "Marthas" through which to capture a feeling for the complexities of the character (see Figure 2.1).

Overall, while Nixon relied on her childhood and personal life for the raw materials of the story of *Jarrettsville*, she learned through her training as a writer how to structure these materials into a novel, and she extended beyond this through vigorous research. Essentially, Nixon started with a family story, and then built it up through historically accurate details, which she then used to write with a feeling, only to then engage in an iterative process of history, art, and writing until she was satisfied that they all worked in harmony. Within the field of creation, however, rather than reaching a stopping point Nixon had reached a new starting point: she had completed a first draft.

FROM SOCIAL CIRCLES: REFINEMENT, COMMUNITY, AND ARTISTIC EXCHANGE

While on one level the *practice* of writing is dependent on things like background experiences and training, in the field of creation it is also deeply influenced through direct social interaction. As Kurtzberg and Amabile summarized the undersocialized view of creativity, "The focus has rested squarely on the individual, highlighting individual cognitive processing, stable individual difference, and the effects of the external environment on the individual. Relatively little attention has been paid to team level creative synergy, in which ideas are generated by groups instead of being generated by one mind."[11] Others, such as Michael Farrell, refer to these group formations in the field of creation as "collaborative circles" in which an initially weakly tied network of individuals who share a common interest come to increasingly rely upon each other until their creative processes become increasingly complex and mutually dependent.[12] Rather than the "temporary partisans" or "support personnel" of the field of production, in the field of creation collaborative circles are made up of other writers, friends, family members, romantic partners, confidantes, and so on all at once.

Novelists often find collaborative circles across several locales: with friends and family members who are also writers, in quasi-formal writing pairs or writing groups, and through participation as instructors or students in MFA programs in creative writing.[13] As collaborative circles enmesh both creative and social relationships, their sources and memberships are often overlapping and fluid. When working on *Jarrettsville*, members of Cornelia Nixon's circle, for instance, came from all three categories.

The influence of Nixon's spouse, the poet Dean Young, is impossible to untangle from the creation and re-creation of *Martha's Version* and then *Jarrettsville*. More generally, their marriage could be typified neither as a marriage that was sometimes also an informal creative relationship or as an informal creative relationship that was sometimes also a marriage. It was instead, according to Nixon, always *both* of these things: "Dean was my first reader always. Because that was . . . a big part of our marriage that we read each other's work. . . . All the humor [in *Jarrettsville*] comes straight from Dean. The epigraph for *Martha's Version* was originally from one of Dean's poems."[14]

It would be equally inaccurate to characterize Nixon's relationships with other writers as either friendship-based or creative-based, as they are deeply and irrevocably intertwined. This was true of Nixon's friends, the married poets Robert Hass and Brenda Hillman, who read a draft of *Martha's Version* back and forth to each other while driving from the San Francisco Bay Area to the Iowa Writer's Workshop. Upon their return, they shared with Nixon that they had most connected with her descriptive details of the setting. "She was really interested in the character [of Martha] at that point," Hillman recalled, and there was still work to be done beyond the character of Martha to "flesh this out a little bit." Nixon also remembered that Hass and Hillman thought the story started "a little slow," and having been good friends with them for so long and believing Hass and Hillman to be such "fantastic read-ers," Nixon worked to address both of these concerns in her revision of the text. Just as Nixon sometimes let the imagined ghost of D. H. Lawrence guide her hand, she let her friends and fellow authors guide her as well.

The most formally organized component of Nixon's social circle is her writing group, made up of fellow novelists who are also her friends. The members first met each other at Bread Loaf—a prestigious annual writers conference near Middlebury, Vermont—and all being from the San Fran-cisco Bay Area and enjoying each other's company and creative suggestions, they decided to "keep the conversation going" once back home. The group met the second Thursday and fourth Saturday of each month and relied on a turn-taking system in which each member shared work and got feedback.

In the field of creation, as in Nixon's writing group, recompense oper-ates largely within an economy of time and artistic attention, a gift exchange of sorts. Sometimes within the artistic exchange of the writing group "the entire direction of the book" can change, as happened with Nixon for a dif-ferent novel she was working on. In the field of creation writers/friends can sometimes push each other in new directions, as is the case with one member of Nixon's writing group in particular: "She's the one who writes the least like me. It's not because she's romantic, it's because she's more of the super mundane school. No detail is too mundane for her, whereas I'm interested in moments that are really tense and quivering, or beautiful, or somehow a high point. It's the difference [between us], which is why she's a great reader [for me]. I love her, I love working *with* her. She gives me the best advice because she's not automatically buying what I'm doing."

At the time Nixon's writing group was on the more formal side, with its planned dates and predetermined system of taking turns. Other authors' groups are much less formal: the taking of turns is an informal arrangement, and the members are unconnected friends who specialize in collaborating on different elements of their writing practice. As described by Barbara, an author of literary fiction, rather than being members in quasi-formal writ-ing groups, some novelists see themselves as embedded in a collection of creative friends:

> I have two very trusted friends who are also editors, Jeremy and Sarah. When I've finished my first draft I show it first to Sarah who is the more encouraging person. And when I finish my second or third draft I show it to Jeremy who's more rigorous and structured and I find that's very good. . . . He's like "you need more of this, you have a little lack of sym-metry here, I think you need to tie it up more." And sometimes I dis-

agree and I'll convince him, but sometimes he convinces me and even in the third draft the whole novel changes because of him. I don't have a group per se, personally, I just have two people and I know exactly their function.

Patrick, a younger novelist who formed an ad hoc and informal writing group for himself through two friends and one professor he met while attending an MFA program in creative writing, also sees his social circle as made up of friends/artists who help him develop different facets of his work: "John, I sort of consider him my line-editing specialist. . . . Alison, she's always very good with parsing out the characters' emotional journeys, saying this isn't realistic or you need more of this here. . . . David is more like just 'let's look at the events, let's look at what happens and see if that's what should happen.' So they all have their own concerns and it's complementary." While Nixon's writing group initially formed through a writing conference, for younger writers like Patrick, it is often through their experiences as novitiates in creative writing MFA programs that they forge the initial friendships that blossom into collaborative circles.[15]

The rise of MFA programs in creative writing—they have more than doubled in number since the turn of the twenty-first century—has created new outlets for the formation and maintenance of collaborative circles. With MFA programs as hubs, there are these days diffuse networks of authorial creation that span out across the country, mostly beyond the purview of the field of production.[16] While earlier studies of the lives of authors have reported a fair degree of social isolation, in the present-day field of creation, it is through new outlets that today's writers find additional sources of creative community.[17] As a novelist and faculty member in an MFA program explained, "I used to say teaching just interferes with my writing because in terms of time it does. But you can only write for so many hours a day. And it's really lonely just writing. You need to have community and the writers group is great but I only see them like once or twice a month usually. . . . It can be good to write for a while in the morning and then go to school and talk to young people. . . . So it's more about community."

Barbara, whose two editor friends Jeremy and Sarah are instrumental to her creative process, offers an example of the negative case; she neither went to nor teaches in an MFA program, and as a result feels less of a sense of community in the field of creation. While she has a few friends, she feels she lacks a collaborative circle upon whom she can rely: "I'm happy [with my career], but I envy people who have a circle; I envy people who were in MFA programs together where they bonded. I envy people who were in

MFA programs because they have mentors. . . . I'm missing the context. I'm not saying I feel uneducated . . . I mean I don't have a certain sort of [social] structure in place that some people do that are tremendous resources for writers."

In the field of creation, it is within a looser network of weak ties that a novelist may feel a broader sense of participating in a writing community. Within a denser network of multiplex ties, a novelist becomes enmeshed in a collaborative circle. These collaborative circles, however, are most regularly activated in the privacy of homes, via email, phone, or Skype, or go unnoticed in coffee shops, in restaurants, or on walks. They are, as a result, outside the scope of studies of industries or formal organizations. As such, while the physical act of writing may often be done alone, the broader practice of creative writing snaps back and forth from the individual act of writing to the mutually constitutive creative actions that take place in social interactions.[18] In this way, rather than writers always writing alone, it is through their social circles with other writers that they push their creative practice into new and previously unforeseen directions.

HOW *JARRETTSVILLE* CAME TO BE CALLED *JARRETTSVILLE*

Cornelia Nixon's writing group never read *Martha's Version* or *Jarrettsville*. At the time that Nixon needed the most help, the group had just previously finished discussing a different novel she was working on. For that reason, if Nixon had asked the group to read *another* entire manuscript for her, she would have upset both the semiformal turn-taking system within the group, and the local norms around how much to ask of author-friends. Put another way, to her writing community Nixon had artistic debts that had to be repaid before she could extend another line of credit.

Beyond needing to repay her artistic debts to her writing group, the problem Nixon was having with *Martha's Version* was that during her redrafting of it—in response to both the suggestions from trusted friends and a "come to Jesus moment" that is the topic of chapter 4—the story itself had fundamentally changed, so much so that she needed a revised title. This new draft was no longer just Martha's version of the events, so the title *Martha's Version* no longer fit, and Nixon had never been particularly attached to it either: "I think I did it [i.e., titled it that] because of Martha's Vineyard. I just like the sound. I realized later, 'that's probably why you're doing that, okay?' But my agent liked it, and yeah, [that title was] just wildly literal. I had the hardest time coming up with a title for this book." Nixon had toyed

TABLE 2.1: List of Possibilities for Retitling *Martha's Version,* Cornelia Nixon, January, 2008

On Middle Ground	*Debts of Honor*	*Funeral Season*	*Last Songs*
Verdict in May	*The Acquittal*	*No Fury Like*	*The Secret War*
Peace Falls	*Leaving Jarrettsville*	*Imperfect Union*	*Ruined Union*
No Middle Ground	*Blood on a Rosebud*	*In Jarrettsville*	*Justified*
The War that Would not End	*War's End*	*The Aftermath*	*Where Armies Meet*

around with the title *The Error Is Not to Fall,* a line from one of her husband's poems, but she never took it seriously: "It had to be liberated from that . . . the idea was going to be nice, you know, like a little reflection of each other, but that's all it was." Nixon experimented with other titles; something with "justified" in it she thought, because Martha Cairnes had been acquitted of the murder of Nicholas McComas on the ad hoc grounds of justifiable homicide. She experimented with variations on *"Blood and . . ."* but they never felt quite right, rather "gnarly and-over determined" she figured. But Nixon's agent was waiting for the manuscript, so she wrote out twenty potential titles, hoping she could settle on one by the time the manuscript was due (see Table 2.1).

Fortunately, her writing group had planned a tea. Teas, rather than formal meetings, had more free-form exchanges of half-thought-out ideas and collaborative suggestion making. While Nixon couldn't ask the group to read the manuscript, at earlier teas and in casual conversation they had all heard about *Martha's Version* and the changes it had gone through; a tea meeting was the perfect setting in which to ask for advice. Nixon decided that at the next tea she would bring her list of twenty potential titles.

Nixon had assumed that the group could help her pick from this list. But once together at the tea, the group's response to the proffered options was tepid. Going around the room, they began to discuss the changes that the novel had undergone. What had once been a story told entirely from Martha's perspective had become a story told equally from Martha and Nick's perspectives, bookended by twelve narratives from other residents of the town. From her historical research Nixon had completed a genealogy of the area, and the group talked about all the people in 1860s Jarrettsville who "had married their first cousins, and this whole family really having a presence that extends past any nuclear family. . . . There was a whole web that held the place together, and the former slaves were part of that web, and even at the time people thought that way. They were there. And the betrayals of the war were there, when people were closely connected to each other in many ways and they were fighting on opposite sides, and even after the war was over you still see them fighting each other. The whole place, it was like a terrible familial battle."

According to Nixon, it was either Lisa Michaels or Vendela Vida who said, "how about just plain *Jarrettsville*?" The manuscript, her writing group explained to her, had become something that was as much about the place as about the people, to the degree that the two could even be separated. The group talked about other novels they loved that had place names as titles, and how well it fit for *Jarrettsville*. "It was just so wonderful," Nixon recalled. She was grateful for both the new title and the new clarity of creative vision for what the newly titled *Jarrettsville* really was. As Nixon explained it, her friends, as both friends and artists in their own rights, had "saved me from myself."

By the end of the process, it seemed like *Martha's Version* was in some ways Nixon's version, whereas *Jarrettsville*, in its creation, was a story that had ultimately been written by Nixon but had been collaboratively crafted by many people. Those people, to Nixon, included everyone from her eighth-grade teacher who inspired confidence in her as a writer to her mother who shared the family secret because she knew Nixon wanted to write. They included the friends and acquaintances whose personalities and experiences drifted in and out of the text as well as the teachers who taught her how to write, and the authors she had admired and from whom she had to wrestle her hand back. They also included the members of her social circle who brought humor to the novel, told her what was working and what was not, suggested broad changes, or determined what the book was *really* about and retitled it. All in the all the creativity that went into *Jarrettsville* was an irreducibly social one.

In the crafting of *Jarrettsville*, "Cornelia Nixon" had become a bit of a collective noun; the figurehead undergirded by a long acknowledgments page, and an even longer list of unnamed people who she believed should be acknowledged. It was in the field of creation, behind the scenes and beyond the purview of publishers and readers, that much of the collaborative work of *Jarrettsville* was done. Put another way, for all of Nixon's creative actions, the book was born through an equal number of interactions. Were we to reduce the creation of *Jarrettsville* to Nixon sitting alone in a coffee shop, we would miss much of the point of how *Jarrettsville* became the novel that it is. This is true of the story and style in which it was written, just as it is true of the development of its characters and even the title *Jarrettsville* itself.

AUTHORIAL CAREERS

OR, HOW $6,000 BECOMES A

MIDDLE-CLASS INCOME

STARBUCKS REVISITED

If you were to go back to Starbucks on the corner of Oxford and Center streets in Berkeley, Cornelia Nixon would still be upstairs, writing on her laptop with her headphones on. On most days between 1998 and 2004, she would have been there for two hours, until the parking meter ran out. On good days, although most days were not good days, she'd put more money in the meter and stay for another two. Nixon's writing ritual is a story about her creative process, but it's also a story about money. To make sense of Nixon's creative process, there are two small economic transactions and one broader economic reality that must be accounted for: (1) paying for parking, (2) buying tea, and (3) affording to have good days and bad days at Starbucks.

Nixon lives in a handsome condo in the Berkeley Hills. From her bedroom window in the early evening she can look across the bay to see the sun setting behind the Golden Gate Bridge and the San Francisco skyline. Her condo sits less than a five-minute walk from the Berkeley Rose Garden, a terraced amphitheater with over 250 varieties of roses, tennis courts, and tourists taking selfies before one of the East Bay's most stunning views. If Nixon wanted, she could write at her dining room table, or better yet the desk she has *for* writing in the room adjoining her bedroom. Nixon also has a proper office, also with a desk for writing, at which she also does not write. Instead, Nixon wrote *Jarrettsville* at a coffee shop for two hours a day, and sometimes for four.

For Nixon there were several attractions to working at Starbucks. First, unlike if she were to write at home or in her office, being surrounded by others could stave off the loneliness of the *act* of writing. Second, Starbucks was free of the domestic distractions that lurked at home and the social distractions of her office. Third, to work at Starbucks Nixon had to pay for street parking, which she used as a commitment device, a way to orient her toward long-term goals (i.e., writing) rather than short-term impulses (i.e., the common stalling tactic among writers, best termed "anything but writing"). For Nixon, who was financially comfortable, the actual cost of paying for street parking near Starbucks was trivial, but she had *paid* to be there, so she owed it to herself to get work done. On most days Nixon could spend all day at Starbucks if she chose, but by paying for parking she also imposed an artificial two-hour limit on her work; time spent on "anything but writing" was wasted. The two-hour time limit also allowed Nixon to contain "bad writing days" to just two hours of her day, preventing full days of agony. On "good writing days" she could take a break at two hours to feed the meter for another two.

The second economic transaction in Nixon's creative routine is paying for tea, again a trivial expenditure for her, but not without meaning or import. Anthony Trollope would wake and write each morning at five thirty, finishing his daily session before he dressed for breakfast. Trollope's ability to keep this schedule was dependent on a servant, whom he paid an extra five pounds per year to make and bring him coffee at that early hour. As Trollope wrote of his servant in his autobiography, "I do not know that I ought not to feel that I owe more to him than to any one else for the success I have had."[1] For Howard Becker, Trollope's attribution of success to his servant is an ideal example of support personnel: someone who does the little things that allow an author to write. Nixon does not have a servant, but she does have people who make her beverages as she writes. Unlike the cleanly transactional exchange in Becker's retelling of Trollope's servant, however, Nixon's relationship with the employees at Starbucks is a more complicated one, which can often be the case in even the most seemingly mundane of repeated economic exchanges.[2]

If Nixon were to attribute her writing success to any one such provider of beverages, that attribution would go to Maggie, the manager at Starbucks. Over time Nixon and Maggie grew to know each other. Nixon liked that Maggie offered a friendly and encouraging face, and that she would ask for updates on *Jarrettsville* and check in on Nixon's progress. In fact, Maggie knew the whole story. She wanted Nixon to a do a reading of the novel at Starbucks when it was complete, and one day presented Nixon with a gift: a personalized mug to drink from as she wrote (see Figure 3.1). Nixon, for her part, knew Maggie's story, where she had come from, what she was up to, and where she hoped to go. It is unknown if during their coffee transactions Trollope and his servant also talked about Trollope's writing. It is an important detail about social support that, although perhaps identifiable to the authors who receive it, is not often captured when thinking of a coffee provider as support personnel: the provider of transactional service *x* that allows the

FIGURE 3.1: Maggie's Gift to Nixon.

artist to accomplish artistic *y*. Yet Maggie was more than this to Nixon; her encouragement and the thoughtfulness of her gift—encouragement converted into physical form—stuck with Nixon. Once *Jarrettsville* traveled through to the field of production, Nixon would experience the classic support personnel of Becker's account—a cover designer she never met, a copy editor whose name she at most heard only in passing. While still in the field of creation, however, her relationship with Maggie, albeit limited, meant much more to Nixon than a simple exchange of money for tea.

The bigger economic reality of Nixon's daily routine is more complicated, and concerns how Nixon is financially able to hold herself to a workday writing routine at all. For *Jarrettsville* Nixon received a six-thousand-dollar advance for many years of writing. For her previous novel, published nine years prior, she had done a bit better, ten thousand, but still far short of a living income. Given such small financial returns and the irregularity of her output, how did Nixon afford her parking, her tea, and, most vitally, her condo? How did Nixon afford to write at all?

TALKING MONEY

Novelists, like other artists, are hesitant to talk about money with outsiders. Those who write literary fiction may be particularly reluctant to engage in these conversations as they have what Bourdieu calls an "interest in disinterestedness" when it comes to talking money.[3] Yet between novelists money is no less common a topic of discussion than it is among anyone else, and given the financial realities of writing novels, it may be more common. Until recently, for the most part, there were only several ways that the vast

majority of novelists could afford to be novelists at all: they could be independently wealthy, couple with partners who worked in more stable and
financially remunerative occupations, or work day jobs and write on the
side. Although it's mostly beside the point for publishers or readers, making a living while writing was not beside the point for Herman Melville the
customs inspector, William Faulkner the postmaster, Kurt Vonnegut the car
dealership manager, Octavia Butler the telemarketer and potato chip quality
control inspector, James Patterson the advertising executive, or Arundhati
Roy the aerobics instructor.

Others who could not successfully balance their novelistic aspirations
with full-time paid employment had to rely on the largesse of family and
friends. This was the case for Harper Lee, who had wanted to be a writer
since her days as an undergraduate student in Alabama. Yet this aspiration
seemed to be on hiatus for her throughout her twenties as she worked as
an airline ticket agent in New York. While there she reconnected with a
childhood friend from her hometown of Monroeville, Alabama, who had
become a celebrated author. Her friend, Truman Capote, introduced her to
his friends Michael and Joy Brown (he a Broadway composer and lyricist
she a former principal ballerina), both of whom she soon grew close with.
Knowing of Lee's desire to write, and with the financial capacity to support
her goal, as a Christmas gift in 1956 the Browns gave Lee a card that read,
"You have one year off from your job to write whatever you please. Merry
Christmas."[4] It was with this year of financial support from her fellow artist
friends that Harper Lee wrote *To Kill a Mockingbird*. The novel, a mass success and Pulitzer Prize–winning classic, may likely have never been written
without the money of financially well-off friends.

Relying on the largesse of friends is not always feasible, so many other
novelists couple, or end up coupled, with partners whose incomes can cover
daily expenses. This is not to suggest that would-be novelists regularly seek romantic partners based on their ability to provide financial stability, although
some perhaps do, but instead is meant only to suggest that those who already
possess or go on to find financial stability are more able to pursue work as
novelists than those who do not. Unsurprisingly, the financial solvency and
stability required to be a novelist often comes from generational wealth. Ann
Bauer, a novelist who describes her writing career as "sponsored" by her husband, retells one such instance:

> I attended a packed reading . . . about a year and a half ago. The au-
> thor was very well known, a magnificent nonfictionist who has, de-
> servedly, won several big awards. He also happens to be the heir to a

mammoth fortune. . . . He's a man who has never had to work one job, much less two. He has several children; I know, because they were at the reading with him, all lined up. I heard someone say they were all traveling with him, plus two nannies, on his worldwide tour.

None of this takes away from his brilliance. Yet, when an audience member—young, wide-eyed, clearly not clued in—rose to ask him how he'd managed to spend 10 years writing his current masterpiece— What had he done to sustain himself and his family during that time?— he told her in a serious tone that it had been tough but he'd written a number of magazine articles to get by. I heard a titter pass through the half of the audience that knew the truth. But the author, impassive, moved on and left this woman thinking he'd supported his Manhattan life for a decade with a handful of pieces in *The Nation* and *Salon*.[5]

Left out of this description of how most novelists made livings throughout the latter half of the twentieth century—working day jobs, being sponsored by spouses, friends, or generational wealth—is the sometimes financially remunerative activity that many novelists most regularly engage in: writing novels. While Nixon takes longer to write a novel than many and her advances are not large, the fact that she cannot live off her advances is the general rule among novelists. For almost all writers, writing novels is not a way to make a living, and this is not a new phenomenon.[6] In 1946, the novelist Malcolm Cowley described the effect on authors' incomes from the growing book market and rise of the Book of the Month Club: "Most writers lived as before, on crumbs from a dozen different tables. Meanwhile a few dozen or even a hundred of the most popular writers were earning money about at the rate of war contractors."[7]

Today, this general principle still holds, and it is true across a wide range of artistic occupations. Yet there are two challenges to defining novelists' incomes.[8] First, one has to define who counts as a novelist, and the more restrictive one's definition, the less income inequality one is likely to find.[9] Second, as Alison Gerber argues, in defining a novelist's income one must pick between taking an "object-centered" view of income generated from novel writing (e.g., advance plus royalties, minus expenses for novels authored) or a more holistic approach to the lives of working novelists and how they actually afford to live.[10] A novel-centered view overlooks how most novelists actually generate income, as writing is what John B. Thompson refers to as a "winner-takes-most" affair.[11] As a result, when talking author income, although the slope of the curve may change based on definition, the shape of it remains generally the same: there are very few authors at the very top earning at very high rates, a still very small but larger pool of authors earning enough to make a living, and the vast majority earning crumbs from their books and getting by through other means.

Yet three major shifts in the past forty years have made novel writing in the United States perhaps more profitable than ever before. For top-selling authors, a decline of informal restrictions on how much they publish—and perhaps more importantly, to what extent they're actually writing the books they author—has created a Matthew effect, and the rich have gotten even richer.[12] For midlist authors too life has gotten better through two different channels. And down at the bottom, with the rise of eBook technologies new distribution streams have opened up avenues for remuneration where few previously existed, although these new technologies have also created new risks for authors.

THE NAME ECONOMY AND LIFE AT THE TOP

At the top of the income curve authors exist in what Brian Moeran calls a name economy: those who beyond their names require no more identification, and who tie products, organizations, and individuals together.[13] Such is the case with James Patterson, who has a sixteen-person team solely dedicated to him at his publisher, Little, Brown and Company, where Patterson estimates that he is responsible for about one-third of total revenue.[14] From 2006 through 2010, one out of every seventeen novels sold in the United States was authored by Patterson, and although he has received criticism for it, he has taken the name economy at the top of the author income curve to its natural conclusion: he no longer writes many of his books, or at least in the way that other authors write their books.[15] Instead, Patterson, who is credited with over 130 full-length books and will have started and finished a twenty-four book contract at his publisher in less time than it took to write this book, has a stable of about twenty-five coauthors. He provides detailed outlines of characters and plots, leaving the writing of the story itself mostly up to them. It is through his coauthors that Patterson's "productivity" has increased from several books a year in the early 2000s to eighteen full-length books released in 2015 (see Figure 3.2). Adding to his "output," starting in 2016, Patterson began "writing" novellas through his "BookShots" program, aiming to release two to four of them per month, with twenty-one slated for release in the first year of the program.[16]

Among name-economy authors, Patterson is not alone in coauthoring. Just as Patterson views writing "the way Henry Ford would look at it," there

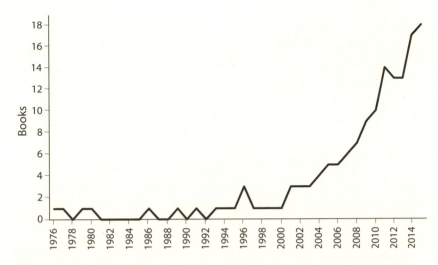

FIGURE 3.2: Number of Full-Length James Patterson Books Authored per Year: 1976–2015.

is Janet Evanovich's "assembly line" and James Frey's "fiction factory."[17] Although the novelty in these examples is that these are name-economy authors who are primarily known as authors, the name economy also draws on books credited to known entities from other arenas—art, politics, sport, etc.—with the actual labor of writing accomplished by ghostwriters. Such was the case with *The Philosophy of Andy Warhol*, for which Warhol is attributed as the sole author, despite general acceptance by all involved that that he wrote exactly none of the book. As recounted by Bob Colacello, a coauthor, "When I finished the chapter . . . [Warhol] took it home . . . and read it over the phone to Brigid Berlin, taping her reaction. Then he gave the tape to Pat Hackett, telling to her 'make it better.' So now the ghostwriter had a ghostwriter."[18]

Making it into the name economy provides great financial rewards for some authors in the field of creation. The power of their names, and what makes them powerful across production and reception (and sometimes viewed with suspicion in the field of creation), is that they offer a rare degree of predictability in fields otherwise characterized by rampant uncertainty, as "everything else is highly speculative."[19] In the case of Stephen King, a name-economy author who does actually write all of his books, that a new book has been authored by him comes with expectations for what "type" of thing it is, be it a rough estimate for sales in the field of production, or a promissory note to readers in the field of reception about what they're buying. It is this name-based promissory note to readers that causes author Eleanor Robertson to write under different pen names in different genres: she is Nora Roberts when writing romance, and J. D. Robb when writing suspense and science fiction.

Yet for some authors in the name economy, it is the predictability of name-economy authoring that they find troubling, according to a logic unique to the field of creation. For name-economy authors whose time and identity are tethered to their writing, there can be fear that in the fields of production and reception the guarantee of their names overshadows any true engagement with the quality—or lack thereof—of their work. For the famed novelist and playwright Doris Lessing, this was a big enough problem that she decided to surreptitiously write two novels under the pen name Jane Somers to see if her publisher, Jonathan Cape, would accept her work for publication without knowing that she had written it. The publisher passed on the novels. As she described her experiment, having already known what the outcome would be, "I wanted to highlight that whole dreadful process in book publishing that 'nothing succeeds like success.' If the books had come out in my name, they would have sold a lot of copies and reviewers would have said, 'Oh, Doris Lessing, how wonderful.'"[20]

A similar story about publishing under the cloak of anonymity is also true for J. K. Rowling, author of the *Harry Potter* series. After the conclusion of the *Potter* series in 2012, under her own name Rowling published *The Casual Vacancy* to weak reviews but over one million copies sold in its first three weeks of release. Rowling's next novel, *The Cuckoo's Calling*, surreptitiously published under the name Robert Galbraith, was received with very strong reviews but sold only fifteen hundred copies before she was exposed as its author. On the experience, Rowling commented that it was "wonderful to publish without hype or expectation, and pure pleasure to get feedback under a different name."[21] Here, Rowling's suspicions also seemed to be confirmed: in the name economy the name of J. K. Rowling was a positive signal for readers in the field or reception and a negative one for reviewers who stand between the fields of production and reception. By changing her name Rowling could perhaps redirect the eyes of reviewers back to the work itself, and direct the eyes of *Harry Potter* fans away from one of her books that may not appeal to them. This was, however, not the first name change that Rowling had undergone. As is the case across many creative labor markets, the name economy of authoring favors not only famous names, but also male and gender-neutral names. The publisher of the *Potter* series, Bloomsbury, changed Rowling's name from Joanne Rowling to the gender-ambiguous J. K. Rowling; other examples include A. M. Barnard (née Louisa May Alcott) and the less gender-ambiguous male given names adopted by Harper Lee (née Nelle Harper Lee) and George Elliot (née Mary Ann Evans).

While the name economy can give even more to those who already have, it can also take away even more from those who have not. The less acknowledged underside of the name economy is the one inhabited by all of those published authors whose names are not common reference points for authors, publishers, and readers. Authors who have successfully published books but have failed to reach many readers—which is most authors—can be punished by the logic of the name economy: they become seen as predictable "bad" rather than good bets. This appeared to be the case for Patricia O'Brien, who had successfully published five novels, but could not sell her sixth, which was rejected by twelve publishers, including the publisher of her last novel, Simon & Schuster, whose editor said that her previous work had not sold well enough to warrant publishing her next novel. Feeling that her client was being blacklisted in the name economy, O'Brien's literary agent suggested she start submitting the novel under a pen name, Kate Alcott, so that the book might get "a fair chance."[22] Within a week, Doubleday, a division of Random House, purchased "Kate Alcott's first novel," which went on to be a best seller. Less overtly deceptive tactics have also been used by publishers to obscure their authors' track records of nonsuccess, such as Algonquin not including mention of Barbara Shapiro's first name or previous five novels in galley copies of her soon-to-be-hit sixth novel *The Art Forger*, while also neglecting to mention Sara Gruen's two previous novels—both poor selling—when promoting her eventual best seller *Water for Elephants*. This tactic, created to mitigate the punishment of poor sellers, is part of the logic described by literary agent Jason Ashlock, who remarked that an author's "biggest enemy today is not piracy, but obscurity."[23]

For those few authors whose names *do* count in the name economy, life is even better at the top in the twenty-first century than before. This is the result of two factors: an institutional transition away from the folk wisdom that the market can support only one title per author per year, and the rise of alternative publishing channels. On the first point, it was believed until recently that there was not a market for more than one book per year by name-economy authors. Even at the end of the 1990s, some highly productive authors would have their manuscripts backlogged or would use pen names to release multiple titles in the same year. This was the case with "Richard Bachman" books—written by Stephen King—which were released only in the years between 1978 and 1997 in which Stephen King books were also slated to be published. The institutional transition away from such folk wisdom is best documented through Patterson's increasingly prodigious output. In 2013, Patterson earned around $90 million, which was not possible in the 1980s or 1990s, when the supply from his assembly line was artificially limited by the institutionalized norms of publishing.

In turn, the rise of electronic self-publishing has also benefited writers at the top. Stephen King experimented with self-publishing on his website in 2000 with *The Plant*, a serialized book project in which readers paid per chapter, which he never finished. In 2010, using Amazon rather than incurring the expense of building his own platform, King spent three profitable days writing the novella *Ur*: "I've made about $80,000. You can't get that for short fiction from Playboy or anybody else. It's ridiculous."[24] Similarly outsized financial rewards have been found by self-published (or formerly self-published) authors such as Hugh Howey, Amanda Hocking, John Locke, and E. L. James. Howey, author of the popular *Silo* series of science fiction novellas, claims to make $150,000 per month through Amazon, compared to the small advances he received when working through a traditional publisher.

Typically, in a slowly growing market with such extreme success at the top, we would expect a hollowing out of the middle or a further draining of income from the bottom. Yet, this is not entirely the case for novelists. Instead, even beyond those few who get rich writing novels, due to indirect governmental intervention and changes in industry norms, the possibility of earning a living from writing novels has increased for a broad cross-section of novelists in the past forty years or so. These market changes have improved remuneration opportunities for novelists at the bottom as well, although those improvements should not be overstated. As a general rule, however, uncertainty has an inverse relationship with authorial income; those who are known, and who write and are published with less uncertainty, tend to make more. Thus, even as income has arguably improved for authors across all strata, uncertainty—in this case, working outside the name economy—is still financially penalized.

Cornelia Nixon has never benefited from the name economy, and if anything, in her career she has fallen victim to it. Her lack of standing in the name economy does not actually hurt her position in the field of creation— her social circle is made up of name-economy and non-name-economy friends and allies—but in the field of production and reception her name is not a promissory note that connects her with publishers and readers. Despite this, critical reception of Nixon's two novels prior to *Jarrettsville* had been positive. This ostensibly helped her standing in the field of production, if not reception. Yet her output was too slow for her to build much momentum for her "name," even off glowing reviews, and to publish a new novel by Nixon meant relaunching her name to reviewers and readers. In the field of creation in which Nixon is principally situated, writing literary fiction "too quickly" induces more suspicion than writing "too slowly," yet according to the logic of the field of production, writing too slowly was an additional problem plaguing her. Even if *Jarrettsville* had been written more quickly it would have still suffered from a momentum problem, as it was dissimilar from her previous novels (neither of which were historical fiction), which for readers could have amounted to a broken promise of her name. Yet rather than being a name-economy author, Cornelia Nixon found her career, and her income, through an entirely different growing income channel for writers.

UNCERTAINTY AND THE EXPANSIVE MIDDLE

With the benefit of hindsight, fans of James Patterson or J. K. Rowling could offer no shortage of reasons for why they deserve their success and are different from other novelists writing similar books. Yet without the benefit of hindsight, as most in the fields of creation and production know, to enter into the name economy is more often than not a fluke, and the result of what to creators and producers can seem like not much more than random chance.[25] Consider for instance that fourteen publishers rejected Patterson's first novel or that Stephenie Meyer sent *Twilight* to fifteen literary agents, and nine of the ten who bothered to respond rejected her. Twelve publishers rejected Rowling's first *Harry Potter* novel, and the publisher that did accept it, Bloomsbury, only believed in it enough to order an initial print run of five hundred copies (three hundred to libraries, two hundred to the market). To this we can also add the story of William Golding's *Lord of the Flies*, which was rejected by over twenty publishers, sold fewer than twenty-five hundred copies in its first year of publication, and within eighteen months was out of print. A similarly safe prediction of failure to reach readers seemed to initially be the case for Anne Frank's *Diary of a Young Girl*, which was first rejected by fifteen publishers, with one even responding that the story was "very dull" and "a dreary record of typical family bickering, petty annoyances and adolescent emotions."[26]

Such was also the case for David Sedaris, likely the most broadly successful humorist and memoirist of the past quarter century, who in 1992, went from being a complete unknown who had been journaling for fifteen years to a member of the name economy through a chance encounter with a local Chicago public radio host: "I had worked as an elf at Macy's Santaland for two years and I had kept a diary. I read parts of that diary, Ira [Glass, who heard Sedaris reading from his journal in a Chicago club, contacted him] edited them and put them on *Morning Edition*. It effectively changed my life within the course of maybe 12 minutes. There was my life before and then there was my life after."[27]

Rather than these being exceptional entry stories into the name economy, that these authors' successes were unlikely and unforetold is the general rule. For published authors to linger in obscurity is the typical experience, with the success of those rare few who do make it appearing to be predictable or logical only after the fact. As a result, almost all novelists write without knowing if they will ever be able to live off of their writing alone. Simply put, left to consumer market devices alone, almost all novelists could not in fact afford to be novelists. Yet for two reasons, finding oneself in the expansive and uncertain middle is perhaps less terrifying than it has ever been before.

The first factor is the rise of advances since the early 1980s. In the second half of the twentieth century, building off the large expansion of the book market and the rise of literary agents who more strongly negotiated for authors' rights, income from writing for the uncertain and expansive middle grew and was more equitably dispersed than at any other time in history. If anything, through the system of literary advances, the earnings at the top have trickled down into the pockets of those in the middle. The modern system of advances in book publishing can best be described as accidentally socialistic; in making bets on the next generation of name-economy authors, publishers have rerouted profits back down into the expansive and uncertain middle.[28] The second factor that provided new income to midlist novelists is a work-around of sorts and, unlike the first factor, resulted from a conscious and clever strategy taken by the National Endowment for the Arts (NEA) to subsidize the lives of working writers who cannot depend on market forces alone. This second factor is the dramatic rise of MFA programs in creative writing.

The first such program, the Iowa Writers Workshop, was founded in 1936 by Wilbur Schramm. This model would not begin to be seriously replicated until the 1960s, or really take hold until the 2000s. In fact, more MFA programs in creative writing have been founded since 2000 than were founded throughout the entire twentieth century (see Figure 3.3). Unlike English or comparative literature degree programs, MFA programs in creative writing mostly provide income to novelists, short story writers, poets, and other creative writers. They may be full-time faculty, fellows, adjuncts, or writers in residence whose income is supplemented—or simply just *provided*—while working on their writing. Some MFA faculty, like Greg, a short story writer and novelist, are comfortable with the arrangement. He explained his tenure-track position in an MFA program as "a job, a way to earn a living while writing."

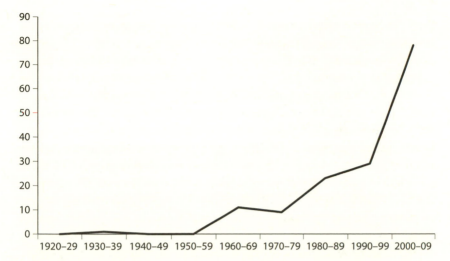

FIGURE 3.3: US MFA Creative Writing Programs Founded per Decade.
Source: Data compiled by Seth Abramson for *Poets & Writers* 2012 MFA rankings.

Yet in the past forty years or so the MFA system of remuneration has become so institutionalized that younger writers, who do not know another way, may end up romanticizing the past. As one such writer-teacher explained, "Most writers now have to teach in universities because it's the way that we support ourselves, and it's a very odd thing to be going on, to have all the people in the country who are recording what life is like now doing this really odd thing, which is the academic world, [and] is not the same as the rest of the world. It would be nice if we could go back to living from writing." Although this novelist references wanting to "go back" to a time when novelists could make their living from writing, he does not specify the time to which he refers, and the historical existence of it is dubious. While the early and mid-twentieth century have been reinterpreted as a "golden age" of literature in the United States, the book market (and concomitantly the returns generated from writing books) in this era was comparatively quite small.

Jonathan, a well-known and respected player in the field of production who has held a range of positions over his long career, thinks that this history of little to no returns for creative writing has been lost and replaced with an assumption that writers have always lived, and should be able to live, off their writing alone: "Certainly Hart Crane never thought society owed him a living. So there was that radical shift . . . and now you have people who are so firmly entrenched in [the] second generation and beyond, so firmly entrenched in the MFA program that they have no other idea, they have no traditional grounding." Some teacher-novelists attribute the growth of the MFA in the 1970s to English departments moving away from the traditional study of evaluating literary works, and leaving a "vacuum for creative writers to rush into." While it is true that curricular shifts in English departments created an opportunity space for the rise of MFA programs in creative writing, this factor created only one of several conditions under which these programs could carve out a specialized educational niche. The conditions for their existence and diffusion in the first place are something entirely different. Instead, the rise of the MFA in creative writing was in many ways the result of a conscious strategy by the NEA, which worked under the goal of funneling income to already working writers. Yet funding MFA programs in creative writing was not the NEA's first attempt to support working writers, as instead it slowly emerged as the most self-sufficient and politically expedient one.

Starting in 1967, under the proposal of novelists and poets Harper Lee, Ralph Ellison, John Steinbeck, and Paul Engle, the NEA began to sponsor individual writers. The first batch of twenty-three writers funded included William Gaddis, Richard Yates, and eventual Nobel Prize recipient Isaac Bashevis Singer. Shortly thereafter, the formal Literature Panel was formed under the directorship of Carolyn Kizer, who continued to fund individual authors, as well as to institute Discovery Awards to fund aspiring writers. As the short-lived Discovery Awards were later summarized by NEA literature director Amy Stolls:

> The Endowment hired "talent scouts" to find these gifted, financially needy, unknown writers. The response from the scouts was "overwhelming," claims a 1967 report to the Council, citing "a young Negro poet who supports her three children by running a general store in Alabama," and another "young Southern writer, blind since birth and seriously crippled in infancy, who has managed to struggle through her teacher's certificate, and is now teaching young children in Tennessee, and writing poems and stories for three hours each evening." Grants were then awarded according to need: $1,000 to the single writer without dependents; $1,500 to the writer with one dependent; and $2,000 to the writer with two or more dependents. Among these recipients one can find the 25-year-old Alexander Theroux and the 26-year-old Nikki Giovanni.[29]

By 1970, Discovery Grants came under fire from the advisory board of the Literature Panel—comprising publishers and editors—under the argument that artistic funding should be granted to authors not on the basis of need but solely on the basis of perceived talent. Yet by the time Len Randolph became director of the Literature Panel in 1970, the NEA had come under fire for funding writers at all. The opening salvo came in 1970 when Aram Saroyan's one-word poem "lighght" was selected by George Plimpton to be placed in the *American Literary Anthology*. Publication came with a $500 reward from the NEA, which conservative senators objected to, using the poem as an example of wasted governmental funds. Then, in 1973, when Erica Jong noted the grant money she had received from the NEA to write her second-wave feminist novel *Fear of Flying*, Jesse Helms "bombarded the NEA with demands that the director explain why he was using public money to fund a 'reportedly filthy, obscene book,'" which despite his objection Helms claimed to have never read.[30]

Jonathan, who served on the Literature Panel at the time, remembers a consistent worry among panelists in the early 1970s that funding individual writers put them at risk: "There was a lot of worry, always at the [NEA] that the General Accounting Office would audit grantees, and that they would discover that these guys [weren't spending the money in ways that would be approved of by those who opposed the funding]. . . . Like, Allen Ginsberg sent us a letter [at the NEA] saying, 'Thank you very much for the $2,500 grant. I bought a Volkswagen bus and gave it to Charlie Plymell, who has been driving around the country giving poetry readings and selling dope.' If [the GAO] got their hands on that it would all be over."[31]

Despite political threats, Len Randolph, who would serve as director until 1978, saw it as his mission to fund working writers. His solution to the problem of critical conservative legislators who could target individual writers and works for attack was to "hide" the funding of writers through institutions. Randolph accomplished this by providing seed and grant money to a wide range of programs and organizations that employed working writers: programs for poetry in the schools, creative writing in the prisons, and MFA programs, "really anything in which writers could be paid for not doing much work," as Jonathan recalls. Because multiple funding sources were attractive to the NEA in proposals, MFA programs, which could also attract matching funds from state governments and facilities and supplies from the universities at which they would be housed, were particularly desirable. If the NEA could provide seed money, it was argued, student tuition would also make MFA programs self-sustaining and self-replicating. Under Randolph's direction, MFA programs were preferable because things like "poetry in the prisons would never be revenue neutral." There was concern expressed by some on the Literature Panel, however, that paying working novelists to teach in MFA programs was cynical, as it would ultimately be program students who would end up paying their salaries. As Jonathan remembers it, "Reynolds Price once stood up at a meeting and said 'We're misleading these people [i.e., students] into believing that if they take an MFA they can make a living as a writer, and we all know that's not going to happen. They can only make a living teaching other people and it's dishonest of us to say otherwise.'"

The cynicism of the remunerative system notwithstanding, MFA programs in creative writing and authorial advances created new income streams—and in the former case *steady* income streams—to novelists in the expansive and uncertain middle. While it cannot be discounted that these income streams are generated at least partially on the backs of MFA students who incur debt in pursuit of their writerly aspirations, by 2009, MFA programs had diffused so widely that they constituted, according to Stanford English professor Mark McGurl, "the largest system of literary patronage for living writers the world has ever seen."[32]

In addition to paying working writers salaries for limited teaching, the wide adoption of MFA programs, although not by design, has also arguably generated revenue to authors through book sales, as unlike primary and undergraduate curricula, which lean on classics and modern classics, MFA programs are oriented toward newer works. As an editor at a publishing house explained, "Maybe unlike English departments which have traditionally not created readers for contemporary work, MFA programs do. . . . These creative writing students who are in MFA programs, they don't read old books. . . . If the AWP newsletter notes a book, they'll see it and you can sell hundreds if not thousands of copies into the MFA market. Not as classroom adoption, it's just the books that everybody's reading that season." While providing income for midlist authors, MFA programs in creative writing have also arguably diversified income to novelists along lines of both race and gender, at least at the top of their respective markets (see Figure 3.4). Although MFA programs, like the fields of creation and production for writing more generally, are disproportionately and often overwhelmingly white, nonwhite authors make up 18 percent of faculty of the top twenty MFA programs in the country, compared to 5 percent of fiction authors who make it onto the *New York Times* best-seller list.[33] There is also more gender parity within the faculty of the top twenty MFA departments than at the top of the book market, although overall parity between the sexes still falls short in both arenas (see Figure 3.4).

In addition to the increased size of authorial advances since the 1980s, MFA programs in creative writing have in effect done what they were intended to do: increased the living incomes for a wider swath of novelists who would otherwise be susceptible to the capriciousness of the consumer

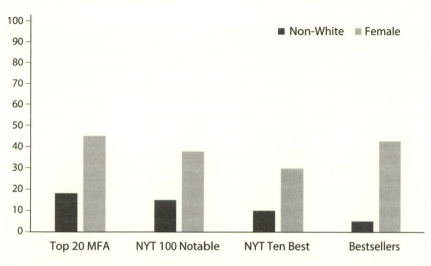

FIGURE 3.4: Percentage Representation Nonwhite, Female.
Source: 2014 MFA rankings *Poets & Writers*. Notable, ten best, and bestsellers Griswold and Wohl (2015).

book market. The stable income from MFA programs is perhaps most important for those who may otherwise not be novelists: those without families and friends who can financially afford to subsidize—and sometimes simply *pay for*—a career as a novelist. While the market has expanded income for those at the top in the name economy and less so for those in the middle, non-consumer-market forces for literature have caused the twenty-first century to perhaps be the most financially remunerative period in American history for authors overall. Albeit almost entirely overlooked by sociologists, as has been written by Chad Harbach, "the university now rivals, if it hasn't surpassed, New York as the economic center of the literary fiction world."[34] While by design this has increased and stabilized the incomes of already working novelists, at the same time it has saddled many of the next generation of novelists with even more debt from student loans.

DOWN AT THE BOTTOM

Market forces have pushed the income of top-selling authors to new heights, and in the expansive and uncertain middle authors have some newfound respite from the unpredictability of the market through larger authorial advances and numerous teaching positions in MFA programs. For writers at the bottom of the income distribution—those below even the expansive and uncertain middle—technological changes have increased their potential income, although these increases should not be overstated. Self-publishing is itself not a recent phenomenon, and just as the technological advancement of word processing in the late twentieth century increased its viability, technological advancements in production and distribution again dramatically increased its viability in the twenty-first century. By 2014, self-published books released in the United States outnumbered industry-published titles, to say nothing of eBooks.

The very bottom of the income heap is still, however, disproportionately populated by self-published authors, some of whom, unlike industry-published authors, even experience negative financial returns on their writing. That does not mean that there are no self-published authors who are members of the name economy or write in the expansive and uncertain middle. If anything, authors who entered the name economy via self-publishing, like Hugh Howey and Amanda Hocking, are black swans; their success has in part exacerbated the conditions under which unknown authors can fall prey to scams in the self and vanity publishing sectors.

Targeting such self-published and would-be self-published novelists are those who are hoping to generate income not from the work of authors but out of the authors' own pockets. This includes classes of "agents" who charge reading or submission fees, "publishers" who charge submission or publishing fees, contests that charge submission fees or are purely in the business of selling anthologies to those who are included in them, and sundry books, self-help courses, seminars, webinars, workshops, retreats, and the like that suggest that there are tricks or insider secrets that, for a fee, can unlock the gates to even a modest income from writing books. That these promises are untrue clearly signals the real business these people are in. More recently these tactics at profit generation have included the selling of author "services" such as developmental editing and copyediting, cover design, typesetting, upload fees, and profit-generating transaction costs on download sales. Historically these types of services have been taken on by publishers that need a book to sell in order to generate returns, whereas today these revenues are generated out of authors' pockets regardless of sales.[35] Generating income from authors is no small business either. With the usual caveats about poor data aside, one recent survey of self-published authors found that the modal author earns less than $500 in sales, while spending on average $685 in direct costs.[36] Howey, the outlier success story and most public face of self-publishing, has suggested that new self-published authors should publish their first books as "loss leaders," taking on writerly debt in the hopes that they will eventually reverse their income stream.[37]

TABLE 3.1: Income from Writing for Self-Published and Contract-Published Authors

	SELF-PUBLISHED(%)	CONTRACT-PUBLISHED(%)
No Income	19	6
$1–$4,999	63	34
$5,000–$19,999	9	22
$20,000–$59,999	5	24
$60,000+	4	14

Source: Weinberg 2013.
Note: *N* = 3,238. Due to self-reports and nonrepresentative convenience sampling, this table should be read as no more than suggestive of general income-level trends across groups, which are found across surveys.

While there are good arguments for authors who are *already* part of the name economy to self-publish, for the modal unknown author simply hoping to be read, most often self-publishing makes sense only when and if all other options have been exhausted (see Table 3.1).

This logic is not lost on those who self-publish, as the majority of self-published authors would prefer to publish with a publishing house.[38] Yet still, while self-published authors must navigate the land mines of opportunistic "allies" who generate revenue by providing them services for which the fees will likely never be recouped, it's difficult to argue that self-published authors today are not better off than those in the twentieth century. From the perspective of the self-published, that they receive any economic returns is an improvement over twentieth-century arrangements, to say nothing of the fact that technological advancements in distribution allow for something that is perhaps even more important to some self-published writers than financial return: to have their creative works widely available to be read at all.

HOW $6,000 BECOMES A MIDDLE-CLASS INCOME

In 1969, Mario Puzo's *The Godfather* was released. Puzo had previously written two novels, *The Dark Arena* and *The Fortunate Pilgrim*. The *New York Times* and other venues gave them strong reviews as nuanced and intimate works of literary fiction, though neither sold well. For both books, on which he spent over a decade, Puzo had earned a combined $6,500. By the time he started *The Godfather* Puzo was forty-five years old and over $20,000 in debt to his family and various loan sharks. He wrote *The Godfather* because, as he later said, he was "tired of being an artist. . . . So I told my editors OK, I'll write a book about the Mafia, just give me some money."[39] Yet like most authors outside the name economy, nobody had predicted Puzo would attain fame. Puzo's publisher, Athenaeum Press, rejected *The Godfather*. "They were courteous. They were kind. They showed me the door," he later recalled.[40] Puzo, fresh off his most recent failure and deep in debt, had decided to give up writing entirely until, on a chance encounter, he ended up contracting *The Godfather* to G. P. Putnam's Sons. While Putnam believed in the book enough to publish it, their hopes were not high, and thus they gave him a $5,000 advance for the manuscript; Puzo's monetary compensation for decades of writing now amounted to $11,500.[41]

Although harder to see in hindsight, the improbability of *The Godfather*'s success, even after it had been contracted, was clear to the entire Puzo family: "I remember one day when I was working on it. My wife sent me to the supermarket; my daughter asked me to drive her to her girlfriend's; my son wanted a ride to football practice. I exploded. I said, 'Jesus Christ, do you guys know I'm working on a book that could make me a hundred thousand dollars?' They looked at me and we all laughed together."[42] Although Puzo would end up entering the hallowed halls of the name economy, these parts of his story—his debt, his despair, his hand being financially forced to stop writing well-reviewed "art," his giving up entirely on his authorial career as his financial failure continued—are rarely told. The nearly impossible odds are omitted from the story of his success.

In 2009, forty years after the publication of *The Godfather*, Cornelia Nixon had, like Puzo, published two well-reviewed but poorly selling novels. Just as Puzo had hoped of *The Godfather*, *Jarrettsville* represented for Nixon her best shot at entering the name economy: "I hoped that [*Jarrettsville*] would lift my career out of the midlist doldrums, of getting great reviews and then not having readers." Nixon, like Puzo, had experience with how unpredictable success is for novelists. In her long career she had seen no shortage of what she believed to be mediocre novels go on to great acclaim and financial awards. She had also seen no shortage of what she believed to be exquisite novels be quickly forgotten, if ever noticed at all. Yet, she still hoped that luck would strike with *Jarrettsville*, and that it would beat the odds. "That's my shot," she thought, "that's my blockbuster."

While there are some parallels between the stories of Nixon and Puzo, there are differences as well. Unlike Puzo, Nixon did not write *Jarrettsville* while being "tired of being an artist," nor did she *need* to write the novel for income. Nixon was not in debt while working on her would-be blockbuster, nor had she ever considered giving up writing entirely. Although some of these differences could be dismissed as quirks of personality, Puzo and Nixon were also writing in different periods and under different conditions. While Puzo wrote in what has been remembered as a golden age for literary fiction, en masse the conditions under which he wrote were actually much more difficult than those today. Puzo's early career predated the rapid growth in authorial advances and the rise of MFA programs. He considered giving up not because he was sick of writing, but because it was no longer financially feasible to write. Nixon, on the other hand, did not feel compelled to choose between making art and making money, or choose between making money and writing at all.

Cornelia Nixon has never had to live off her advances or sales, as across her literary career she has worked as a professor of English and later creative writing. When she received a $10,000 advance for *Now You See It* in 1991, she could use it to buy a celebratory new car, as she already had a stable income as an associate professor at Indiana University, a job from which she made about $75,000 a year.[43] Her poet husband was also a professor earning a steady income, which in the same year that *Now You See It* was released allowed them to purchase "a great house with a big yard on a quiet street" in Bloomington for about $130,000. In 1998, because they spent their long summers off in Berkeley, for about $350,000 they bought the condo in the Berkeley Hills in which she still lived, with its view of the San Francisco Bay and writing desk on which she admittedly did not write. Several years later, in the same year that her second novel, *Angels Go Naked*, was released, with Young she moved full-time to the Berkeley condo after having accepted a professorship at Mills College in Oakland. It's about a twenty-minute drive from her condo to the tranquil Mills campus, and the Starbucks where she writes, across the street from UC Berkeley, is only a two-minute detour off this path. To move from Indiana University to Mills, Nixon had to temporarily surrender her full professorship and regress to the associate level, and the cost of living in Berkeley was also higher, but so was the quality of life, she figured. Moving from Bloomington to Berkeley was the type of decision that a financially stable person could make. While writing *Jarrettsville* Nixon was a full professor at Mills, and during the writing process she also became the director of creative writing, and later was given an endowed chair. By *Jarrettsville*'s release, on paper at least, she was making about $125,000 annually at Mills, and as had always been the case, with the income from her professorship she didn't need the advance from *Jarrettsville* to pay the bills.

To understand Nixon's creative process, from where she writes to how she writes and what she writes, one must understand the indirect route through which she earns income by writing. As a consequence of her novels she earned her position at Mills, and as a consequence of her position at Mills she earns a living. Unlike in previous eras, as a result of a conscious strategy of governmental intervention, Nixon can indirectly earn a stable income through her writing without being under the threat of censure for what she writes and without the continuation of her writing career predicated on a misplaced fealty to the wild and irreducible uncertainty of the marketplace for novels. Nixon is a relatively privileged author in a relatively advantageous time for authors, and her ability to have a career as a novelist is less dependent on luck than would have been the case at any time in the past. For novelists, it is, after all, almost entirely a twenty-first-century phenomenon that irregular $6,000 advances can be turned into a stable and middle-class income.

PART II

FROM CREATION TO PRODUCTION

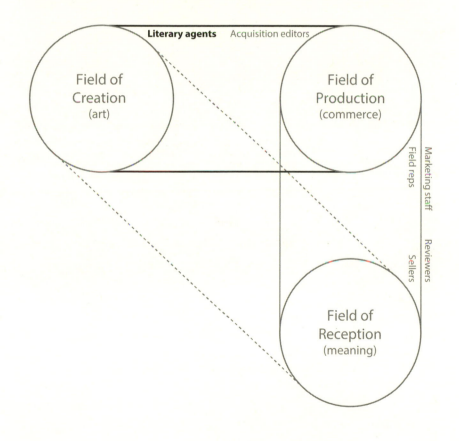

LITERARY AGENTS AND DOUBLE DUTIES

OR, WHY AN AUTHOR'S SUCCESS IS OUT OF HER CONTROL

NOWUCIT, NOW YOU DON'T

In the fall of 1981, when Cornelia Nixon first started her job as an assistant professor in the English Department at Indiana University, she was a literary critic by training with a passion for fiction writing. But before obtaining her PhD in English, Nixon wrote her first novel as an undergraduate at UC Irvine and a second as an MFA student at San Francisco State; neither ever saw the light of day. Despite having an MFA in creative writing, a PhD in English, a prestigious job as an assistant professor, and two early unpublished novels under her belt, she still did not know exactly *how* someone becomes a novelist. She knew how to write a novel, and even how to critically analyze and teach a novel, but how to *publish* a novel was still foreign to her. Nixon's nascent fiction career began when Clint McCown, then editor of the *Indiana Review* literary magazine, suggested she send him something. She sent him the short story "Killing Snakes," which was published in *Indiana Review* soon thereafter. Her colleague Scott Sanders then encouraged her to submit an unsolicited short story to the *Michigan Quarterly Review*; "Snapshot" was published there in 1985. It was also at Indiana University that Nixon met Dean Young, an upstart poet and her soon-to-be husband. Before meeting Young, Nixon was confident in her ability to write creatively, but, as she described it, Young exposed her to the larger field of writing creatively and how one staked one's claim in it. The literary magazines she had been publishing in, Nixon learned from Young, could be used to begin to build her reputation in the field of creation, and more importantly could be catalysts to shepherd her work into the field of production. Although literary magazines had existed in the United States since the early nineteenth century, they had gone through three waves of growth in the twentieth. The third wave, rising during the 1990s, was the perfect time and place for Nixon to make her debut as a fiction writer through them.

The first wave of literary magazines growth occurred in the 1950s, with the rise of small presses and declining printing costs mitigating two of the most onerous barriers to entry. The second wave occurred in the 1970s following the 1967 founding of the Coordinating Council of Literary Magazines (CCLM; now CLMP). Both the CCLM and the second wave of literary magazines it ushered in were funded by a familiar source: seed grants from the NEA's Literature Panel, as chaired by Len Randolph. When Nixon was introduced to the literary magazine scene in the early 1990s, it was in the third wave of growth, as the magazines neatly followed the rise of the MFA programs that housed them. As the number and size of MFA programs expanded, their literary magazines provided legitimacy and outlets for the expanding supply of short stories that were being produced within them. As a result, the rise of MFA programs in the field of creation created both a supply and a demand for short stories as a form of creative writing, in addition to the institutional spaces in which they could be published and flourish.

Although not entirely by design, literary magazines also provided a contact point between unknown writers and literary agents who might read their works and shepherd them into the field of production. In decreasing literary agents' search costs, there was however a mismatch in content. At the same time that literary magazines began their most recent rise, the publishing industry was beginning to move away from investing in short story collections under the belief that collections by non-name-economy authors did not sell well. While for MFA-centered writers publishing short stories in respected literary magazines could serve as a reputational end in itself, for those in the field of production literary magazines were a farm league to be scouted: they were coordinated gatherings of talent, likely containing the next generation of publishable literary novelists.

With the contours, hierarchies, and functions of literary magazines learned from Dean Young, Nixon placed five more short stories over the course of six years, including "Affection" in *Ploughshares*, arguably the top nonprofit literary magazine in the United States, having been supported through NEA grants since soon after its founding in 1971. "Affection" drew interest from three literary agents, all of whom, in straddling the fields of creation and production, understood the rules of both. Knowing that short story collections were on the outs among publishers, all three agents approached Nixon similarly: "They read 'Affection' but did not ask, 'Do you have a collection of *short stories* that I could read?' but [instead said], 'If you have a *novel*, I'd love to see it.'" Nixon sent them *Now You See It*, a novel constructed out of interlocking short stories. Although the "novel in stories" device had appeared as early as 1919 with the publication of Sherwood Anderson's *Winesburg, Ohio* (reviewers didn't know what to make of it), by the 1990s and more clearly into the 2000s, it had become a creative solution to resolve unbalanced interests across the fields of creation and reception. While literary authors were writing short stories and literary readers seemed to prefer novels, the "novel in stories" was a compromise of sorts that publishers used to reconcile intra-field differences.

Nixon signed with the first literary agent to respond to her novel in stories. Her agent intimately understood the field of production, and perhaps even more importantly, was well connected in it. Within two weeks Nixon's agent had secured interest from editors at three major publishing houses. Two of these editors, at Crown and Knopf, were interested but requested major rewrites. The editor at Knopf, the most prestigious of the presses, wanted the "novel in stories" device to be ditched entirely and for the manuscript to be rewritten as a single narrative; might this new author from the field of creation show deference to the fields of production and reception, the editor was asking. The third editor, at Little, Brown, not only understood the story as Nixon herself understood it, but was enthusiastic and ready to publish it without changes. Nixon's agent strongly advised her to sign with Little, Brown and secured her a $10,000 advance. Because Nixon had a steady income from her job as professor, rather than needing the $10,000 for living expenses, she splurged on a red Honda CRX sports car, with a celebratory license plate reading "NOWUCIT."

For Nixon's literary agent, the editor at Little, Brown, Patricia Mulcahy, was clearly the right choice to shepherd *Now You See It* to the field of production. For Nixon's agent, knowing the rules of the game, it was Mulcahy's enthusiasm for the novel that made the decision clear. And she was right. On the wings of Mulcahy's enthusiasm, *Now You See It* made it into the hands of Michiko Kakutani, the book critic for the *New York Times*, and likely the most well-known book reviewer in the United States. As Nixon recalls it, "Mulcahy told me that she hadn't asked Kakutani to review anything for a while. She'd been saving it up [i.e., holding back on asking until she had something special]. She said she could get [*Now You See It*] to the top of [Kakutani's] pile but there was no telling if she was going to review it or not. She heard a little rumor the week before that maybe Kakutani was going to do it. And that's the last we heard until that beautiful Friday."

Even if Nixon had rewritten all of *Now You See It* into a single narrative, would the editors at Crown or Knopf have had enough enthusiasm for it to cash in that chip with Kakutani? Likely not, but validating Nixon's agent's expertise, Mulcahy had. Almost twenty years later Nixon still remembers the day: "March 29th, 1991, it was the happiest day of my life. It was 6:00 in the morning and I was getting screaming phone calls from New York City because it was hitting the doorsteps." In a review that was effusive in its praise, *Now You See It* was, according to Kakutani, "a luminous and compelling book" and Nixon was a "wonderfully talented new writer," with a "thoroughly original voice . . . that moves fluently from the poetic to the visceral."[1] Accompanying the review was a picture of Nixon, taken by her husband, whose help set Nixon down this path. On the signal of Kakutani's glowing review, Nixon's agent secured an additional $10,000 for the paperback rights to *Now You See It*, which, with the red Honda already paid for, "probably got blown at the grocery store," Nixon figured.

Today, a blown-up picture of Kakutani's *Times* review, gifted to her by Little, Brown, still hangs framed in Nixon's office at Mills College. From having read a short story of Nixon's in *Ploughshares*, her agent had taken her from an obscure assistant professor of English to a published and celebrated novelist with book advances in the five figures and a glowing review from the most well-known critic at the most influential outlet in the United States. Nixon's childhood dream had all at once become a reality, and it was her literary agent who had made it happen.

Though Nixon would never forget this and twenty years later was still incredibly grateful for it, she would soon fire her agent. Nixon did not fire her agent because she thought they'd outgrown one another, or because the success of the novel had gone to her head. By Nixon's own account, it was her agent's business acumen that got her to where she was, and it was a business acumen that Nixon still believes is unrivaled. Yes, Nixon's agent had indeed successfully placed *Now You See It*, but Nixon increasingly worried that there were other meaningful things her agent did not see or do. What were they? To understand why Nixon fired her literary agent, one must first understand how agents' role has developed over time, and how they go about their work of constructing bridges across the divide between the fields of creation and production.

FROM SINGLE TO DOUBLE DUTIES

The first literary agency on record in the United States was founded in 1893 in New York City by Paul Revere Reynolds, a descendent of the famed revolutionary Paul Revere.[2] It was Reynolds's son, however, also a literary agent and also named Paul Revere Reynolds, who most succinctly described the job of literary agents with the title of his 1971 book, *The Middle Man*. In the senior Reynolds's time and across the majority of the junior Reynolds's career, literary agents were involved in the "business side" of book publishing. Their primary role was the handling of publishing rights between authors and publishers, and many of them were lawyers engaging in sideline contractual work. In this arrangement, as contractual brokers between authors and publishers, literary agents were the classic "support personnel" of Becker's art worlds, as it was the job of authors to be creative and the job of literary agents to ensure that mostly boilerplate contractual language was in fact boilerplate.

In this older model it was acquisition editors in publishing houses who served as the point people for the safe passage of novels from creation to production. This "double duty" taken on by editors allowed them to work with authors for all matters of artistic concern and with the author's agent for all matters of financial concern; authors and agents could focus on "separate spheres" of art and commerce within the same transaction, while editors navigated relational exchanges with both.[3] Many publishers preferred working on financial matters with agents because, unlike authors, they were well versed in the norms of contracts in the field of production, and could differentiate between the meaningful and trivial, as well as reasonable and unreasonable when making requests. With one set of conversations to be had with authors and an entirely different set of conversations to be had with agents, editors served double duties in a way that mitigated against any cross-pollination of field-specific talk. Throughout much of the twentieth century, however, having a literary agent was not the norm but a luxury mostly reserved for name-economy authors for whom the dollar amounts were larger and ancillary rights more complex. In tracking the rising presence of literary agents between authors and editors, Eric de Bellaigue estimates that 10 to 12 percent of published authors were agented prior to World War II, around 50 percent by the 1960s, 90 percent by the late 1990s, and somewhere closer to 99.5 percent of all authors with books at major trade houses were agented by 2008.[4]

John B. Thompson attributes the rise of literary agents in the late 1960s and early 1970s to a multitude of factors; a primary one was the overall growth of the market for books caused by both the rise of chain bookstores and a growing college-educated population.[5] With the resultant rise in revenues for authors, there was greater need for complex negotiations and rights management due to synergistic media strategies (e.g., television and movie deals) and multimarket global publishing rights. At the same time, the conglomeration and consolidation of publishing firms led to: (1) an increased workload for editors who had less time to hunt for new talent in the "slush pile" of unagented submissions, (2) a pool of laid-off acquisition editors with the cognitive know-how for selecting and revising manuscripts, and (3) increased barriers to entry for employment at publishing firms at a time when literary agents were in need. At the same time that publishing firms were laying off editorial staff, anyone, including a laid-off editor, could call herself a literary agent and sign authors from a home office. Some former editors even preferred their new work as literary agents, and saw it as closer to the work they had done at an earlier time as editors.[6]

As conglomerated publishers grew larger and editors were tasked with taking on more projects, the "discovery" of new talent in the field of creation was almost entirely farmed out to literary agents, some of whom had consolidated into firms. Whereas publishers had, in the past, sometimes recommended agents to the authors of manuscripts they would receive and develop, these roles were now inverted, with agents taking on the task of "discovering" and honing manuscripts before delivering them to publishing houses and editors they might "fit" with. As recently as the early 1980s, Coser, Kadushin, and Powell lamented that some major publishing houses had gone as far as to cease accepting unagented manuscripts, but by the 2000s no major trade publishing houses in the United States would consider such submissions.[7] These shifts fundamentally changed the structural relationships of authors, agents, and editors, as literary agents became the primary boundary spanners across the fields of creation and production.

As the jobs of literary agents diversified, their role also expanded from contract negotiation and rights management to include a new set of services: (1) the discovery of authors in the field of creation, (2) direct engagement with artistic concerns such as the development and editing of manuscripts, and (3) a greater role in long-term career management for authors. As such, literary agents went from solely dealing with contractual rights to taking on double duties and managing *both* artistic and financial concerns with authors. In this arrangement, double duties were taken on by both agents and editors, and over time they developed a localized and blended pidgin language with one another, which may be only partially decipherable to those on either side of them. By way of example, for an editor to tell an agent that her author's manuscript is in a "crowded" space is to euphemistically say three things at once: from an artistic perspective the work is lacking; from a commercial perspective there is too much competition for this work to likely succeed; and from a relational perspective (between editor and agent) declining to offer a contract for the work under question should not be read as a slight or as disinterest in doing future business.

With this transition from single to double duties, former acquisition editors who became agents had the simple advantage of having *already* developed double-duty skills in their previous jobs. The expanding role of the literary agent, at the same time, also created another monetary pull factor from working as an editor to working as an agent, as an agent's share of financial rewards from an author's publication increased. During the 1990s, the customary commission for literary agents for domestic contracts increased from 10 percent to 15 percent, with commission on foreign rights sometimes rising to 20 percent today. As literary agents have fully transformed themselves from serving contractual duties to double duties, which span both art and commerce, their share of the rewards has also increased.

LITERARY AGENTS TODAY

Today, literary agencies are still relatively small-scale operations, ranging from a single agent working from her dining room table to ten to twenty literary agents operating under the same roof with a small support staff.[8] Agents consolidated into agencies for three reasons, two of which were financial, and the third of which was due to their position as boundary spanners between two fields. By coordinating into teams agents could manage their two financial concerns by decreasing each individual's operating costs, while also pooling the risk of all working in an unequal and uncertain market.[9] The formation of literary agencies also ameliorated a third concern over legitimacy, as agents are boundary spanners between two fields and the occupation has always attracted predators. The role of not-quite literary agent is an attractive one for predators, as literary agents allow would-be authors to mostly remain oblivious to standard operating procedure in the field of production. In a generally unregulated occupation that serves a high-desire and often low-information population, it is perhaps inevitable that predators would emerge. For this reason, consolidating into agencies, rather than working out of their homes, also allowed real literary agents to further differentiate themselves from purported literary agents.

In 1901, H. T. Bensonhurst of Long Island, New York, wrote a letter published in the *New York Times* explaining that he had written a manuscript and, not knowing any publishers, replied to advertisements he found in the *Times* from literary agents seeking authors. He was troubled to learn that the agents who responded, rather than working to secure him a publishing contract and taking a commission if the efforts were successful, wanted him to pay up front and out-of-pocket for their services. Sixty-five years later the younger Paul Revere Reynolds remarked on the phenomenon of agents charging authors for services by explaining that "a number of the people listed as agents are not really agents, but predatory sharks."[10] Today, well over a century after Bensonhurst's letter, the game is remarkably unchanged, and if anything it has only intensified in the twenty-first century with the growth of alternative publishing channels. While authors and perhaps even cohorts of authors have grown wise to the ruse, for those who are in fact sharks posing as agents, the seabed down at the bottom of the authorial economy in the field of creation is constantly replenished with an oversupply of hopeful fish, many of whom are generally unfamiliar with the predatory waters they've wandered into.

To lack a reputation for legitimacy comes with great costs for literary agents, and to be a legitimate agent means to be a true boundary spanner between fields. Most simply put, legitimate agents earn income from the future sales of an author's work in the field of production rather than out of authors' pockets in the field of creation. Coupled with the oversupply of authors who want access to the field of production and the uncertainties of working on commission in a fluke-based market, the two rules of legitimacy for literary agents are as follows:

1. Due to oversupply, a literary agent who does not *discriminate* in the projects he or she works on is not actually a literary agent and is in fact a predator.
2. Due to uncertain demand, a literary agent who does not *take on risk* by having his or her long-term income ultimately dependent on the successes or failures of the projects taken on is not actually a literary agent and is in fact a predator.[11]

As a result, those who do not discriminate in the authors they work with and those who derive income out of authors' pockets through reading, evaluation, and marketing fees are not actually literary agents, but merely masquerading as such while working under an illegitimate business model.[12] Put another way, rather than literary agents of the past who dealt only with contractual obligations, literary agents who today *do not* serve double duties by equally investing their time and reputations on artistic concerns are viewed with such suspicion that they're dismissed as not really even being literary agents at all. Unlike their predecessors, agents today not only stake their incomes on the books and authors they represent, but build their professional reputations through them as well.

Given the existence of predators, how do literary agents achieve legitimacy, particularly if they are new to the profession and lack reputation? Many new literary agents achieve reputational legitimacy by having already worked in the field of production prior to becoming agents—about two-thirds of currently working literary agents have previously worked for publishers—or through reputational spillover from the agency or agent they work for.[13] Established literary agents, on the other hand, can also confirm their legitimacy through recounting the name-economy authors they've represented, which signals both *what* they are (i.e., a *legitimate* literary agent) and *who* they are (i.e., a legitimate literary agent who works on certain types of books). Literary agents can also establish legitimacy through membership in the Association of Authors' Representatives (AAR).[14]

Distilled to its simplest function, the strict entry requirements for the AAR and its code of ethics work in tandem to exclude any predators masquerading as literary agents from membership. Achieving AAR membership is no fly-by-night affair, as one must possess: (1) the institutionalized cultural capital of having successfully completed at least ten deals in the previous eighteen months, (2) the social capital required to attain letters of reference from two current AAR members, and (3) the economic capital to pay the initiation fees and dues for membership. The AAR's eight-point code of ethics covers a wide array of business practices, including legitimate and illegitimate charges, the timing and handling of payments to authors, and more general legitimate and illegitimate ways for agents to earn money.[15] While AAR membership can serve as an important signal of legitimacy to authors in the field of creation on one side and editors in the field of production on the other, this does not mean that every legitimate literary agent in the United States is an AAR member. Andrew Wylie, for instance, likely the most well-known US literary agent and famous for ushering in the transition in practice from agents operating as "double agents" for publishers to unapologetic advocates for authors, is not an AAR member.

While legitimate agents may or may not be AAR members, membership and the signal it conveys is most important for younger agents and those at the margins who must find a higher proportion of their authors through unsolicited author queries. Interestingly, it is the sincere and legitimate agents who are most restricted by the AAR's entry requirements who are in fact most *in need* of its legitimating imprimatur. As a result of this phenomenon, AAR membership can be a meaningful signal of legitimacy at the same time that nonmembership is basically meaningless: nonmembers may be way too illegitimate to procure membership, or way too legitimate to bother. Nonetheless, when comparing AAR members to the full population of literary agents in the United States, differences do arise (see Figure 4.1).

Overall, literary agents are overwhelmingly white (94 percent), and AAR members are slightly more so. AAR members are also more likely than nonmember agents to be women, to have offices in New York City, and to represent

FIGURE 4.1: Characteristics of Literary Agents in the United States for AAR Members and Non-members.
Note: *N* = 1,193.

"literary" or "upmarket" fiction. In fact, the modal literary agent is a white woman who works in New York City—a suite of characteristics that describes 38 percent of all literary agents in the United States. Most importantly, however, these demographics of literary agents do not just tell us who agents are, but also correlate with what they do, and how they decide which books to represent.

HOW DO LITERARY AGENTS MAKE DECISIONS?

From the vantage point of the field of creation, and particularly from the vantage point of authors who cannot find an agent to shepherd their work into the field of production, a literary agent is simply a gatekeeper. Like the spectators in a Roman coliseum, an agent's thumbs-up or -down can signal the future or end of a writer's life as a non-self-published author. Within this field transition, getting a thumbs-up is rare. Scott Hoffman, the cofounder of Folio Literary Management, estimates that at his agency for every unsolicited author query that eventually leads to representation, over eleven thousand are rejected. Put another way, all things being equal, Hoffman estimates a 0.009 percent chance that his agency takes on any given unsolicited manuscript.[16] Although agents spend some of their day guarding the gates of the field of production, gatekeeping is only a small part of what they do. For authors who cannot find representation, agents *are* gatekeepers to publishing, but from agents' perspective they are more like explorers or discoverers; rather than keeping people out they are on the hunt for authors they can bring in. In a sympathetic reading of the oversupply problem that agents face due to the winnowing function they serve, Michael Bourne, book review editor for *The Millions*, presents a thought experiment:

> Imagine that one night you have a dream in which you are in an enormous bookstore lined with shelves upon shelves of books, each bound in the same plain white cover displaying only the author's name, the title of the book, and a brief description of the book and its author. This is an anxiety dream, so it turns out that your livelihood depends on your ability to search this enormous bookstore and figure out which books are good and which aren't. The thing is, in this bookstore, the vast majority of the books are bad—trite, derivative, poorly written, or simply the sort of book you would never read in a million years. You know there are some really good books in this store, maybe even one or two genuinely great ones, but from the outside they're indistinguishable from the terrible ones.[17]

With this predicament simply a part of daily life for literary agents, as Bourne suggests, the only feasible solution for literary agents is to look for shortcuts: are there authors whose names are recognizable to the agent, and have some of the submissions come with recommendations from others whose judgments the agent trusts? Rather than dedicating their entire working lives to finding needles that may or may not exist in haystacks, literary agents employ two other strategies: (1) avoiding the haystack as much as possible by proactively looking for authors instead of only reactively receiving their queries, and (2) decreasing the size of the haystack through specialization. In this way, while literary agents are in fact gatekeepers into the field of production, they strategically work to reduce the amount of active gatekeeping they have to do; they'd prefer to act as the liaison between authors and editors who might fit together.

As it is the job of an agent to pitch novels from the field of creation to production, agents keep a foot in each field, and spend significant amounts of their time familiarizing themselves with the local terrains of both. In order to avoid the haystack, agents regularly venture out into the field of creation, and through their search strategies, learn its subtleties and arrangements. For an agent who represents literary fiction this means knowing where and how to find new fiction authors who match the agent's specialization and sensibility, and hopefully having a stable of authors who keep their ears to the ground and can refer new talent. In the particular case of literary fiction, the rise of MFA programs in creative writing has made this task easier. Rather than being hidden and diffuse in the field of creation, many if not most of the next generation of literary fiction writers are now congregated into clusters that can also sometimes be further winnowed by creative writing professors, either with whom an agent works directly or whose taste and evaluations the agent trusts.[18]

Specialization is a second tool by which agents reduce the size of their haystacks. As agents are already inundated with too many manuscripts and not enough of what they believe to be the "right" manuscripts, through specialization they can exclude the majority at the outset. In Bourne's thought experiment, perhaps romance novels come with green covers and science fiction novels come with red covers; an agent who specializes in romance but not science fiction can exclude all the red covers before the real decisions have to be made. Specialization also allows agents to narrow down their skill set and expertise into representing the types of manuscripts for which they have an *emotional* connection.[19] The enthusiasm an agent hopes to feel for a manuscript is not simply a matter of preference or unchecked bias, as it also serves two key utilitarian purposes. First, as discussed above, it allows an agent to further specialize within the still too broadly defined realm of genre into the more amorphous realm of "taste" within genres. Second, unlike the agents of previous generations who handled only contractual obligations on the business side of publishing, because agents today serve double duties, having an emotional connection to the books they work on better allows them to work with authors to improve their manuscripts, be it through tweaking or radical rewriting. It is for this reason that literary agents must be familiar with the field of creation, not only to have the networks and social and symbolic capital to *find* and *impress* authors they'd like to represent, but also to fully immerse themselves in authors' creative processes, to be enthusiastic supporters of their work, and to intuitively understand their artistic intentions.

A reliance on emotional connection—most frequently operating through an agent's own tastes, interests, and experiences—is part of a three-prong strategy by which literary agents make evaluative decisions in their filtering from the field of creation to production (see Figure 4.2). The other two prongs are evaluative judgments on artistic ability (a logic afforded by keeping one foot in the field of creation) and evaluative judgments on market feasibility (a logic afforded by keeping one foot in the field of production). As the literary agent Jeff Kleinman describes his decision heuristics when

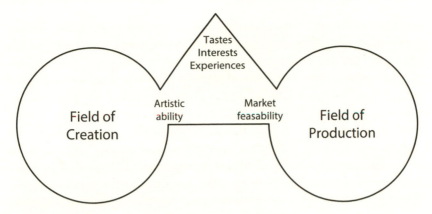

FIGURE 4.2: The Three Prongs of Agents' Evaluations.

taking on a new manuscript, "I have three criteria. The first is missing your subway stop. The second is gushing about it to any poor slob who will listen. The third is having editors in mind immediately."[20]

Sometimes these prongs can be complementary (e.g., an exceptionally well-written work of literary fiction might improve perceived market feasibility while also engaging an agent's fandom), although they are not always so (e.g., a book is artistic but hard to categorize, making market feasibility hard to predict; or it has great market potential on a topic the agent finds uninteresting). In turn, not all three prongs must bear equal weight for any book pitched, but two of the three legs must be strong and the third must at least bear some weight for an agent to consider a manuscript worthwhile. By way of real example of the role of tastes, interests, and experiences as a meaningful evaluative mechanism, consider an agent who in her profile on her literary agency's website explains to would-be authors that she would take keen interest in anything about her favorite baseball team, and stories set in one of the five places she has lived, including Brooklyn, where she now resides. It is far from irregular for this agent to prefer working on novels that overlap with her own interests and experiences, even if her public forthrightness and stated level of specificity is less typical. This need not be a problem in agents' filtering of novels from creation to production, as long as agents' tastes, interests, and experiences are diversified enough to match the diversity of those of would-be authors, publishers, and readers. Put another way, in selecting novels for pitching, that agents rely on a "cultural matching" of themselves to novels they work on need not by definition pose a problem, so long as agents are themselves diverse.[21] As highlighted in Figure 4.1, however, this is not the case, as at least for the cases of racial background and geographic residence, literary agents are overwhelmingly white and the plurality work in New York.

To the degree that these types of demographic characteristics map onto agents' tastes, interests, and experiences (or even map on to a *perception* of shared tastes, interests, and experiences based on race, gender, region, and so on), the lack of diversity among literary agents can pose problems for both authors who will end up underrepresented in the field of production and readers whose taste may be underserved in the field of reception. While there is a certain amount of felicity in an author finding an agent who is enthusiastic about her work, some authors, due to cultural matching, may find themselves with fewer spins at the wheel than others. Consider for instance a hypothetical white female author whose experiences and background are filtered through her fiction. This hypothetical author has nearly eight hundred literary agents in the United States who might connect with her work due to the shared experience of being a white woman in the United States, or a perception of shared experience based on shared background.[22] For Black male authors, however, in 2015 there were two findable Black male literary agents in the United States (fewer than one-fifth of 1 percent of all agents) who might connect with the manuscript due to the shared experience of being a Black male in the United States, or a perception of shared experience based on those demographic characteristics.

In this arrangement, in which authors are writing and agents are selecting manuscripts from the perspectives of their respective experiences, inequalities between groups are not created directly between people, but instead are filtered through novels themselves. As a result, nonwhite authors, whether they start out intending to or not, end up disproportionately competing for representation by the 6 percent of agents who are nonwhite. Consider for instance the Lebanese-English literary agent Nicole Aragi, who *New York Magazine* proclaimed has "done more [than anyone] to introduce us to this past decade's greatest young ethnic writers." Aragi openly acknowledges how her background imputes onto her tastes, experiences, and interests when selecting manuscripts: "In literature I was looking for something which reflected, in some way, my own experiences of living between different cultures. I think people read books in order to be entertained, but they also read books to understand themselves."[23] Although the basic process by which Aragi uses her own tastes, interests, and experiences in making selection decisions is normative among literary agents, it differs in effect because she is a woman of color in a white-dominated industry.[24] She describes possessing the experience of living "between different cultures" and

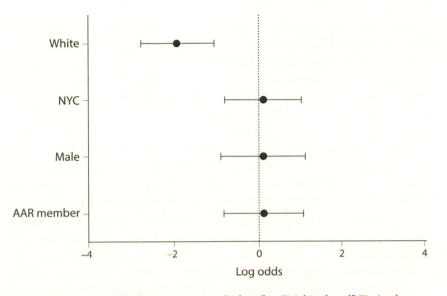

FIGURE 4.3: Log Odds for Representing "Ethnic" or "Multicultural" Fiction by Literary Agent Characteristics.
Note: $N = 1,131$. All controlling for total number of genres represented.

takes special interest in manuscripts that tell those stories in ways that feel real according to her experiences, just as the literary agent described above takes special interest in stories concerning her favorite baseball team, or set in cities in which she has lived.

As a result of the usage of cultural matching as a winnowing strategy, tool of specialization, and device through which to imbue enthusiasm into one's work, the demographic characteristics of literary agents can end up correlated with the types of fiction they seek to represent. Coupled with the demographic divergences of literary agents from the general population, literary fiction in the United States ends up disproportionately speaking to and about those who select it: New York–centered, middle- to upper-class, and white. This is seen clearly in Figure 4.3, as white literary agents are significantly less likely to self-report an interest in representing "ethnic" or "multicultural" fiction than are nonwhite literary agents. While this could alternatively be read as nonwhite agents being significantly more likely to be interested in representing ethnic or multicultural fiction than are white agents, the point remains that agents use their own tastes, interests, and experiences—including their ethnic racial backgrounds in the white/nonwhite binary space of "ethnic" or "multicultural" fiction—as one of three prongs when deciding which manuscripts to accept.

While this type of cultural matching is regularly expressed through the emotionally charged shorthand of *enthusiasm*, the other two prongs through which agents evaluate novels for passage from the field of creation to production can be just as important, as they map onto both sides of an agent's "double duties." In practical terms an agent's evaluation of a novelist's "artistic ability" is also a projection of her own creative time investment with the manuscript, and her evaluation of a novel's "market feasibility" is her projection of her business time investment. In these cases emotional connection to the material can be pitted against more pragmatic concerns: How much work is needed on the manuscript, how much emotional management does the author require, and how productive is she? If on balance the answers to these questions are "a lot," "a lot," and "a little," the emotional connection to the work must be exceptionally strong to reweight the project as one worth adopting.

As agents must work under conditions of uncertainty—they must invest time in a novel before knowing if they will be compensated through a cut of the author's advance if they can secure her a publishing deal—believing wholeheartedly in the potential of a novel is often a prerequisite to working on it. If an agent does not believe in a novel, her time could be better spent finding another novel she believes in more. As a result an agent may end up rejecting a manuscript he has strong enthusiasm for because he believes the artistic time investment is too large and the chance of market return too small. Damon, now a celebrated fiction and nonfiction author, remembers the first time he spoke to his agent over the phone, and how straightforward his agent was about his own calculations: "I remember when he called me that morning . . . and was like, 'I want to do this, and this, and that.' And I was young, I was like twenty-six or something. And I was like, 'Are you for real?' Because that was a fairly big agency. And then he was like, 'But I'm just going to let you know, if I can't get an advance of $30,000 it's not going to be worth it for me.' And, honestly, I didn't even know what that meant."

For Damon's agent, when weighing how much work he believed was necessary on the manuscript, the other projects he was or could be working on, and the likelihood of sale to a publisher, he valued his projected time investment at $4,500, or his 15 percent of the advance in the case of sale. For Damon, however, a Black Southern writer whose fiction was about the lives of Black Southern characters, the $30,000 advance that would make the project worth his agent's time eliminated the independent literary presses that Damon thought could better connect with the readers for whom he was writing: "He won't even look at Algonquin. He won't look at Graywolf. He won't look at a lot of these presses that I actually think would grasp what I'm trying to do a lot better. [With those presses] you don't have to synthesize much [i.e., translate yourself for a different audience] because that is their market, and they're good at marketing literary fiction to Southern people."

While an agent must weight her own enthusiasm and projected time investment in a new manuscript, she also must weigh her likelihood of matching the manuscript with a similarly enthusiastic editor, who is making his own calculations based upon perceived artistic ability, personal enthusiasm, market feasibility, and publisher fit. In these instances literary agents aren't so much gatekeepers as they are matchmakers for authors in the field of creation and editors in the field of production. When it comes to appropriately pitching and placing manuscripts, a literary agent is only as good as her connections, both superficial (i.e., a weak tie; does she know of the right editors to match manuscripts with, and do they know of her?) and deeper (i.e., a strong tie; do they *like* each other, *trust* each other, and, most important, *share* similar tastes and enthusiasms for some work over others?). As an editor described, "You're using the agent as a piece of information that describes something about the author and the project based on having worked with them. . . . So it's a trust. Trust is the basis for having a good relationship."

Agents tend to talk about their relationships with editors in concentric circles. Closest to the agent are several editor/friends with whom they do business on a semiregular basis. Another rung out is a circle of editors with whom they've sometimes done business and whose tastes, wants, and needs they can predict reasonably well. Last is a larger and more amorphous circle of editors with whom they have made deals once or twice and are not close. Rather than agent and editor relationships being based purely on shared dispositions or networked relations, it is a bit of both: agents and editors who trust and understand each other tend to work more together just as agents and editors who tend to work more together also increasingly trust and understand each other. When things are working well, their relationships deepen through repeated transactions and they can increasingly anticipate each other's needs and sensibilities, becoming not only simpatico but also more mutualistic in their dealings with each other.

With most literary agents and all of the major publishing houses located in Manhattan, agents and editors have historically developed their relationships face-to-face over long lunches and after-work drinks. While outsiders often viewed the bygone era of the "three martini lunch" as a symbol of profligate largesse, for agents and editors long lunches still serve the purpose of relationship building to smooth and refine the repeated exchange of manuscripts. In addition to getting to know one another—agents want to know editors so they can send them the *right* books (and not waste time on the wrong ones) and editors want to know agents so they can be sent the *right* books (and not waste time being sent wrong ones)—long lunches between agents and editors are infused with recreational information swapping. Between the boundaries of creation and production, agents and editors are able to swap information freely, as to do their jobs well they are both dependent on new information, and in working on one-off cultural goods such as novels, for the most part they do not have to be fearful about disclosing mostly nonexistent proprietary concerns.[25]

Networking with editors and other agents is still important for younger literary agents, but due to their lack of established relationships, they must also garner information through other means. Simone, an agent's assistant who would go on to become a full-fledged literary agent and AAR member, described how she used the daily Publishers Lunch email blast to garner the same information that more established agents and publishers swap over lunch: "It's good to keep up on what's happening in the business, and the daily deals are really great for knowing who is buying what [i.e., which editors are purchasing the types of books she hopes to someday represent]."[26] For a young agent's assistant like Simone who is not yet regularly having lunches, the insider knowledge she garners through Publishers Lunch while eating lunch alone at her desk is invaluable.

Another channel through which the "three martini lunch" has been supplemented can be found in the AAR newsletter, which in its "Up and Coming Editors" section publishes multipage profiles of new acquisition editors, which go into extraordinary detail about editors' backgrounds before mentioning what books they're looking to acquire. In a recent issue, for example, a literary agent could learn that one such new editor had, in sixth grade, moved to Chicago from Minnesota as his father finished up his PhD coursework, and grew up playing violin and guitar before spending a year in the Air Force Academy, where he had been recruited to play football. Not wanting to go to law school, to medical school, or into finance upon graduation (as all of his friends were, he stated), the new editor packed up his car and drove to New York, where he stayed with family and waited tables until his father (now a professor and writer) set him up as the assistant for an editor at the publisher that would eventually hire him. An interested agent could also learn that this editor, when not looking to acquire manuscripts dealing with "history, tech, music, sports . . . science, and pretty much anything that isn't memoir or fiction," spends his free time "liv[ing] out his unrealized NFL dreams" by playing Xbox—"I get embarrassingly sad when I lose," he shared. This editor, an agent could learn, was also looking to join an eighties cover band, although in his new job he did not have as much time to dedicate to music as he did before.

While it is easy to make light of the level of detail contained in the AAR's "Up and Coming" editorial biographies—they can feel like overly indulgent dating profiles—they contain, in effect, the types of things one might learn about someone over a long, slightly intoxicated and rambling lunch.[27] And due to the reliance on shared taste, interests, and experiences between agents and editors, the information contained in the AAR's editorial biographies is not superfluous. Instead, if an agent was representing a manuscript that was a history of the Air Force, an inside story of the Minnesota Vikings, or a history of music in Chicago, she would know that the profiled editor might be interested in seeing it, as long as it was not a work of fiction or a memoir.

In instances like these, rather than acting as a gatekeeper, a literary agent is not just a matchmaker, but also a translator. Unlike an author, an agent can take the logic of a manuscript from the field of creation and convert it into the language of shared taste and market feasibility with an editor. While an author might believe that her nonfiction book on gender relations in the Air Force is really an examination of gender relations more broadly, in pitching an editor an agent might repurpose the meaning of the book to be "really" about the inner workings of the Air Force, if just through the lens of gender relations. Or maybe the agent knows to skip some military enthusiast editors all together and head right to editors with an interest in gender relations, an entirely different suite of editors of whom the author also need not be aware.

From all their social interactions and due to all the blended languages they use in making sense of manuscripts, agents and editors are more like each other than anyone else who works on books, even though they metaphorically sit on opposite sides of the negotiating table. Good literary agents, just like good editors, due to their position between the fields of creation and production, possess equal fluency in the languages of art and business. Although Cornelia Nixon never doubted her literary agent's business acumen, she started to doubt her agent's fluency in both languages, which was what caused her to move on from the agent who had made her career.

WHY CORNELIA NIXON FIRED HER AGENT, AND HOW SHE FOUND HER NEXT ONE

It is undeniable that it was Cornelia Nixon's literary agent who had taken her from obscurity in the field of creation to celebration in the field of production. On her agent's advice Nixon's short stories became a much more saleable "novel in stories," and in a matter of weeks Nixon's agent had been able to use her prior experiences and connections to get *Now You See It* to the right publishing houses and editors. Three editors responded quickly and positively. Knowing the importance of enthusiasm in making selection decisions, Nixon's agent guided her to the most enthusiastic editor, a smart decision by a savvy insider as that enthusiasm was eventually converted into a *New York Times* review by Michiko Kakutani, who also shared in it.

Yet despite her newfound success, Nixon still had lingering doubts about her agent. As Nixon recalls, "she was the business manager type," an agent from a bygone era who, according to Nixon, was not skilled in the double duties that agents at the borderlands of creation and production must take on. The breaking point for Nixon was a short story she had written titled "The Women Come and Go." Nixon loved the story and told her agent that she believed it to be the best thing she had ever written. She asked her agent to submit it for her to the *New Yorker, Harper's,* or *Esquire.* As Nixon remembers it, her agent sent back her story with a note: "She sent it back and said, 'This may work as part of a novel, but I don't think it's successful as a story.' Which just crushed me, it was horrible." This confirmed for Nixon that she and her agent didn't share a feeling or taste for literature, and although her agent was good at business, she was a bad match for Nixon in the other part of her job, situated closer to the field of creation. Her agent lacked, Nixon thought, the artistic ability and sensibility to be a true shepherd for her career. Despite her agent's disinterest in the story, Nixon still believed that "The Women Come and Go" was one of the best things she had ever written and was undeterred:

> *New England Review* had solicited me. They had written me and asked, "if you ever have anything please show it to us." Immediately that day I sent it, the same copy that [my agent] sent back to me, I sent it to the *New England Review.* One week later I got a contract in the mail from the *New England Review.* They got it into print that fall and about a year after my agent had said to me, "this doesn't work as a story," I got the letter from Doubleday congratulating me because I won first prize in the O. Henry Awards for "The Women Come and Go." For that great story. First prize in the O. Henry Awards, that's the best story in the English language published in the last year. And I called my agent and told her. I said, "I'm sorry I can't work with you anymore. You just can't read."

With the benefit of experience, Nixon knew she needed an agent who not only had the business acumen in the field of production to get deals done, but also shared her sensibilities about what "art" was, and found enthusiasm through shared interests and experiences. This person was the literary agent Wendy Weil. Nixon had first read about Weil in *Poets & Writers*, the trade publication for the field of creation that had been founded with seed money from the New York State Council on the Arts, with funds that had filtered down from the NEA Literature Panel. Weil had spent twenty-five years in book publishing before founding her own literary agency in 1986. It was a small shop, just Weil, two assistants, and her dog, but she had represented authors whom Nixon admired: Alice Walker, Rita Mae Brown, Susan Brownmiller, and Paul Monette. In addition to unapologetically literary works, Weil also represented unapologetically commercial works, such as Fannie Flagg's *Fried Green Tomatoes at the Whistle Stop Cafe*. Most important to Nixon, however, was an agent who respected and understood her identity as a short story writer, and Weil had represented Andrea Barrett's *Ship Fever*, a book of short stories that won the National Book Award. "I read *Ship Fever*, and I loved it," Nixon would later recall. "I just pined for Wendy Weil."

Nixon sent Weil a letter asking for her representation. With it she included *Now You See It* and all of her positive reviews, including Kakutani's. They corresponded for a year, and seemed to match in interests and sentiments, as well as background and experiences. Weil asked to see more of Nixon's writing, so Nixon sent along a second novel in stories she had written, *Angels Go Naked*. Under Nixon's prior agent there had been an editor, Jack Shoemaker at Counterpoint Press, who wanted to purchase *Angels*, but the deal quickly soured due to Nixon's agent's aggressive business stance. "She wanted [a] $60,000 [advance], or some ungodly number that was far beyond what we could have done," Shoemaker recalled. So *Angels Go Naked* had remained in a drawer, until Nixon sent it on to Weil:

> And she liked that. But she still hadn't taken me on. And then I told her about *Jarrettsville*, the novel that I always knew I was going to write. And I said, "I'm going to write this novel, I'm really going to do this now. I'm doing the research, I'm going to do it." And she said, "All right, write me the first chapter." And she read the first chapter and said, "Okay, I'll take you on. But only if you send me a chapter every month." Every month. She said, "I will try to place *Angels Go Naked* for you while you're doing this. But you have to send me a chapter every month." And I did. I did. And she read it and responded to it. I mean, I've never heard of an agent doing this before. I've told this to other writers and they're just flabbergasted. Agents are just like business managers. But she's really a literary agent. She reads. And her response is fantastic. She was smart and a good reader.

In addition to being a smart and good reader who shared a sensibility for literature with Nixon, Weil also had to weigh business concerns, such as her own time investment as it related to Nixon's productivity. Weil's "chapter every month" was a test. Could Nixon be prolific enough to make taking her on worth the time investment? In turn, while Nixon's previous agent had valued her time working on *Angels Go Naked* at $9,000 (15 percent of a $60,000 advance) and as a result would not work with an independent press like Counterpoint, Weil, who understood Nixon's work and the long-term promise of it, did not share Nixon's first agent's outsized expectations. Shoemaker and Weil were also a better match with each other, and fell into the second concentric circle of agent-editor relations: they weren't close but understood and admired each other's tastes, doing business with some regularity.

As Shoemaker recounted his relationship with Weil, "She's one of the people [i.e., agents] that shows me things I pay attention to. She knows my taste and she shows me things that she has a reasonable expectation that I'm going to enjoy, which is the trick. So many of these agents are just sending things to everyone and they have no sense of what we are publishing here or what my taste is. But the agents that I really admire and work most with are those who can say when they look at a book, 'gee, Jack, I really like this,' and I have something to go on when they say that." Shoemaker, in addition to his connection to Weil, was also a close friend of a key member of Nixon's collaborative circle, the poet Robert Hass. As Nixon recalls of her experience with *Angels Go Naked*, once Weil was on board, she had two allies, one from the field of authorial creation and one whose formal job it was to stand at the borderlands of creation and production: "Wendy Weil was there and Bob Hass was there."

With an O. Henry Award for "The Women Come and Go," an agent she adored, and a signed contract for *Angels Go Naked* to be published, Nixon continued to work on *Jarrettsville*, which at the time was still called *Martha's Version*. It was Wendy Weil's job to place the manuscript in the right hands. Those hands, unbeknownst to Weil at the time, would once again be at Counterpoint Press, though they belonged to an editor Shoemaker had hired rather than Shoemaker himself. The path back to Counterpoint, however, was not a straight or easy one.

PART III

THE FIELD OF PRODUCTION

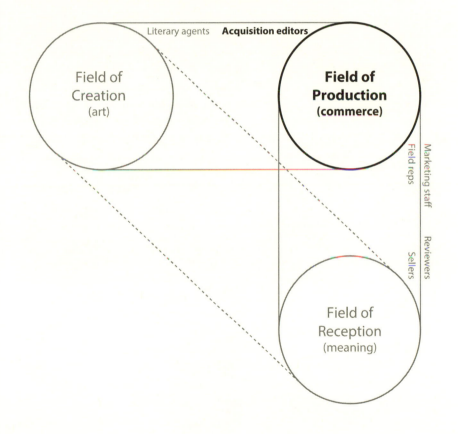

Literary agents **Acquisition editors**

Field of
Creation
(art)

**Field of
Production
(commerce)**

Field of
Reception
(meaning)

Marketing staff

Field reps

Reviewers

Sellers

DECISION MAKING, TASTE, AND FINANCIAL COMMITMENT TO CULTURE

OR, WHY COUNTERPOINT PRESS ACCEPTED *JARRETTSVILLE* AFTER REJECTING IT

FROM GOOD MATCH TO BAD MATCH TO NO MATCH

As a precondition for representing Cornelia Nixon, Wendy Weil asked her to write and send one chapter per month of the novel that would eventually become *Jarrettsville*. Weil thought she could place *Angels Go Naked*, but for both Nixon and Weil, *Jarrettsville* was the brass ring; it was the novel Nixon always knew she'd write, and although still just a story about a story and not yet on paper, it was the novel Weil wanted to represent. Despite her interest in *Jarrettsville* (still called *Martha's Version*), the slow pace of Nixon's output was a concern for Weil. While she was enthusiastic about Nixon's ability, she still needed to satisfy her own double duties as both a trusted evaluator of art and translator of art into commerce. In "testing" Nixon's output, Weil was looking for harmony between these two concerns. Along the way, as Nixon worked on *Martha's Version*, Weil worked on placing *Angels Go Naked*.

Jack Shoemaker at Counterpoint Press had already shown interest in publishing *Angels*, but Nixon's old agent had turned down his offer. At that time, with Kakutani's glowing review of *Now You See It*, her agent was targeting large conglomerate publishers, not smaller, independent literary presses like Counterpoint that lacked the on-hand cash reserves to offer large advances or enter bidding wars. But for Nixon's new agent, securing a large cash advance for *Angels* was far less important than getting the novel published. Weil hadn't been Nixon's agent on *Now You See It* and thus could make a clean start representing her author's next manuscript. Weil also did not have an aversion to small presses; if they were the only option, the advance would be low but they could keep her authors in the game. If she could place *Angels*, Nixon could continue to build on her career and reputation as a literary author while writing *Martha's Version*. Yet most crucially for Weil, her primary interest in signing Nixon was always *Martha's Version*, and to get *Angels* "out of the drawer" and published could funnel Nixon's energy to the manuscript they were both most interested in.

Counterpoint made sense as a home for *Angels Go Naked*, even beyond Shoemaker already having wanted to publish it. The trio of Nixon, Weil, and Shoemaker formed what Viviana Zelizer calls a "good match": they were good partners in economic exchange because they all had established their reputations for working on and with "quality" literature and all understood *Angels* along the same lines.[1] In turn, there was a preexisting economic relationship between Weil and Shoemaker that was already infused with interpersonal know-how and mutual admiration, and there was a strong two-step tie between Nixon and Shoemaker, who shared a close friend in Robert Hass. Yet, although nobody knew it at the time, with *Angels Go Naked*, the "good match" between Nixon and Shoemaker would ultimately turn bad.

Counterpoint released *Angels Go Naked* on April 1, 2000. A novel in eleven interlocking stories, *Angels* was about the tumultuous relationship between a musician, Margy, and a scientist, Webster. It was favorably, if not always glowingly, reviewed. Writing in the *New York Times*, the novelist Beverly Gologorsky concluded that "Nixon's great achievement in *Angels Go Naked* is in transforming the ordinary events of Margy and Webster's daily existence into exquisite dramas. Life courses through her stories, dominated as they are by two characters who insist on being themselves, even as they force Nixon's readers to look inward."[2] Yet for some reviewers the novel in stories device used by Nixon in *Angels*, unlike *Now You See It*, erred too far in the direction of stories. While in the *Times* Gologorsky noted that "surprisingly sturdy threads bind the 11 sections of this 'novel in stories,'" an anonymous reviewer in *Publishers Weekly* wrote that "although subtitled 'a novel' . . . [*Angels*] is really of collection of 11 related short stories." Another anonymous reviewer, in *Kirkus*, concluded that *Angels* was "elegant but disconcertingly episodic" and its pleasures were "blunted by the elliptical format." Although overall the reviews were positive and furthered Nixon's literary reputation, the same novel in stories trick she had previously used to translate her work from the field of creation to production had this time not worked as well. More worrisome for Nixon was something else that *Angels Go Naked* had in common with *Now You See It*: despite positive and well-placed reviews, it did not sell well. *Angels* sold so poorly that Shoemaker felt forced to make a difficult decision:

I love that book. I think *Angels Go Naked* is just a wonderful novel. And so we published [it] in hard cover. It frankly did not do well commercially . . . we just couldn't make it happen in the marketplace. Part of that had to do I think with the beginning of Counterpoint, that we weren't maybe as adept at some sorts of marketing ideas or strategies as we became later. . . . And we weren't able to successfully do it in paper[back], that is, I could never justify it. The sales of the hardcover were so light that we couldn't come back and do a paperback so we ended up remaindering it [i.e., sold at dramatically reduced prices, with the leftovers destroyed] . . . and then keeping a small quantity in print . . . and I think Cornelia was very hurt by that, understandably so.

Nixon *was* quite hurt. A paperback release for *Angels* would have offered a second chance to connect with readers in first-run bookstores, and to extend the book's life beyond those hardcover editions found at discount bookstores. In regular bookstores sales of *Angels* could beget new sales, whereas in discount bookstores sales would yield only empty shelf space quickly refilled with a shipment of someone else's orphans. Nixon did not need to know the details of how this process worked to feel the hurt.

For Shoemaker, however, it was not a lack of belief that caused the relationship between himself and Nixon to break down. Instead, he still spoke fondly of *Angels* a decade later, and secretly harbored new plans for it. But like literary agents, an editor and owner of a publishing house also faces double duties, and what Shoemaker *wanted* to do did not always align with what he could justify doing; even his own taste, beliefs, and social ties had to butt up against the reality of the marketplace at some point. As the good economic match between Nixon and Shoemaker became bad, the relational match faltered too. Over the course of the production of *Angels*, Nixon had grown close with Shoemaker's wife, a memoirist and novelist, and "we were sort of independently friends for a while until [Counterpoint] didn't do the paperback." For Nixon, as it was for Shoemaker, the falling out was based not on hostility but on their economic and social relationships being inextricably linked; for one to sour was for both to sour.

Despite this good match gone bad, Shoemaker still had other books to publish, and Nixon and Weil still had another book to work on. Weil had two assistants, both young women and recent graduates from Sarah Lawrence, who also aided in the writing of the novel. For Nixon, "they were at the time who I imagined my readers [for *Martha's Version*] to be. And they said it was appealing. So I was kind of thinking of them as I wrote it." Yet *Martha's Version* did not come at the pace that Nixon had promised. Instead of sending Weil a chapter per month, it took five years for Nixon to finish the first draft, with most of that time taken up by research. Yet by the end of the process Weil and Nixon were both enthusiastic about the book's promise.

Counterpoint passed on the novel, as an internal reader report had not been as enthusiastic as Shoemaker was hoping. It was a blow for Nixon and Weil, but a glancing one, as Weil was both well respected and well connected and at the time was looking to swim in deeper waters with *Martha's Version*. So began the iterative rewriting of *Martha's Version*, which was sent to five editors in 2002, and then reworked, before being sent out to another sixteen editors from 2003 to 2005. Those sixteen editors all also rejected *Martha's Version*. As a result, Nixon and Weil, over the span of several years, found themselves having gone from a good match to a bad match at Counterpoint and then, seemingly, to no match at all. Yet editors, like agents, are not simply gatekeepers to the field of production, and it was instead partially through the rejections themselves that *Martha's Version* began to take shape as *Jarrettsville*. To understand why Counterpoint would eventually accept the manuscript after first rejecting it requires understanding how both *Martha's Version* and Counterpoint changed during that time.

FROM SURROGATE CONSUMERS TO DOUBLE DUTIES

The formal role of the book editor, like that of the agent, first emerged around the turn of the twentieth century, and was one of two solutions to a more general problem. Before World War I, many publishing houses were in both the book and magazine business, serializing their authors' works first in magazines before releasing them as bound books. Magazines were pitched to a general interest reader, meaning their contents had to remain unobjectionable to even the most delicate of sensibilities. As Marc Aronson recounts of this era, "if [a] magazine couldn't sit out on the coffee table to be enjoyed by the whole family, it could not be published."[3] Rather than entrusting authors to never stray beyond the delicate moral standards of an imagined "whole family," publishers looked to what Paul Hirsch calls "surrogate consumers," people who could stand in for the general market.[4]

In one solution to this problem, the publisher Macmillan contracted out the reading of submissions to a group of elite and respected women who could check the work against their own moral standards; the surrogate consumers were themselves consumers, albeit a shallow pool of elite ones. Charles Scribner's Sons, in contrast, used another model and brought their surrogate consumers in-house, looking for full-time staff who could both check works for decency and work with authors to bring their manuscripts back out of moral gray zones. It was in this second reaction to the general problem of maintaining decency standards as demanded by general interest magazine serialization that the specialized role of the editor was first born. Yet even beyond this innovation, at Charles Scribner's Sons the role of editor would continue to develop even further.

Maxwell Perkins began his career in book publishing in 1910, working in Scribner's advertising department. Riding the wave of the rise of the editor in publishing houses, he transitioned roles. The escalation of his fame, at least among those in the field of production, began in 1919 with a submission titled *The Romantic Egoist* by an obscure writer from Minnesota. Scribner's editorial staff was unimpressed by the work and rejected it, despite Perkins's protestations. Yet Perkins continued to work with the novelist, and helped him turn eighty pages of *The Romantic Egoist* into a newly titled novel that was resubmitted to Scribner's and again nearly rejected. This time Perkins again lobbied hard for the value of the novel, and used a form of capital that is still today the sharpest arrow in the editor's quiver: his own enthusiasm for the work. The novel, retitled *This Side of Paradise*, was released in 1920, and its three-thousand-copy print run reportedly sold out in three days, with an additional eleven printings to follow over the next two years. Because of Perkins, F. Scott Fitzgerald entered the name economy and five years later would publish *The Great Gatsby*, also with the help of Perkins at Scribner's.

Perkins would go on to be the lifelong editor and friend of Ernest Hemingway, and was also the editor for Marjorie Kinnan Rawlings's best-selling and Pulitzer Prize–winning *The Yearling*. Yet Perkins's reputation among editors is not based as much on who he worked with as on *how* he worked with authors. With Perkins leading the charge—or at least in retrospect being bestowed with the lion's share of the credit for the charge—editors transformed from support personnel who checked works against decency standards to authors' allies and friends who were actively involved as silent partners in the creation and reformulation of novels. Nothing did more to cement Perkins's reputation—and the transition in how the job of an editor was understood—than his work with Thomas Wolfe.

Under Perkins's guidance, Wolfe's eleven-hundred-page manuscript *O Lost* was significantly cut down to center around a single character and retitled *Look Homeward, Angel*. Wolfe's follow-up, due to Perkins, was transformed from "a four-hundred-thousand-word tangle of unnumbered pages packed into three cartons" into *Of Time and the River*, which Wolfe dedicated to Perkins.[5] Yet over time Wolfe soured on Perkins as assorted literati had raised his standing from a silent partner in the creation of Wolfe's novels to perhaps being more deserving of the credit for the novels' success than Wolfe himself.[6] Bernard DeVoto went as far as to suggest that *Look Homeward, Angel* had been "hacked and shaped and compressed into something resembling a novel by Mr. Perkins and the assembly-line at Scribner's."[7]

Over the span of several decades, Perkins had gone from maintaining market-based decency standards for Scribner's, to being a silent partner in the production of award-winning literature, to essentially being credited with the *authorship* of his authors' work. Alongside contemporaries such as Hiram Haydn and Saxe Commins, Perkins transformed what it meant to be an editor. By the 1930s, "a cultural mythology had formed around editing: the editor as savior, finding the soul of a manuscript; the editor as alchemist, turning lead into gold; the editor as seer, recognizing what others had missed."[8] This romantic mantra of editor as multiplex everything to authors was taken up by the next generation of editors who emerged after the Second World War. Editors such as Robert Gottlieb and Roger Straus were credited with adopting the mentality of an editor as an author's savior, alchemist, seer, and, perhaps most important, friend. Yet still today, it is Maxwell Perkins who is the platonic figure of the occupation, with a volume of his collected letters *Editor to Author* serving as the totemic object of the editorial ideal.

Today, concerns are frequently evoked about how a market orientation has invaded the once noble, artistically oriented practices of editors. Some editors now cite the 1950s and 1960s as the golden age of editorial autonomy and art-based editorial practice—two things that they believe have been lost—and the figure for which these elegies of editorial autonomy are sung is Perkins. Yet Perkins himself retired *before* this retroactively constructed golden age is believed to have started, and upon his retirement he cited the same concerns over autonomy and editorial practice that are cited today by editors as having become problematic long after Perkins's exit. What today's editors believe to have been lost post-1960s, Perkins believed to have been lost pre-1950s, if it had ever existed at all: "Materialism was ruling America," Perkins wrote, and "some book people were choosing expediency over literary values."[9] Without the benefit of hindsight, for Perkins himself, the "good old days of Maxwell Perkins" were quite similar to the purportedly bad new world with which he is commonly juxtaposed.

For today's editors, the turning point in the encroachment of market forces occurred in the 1970s and 1980s, when international conglomerates purchased and consolidated publishing houses to diversify their portfolios. It was in this era that some editors, laid off or disheartened, began to transition to the emergent role of literary agent. While editors lament a decline of an art-based focus in editorial work (and surely some of that occurred during the first wave of conglomeration), at the same time literary agents were converting from handling only contractual obligations to *taking on* an art-based focus in their work. Put another way, to some degree the simpler past as told by today's editors is an imagined one, and to the degree that these narratives are accurate, there has been a shifting of roles as much as or more than there has been a total loss. To the degree that editors now focus on "commerce" rather than just "art," agents have picked up the slack in the system, as they've taken on artistic concerns, resulting in a new structure in which both agents and editors take on dual roles.

THE INTERDEPENDENCIES OF AGENTS AND EDITORS

As agents and editors share the double duties of artistic and financial consideration, they are the conduits through which novels are translated into the language of the field of production. In the process, what a manuscript "is" must be interactively and conversationally constructed through shared understandings about what different books "are." Between agents and editors, adjectives for fiction such as "gripping" and "thrilling" mean "moneymaker," and adjectives like "intimate" and "careful" mean "art." For an athlete's autobiography, "well written" means "readable," whereas an agent or editor would only very carefully refer to a work of literary fiction they supported as "well written," as to be anything less than "wonderfully" or "beautifully" written would introduce doubt about its quality.

Part of the transition work between fields that agents and editors undertake is converting the incomparable to the comparable. In the field of creation for a novel to be "unlike anything else" is a mark of accomplishment between authors, whereas between agents and editors for a novel to be "unlike anything else" is anathema; the simple untruth of the claim would introduce doubt about the trustworthiness of the speaker, and neither an agent or editor would know *what to do* with a book that cannot be compared. In the field of production, between agents and editors comparison is shorthand both to mitigate against uncertainty and to explain why a book is worthy of time or financial investment. For this reason, to be "similar" to another book is not just a statement about story or style (there are *many* books that are similar in story or style), as it is more regularly a statement about market potential. It is in the transition of cultural objects across fields that categorical comparison rises to prominence, and once fully immersed within any one field, the necessity for categorical comparison recedes.[10] In the transition between fields, category talk is a machete used to hack through the oversupply of potential manuscripts, and to set cultural objects down paths.[11] Upon entry into the field of production, literary fiction and romance fiction, for instance, are sent down different paths, and agents and editors devise the maps and set the coordinates for their proffered, and preferred, destinations.

If an agent is doing her job well, to send a book to an editor means not only that she believes in the book but also that she feels the receiving editor will believe in it too. As it requires the shared belief of agents and editors to shepherd a manuscript into the field of production, they are interdependent. Through their interdependence they are also allies of sorts, but allies that in the case of "good matches" will eventually square off over contract rights. In the case of good matches, that this squaring off happens between the two parties who most need each other tends to keep negotiations from getting too acrimonious. In the case of bad matches (i.e., an agent has misread an editor's interests, is not up to date on an editor's needs, or has expanded the breadth of her search in the hopes of a contract), this interdependency also creates an imperative to be exceedingly gracious in discussing why the match *temporarily* can't work so that the relationship can remain intact. Editors maintain good relations with trusted agents in the presence of bad matches in several ways: when rejecting manuscripts, they are as generous with praise as they are with criticism; they make a point to note that although the match under question wasn't right, they hope to do business again; and to reiterate the point, they sometimes even reference interpersonal relations and fond memories with the agent while rejecting the manuscript.

This imperative to maintain good relations with trusted allies is so strong that it can even cause moments of cognitive dissonance, or false memories to keep the overall match a good one. An editor recounted a story of many years ago when a literary agent with whom he had a continuing relationship made demands for a manuscript that were simply impossible to meet. It was a very frustrating situation for him. The editor, in recounting this story, corrected himself halfway through, saying, "You know what, it must have been somebody else, I can't . . . that doesn't sound like him." But the story *was* about him. Rather than having to reconsider his relationship with the literary agent, the editor concluded that he must have been wrong not about what happened, but with whom it happened.

The interdependence of agents and editors also serves two other purposes, both related to mitigating uncertainty when evaluating one-off cultural products for which quality is subjective. First, having an agent and editor who have both put the stamp of their approval (and reputations) on a manuscript provides a check of sorts that belief in the work is not entirely idiosyncratic. Second, by both agents and editors performing boundary-spanning double duties, the business side of a publishing house need never speak directly with an author about financial concerns (that's what an agent is for) and an author need never speak with the business side of a publishing house about artistic concerns (that's what an editor is for).[12]

Because of the interdependency of agents and editors, questions of how editors decide which books to publish can be a bit overstated. Rather than wholly making their own decisions about what to publish from what's out there, they rely on agents to hack through the underbrush of poorly fitting manuscripts. As a result, editors, for the most part, decide what to publish from an already well-pruned list of what agents have prescreened for them, and it is only after an agent has done her job that an editor's work of deciding what to publish truly begins.

HOW EDITORS MAKE AND LEGITIMIZE DECISIONS

Editors, like agents, use multipronged heuristics in making decisions about which projects to take on. Rather than being formally weighted or consistently applied, there is a catch-as-catch-can approach to these tools, as they can be used to inform an editor's decisions, or used after a decision has already been made as an account or justification for that decision. For editors there are four prongs through which they decide what to publish: perceptions of artistic ability; their own tastes, interests, and experiences; perceptions of market feasibility; and perceived fit with the publisher, or ease through which they can get others in the publishing house on board with the project (see Figure 5.1). Not every prong need bear equal weight in every case—they rarely if ever do—but it is rare that an editor will take on a project if she finds no redeeming qualities according to the logic of any one prong. For all prongs, editors rely on agents to know both their dispositions (i.e., what counts as "good" to them, as well as their tastes, interests, and experiences) as well as their positions (what counts as market feasibility where they are, and what fits with the publisher or imprint they work for). None perhaps is more important than an agent's evaluation of artistic ability matching that of the editor, only closely followed by an editor's own interests, tastes, and experiences. As editors are for the most part beholden to agents to sift through the entrants from the field of creation and bring them the manuscripts with the best chance of being published, according to the editor's own grab bag of heuristics, it is the "softer" matches such as artistic ability that are harder to know in advance.

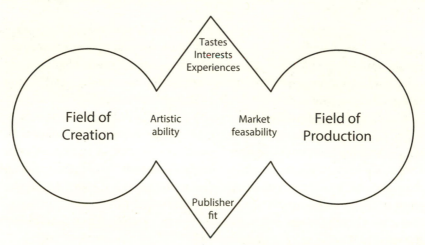

FIGURE 5.1: The Four Prongs of Editors' Evaluations.

Editors, like agents, also use their own tastes, interests, and experiences when selecting manuscripts. As has been the case since the days of Maxwell Perkins, editors are granted latitude and (to outsiders) a surprising amount of autonomy in their purchasing decisions. Instead of being told what to do, they more often face relatively open-ended ceilings and floors: they cannot offer *above* a certain amount of money for a manuscript without attaining approval from several rungs up the hierarchy, and they cannot take on *fewer* than a certain number of manuscripts per year without facing disapproval.

As an editor described the importance of personally connecting with novels in deciding to publish them, "I go for a pretty simple criteria, but there are very few manuscripts that meet it. It's just whether it's something that impacts me emotionally. And that can be laughing or crying or what-ever, getting pissed. So yeah, just emotional impact I think." The impor-tance of emotional impact is not idiosyncratic to this editor, nor is it simply a mark of status to claim that personal connection is the metric used, al-though there is some of that. Instead, the reliance on emotional connec-tion for editors—and power derived from it—is long-standing in the field of production.

Over twenty years ago, Faith Sale, senior executive editor at G. P. Putnam and Sons, similarly described the power of emotional connection to a manu-script: "Once I have been captivated by the voice of a novel, I am prepared to do whatever I can to escort that novel to its maximum readership, whether that means simply walking it through the successive stages of the publishing process or presiding over total reconstruction and banging heads in-house to get attention for it. . . . But I can't fake it: my devotion to fiction is born more out of instinct than intellect, based more on emotional response than calculated judgment. The moment of connection is the moment I become a book's (or an author's) advocate."[13]

While there are upsides to editors having the relative autonomy to publish books they truly believe in, the downside of this arrangement, however, is that like literary agents, editors may overlook or look past manuscripts that do not match their own experiences. As a result, editorial autonomy diversifies what is published only so much as editors are diverse, which is not much.[14] With regard to racial diversity in the occupation, in the 2014 *Publishers Weekly* Salary Survey, 88 percent of responding editors identified as white, with 3.7 percent identifying as Asian, 2.8 percent as Hispanic (any race), 2.8 percent as mixed race, and 1.4 percent as Black. While the lack of racial diversity among editors can be attributed to a variety of causes, the result is a highly stratified population of editors who are at least partially selecting manuscripts based on works that match their own tastes, sensibilities, and experiences.[15]

Paradoxically, however, although this is widely viewed as a problem in the industry and even among editors, to rely on one's own tastes, sensibilities, and experiences when picking manuscripts is what it means to be a "good" editor, and to *not* do so is to be a "bad" editor.[16] James Wade, then executive publisher and vice president of Crown Publishers, wrote in advice to young editors, "If you suspect you are going to distort, even unwittingly, the author's ideas and expressions for whatever reason (your 'expertise' or your moral evaluation or even hazy issues like taste), then you have no business editing that book."[17] As a result, more often than not editors shy away from works of literary or popular fiction with characters or stories they do not feel they can intuitively and intimately understand, and instead gravitate toward projects for which they feel they are the "right" people. In support of this general principle in the occupation, when asked about which book she was most excited about, one editor described one of her current projects: "I could just tell instantly [that I would publish it]. . . . [The author] grew up in New York like I did and we went to similar schools and it was like, hanging out with one of my friends who's an amazing storyteller. So that's something I'm very enthusiastic about. I knew right away."

Yet as the fields of creation and production are interdependent, for authors for which there is an undersupply of the "right people" in editorial roles, an editorial reliance on tastes, sensibilities, and experiences can also pose challenges. Such is the case for Damon, the Black Southern writer discussed in chapter 4 who acknowledges that his work in the field of creation is partially conditioned on the realities of how editors operate in the field of production:

> I think writers in a lot of ways write to the acquisition editors. Like, we are aware. And that can just tear up your imagination. Which means that a lot of times if you're writing a book like mine, which is not peopled at all by people who are like acquisition editors, I have to synthesize . . . that experience for these other people [i.e., acquisition editors] who have no understanding of the nuances of the rituals, and routines of these folks [i.e., the characters]. . . . And that's what's happened. Even with this rewrite that I did, I did the best I could do, and it was humbling because that's what I did. I had to sell out.

Such is also the case for Maxine, a Jamaican American romance author who writes while being mindful of her publisher's expectations: "Wealth is a requirement most of the time. No drug use, no cursing, the sex has to be romantic. It feels like they're trying so hard to be opposite to street lit. It's like White Harlequin in blackface. But with greater restrictions. It can feel like the policing of Black sexuality." While editors are more prone to share stories of when there are taste-based and experientially-based matches ("I knew right away"), the imperative to do "good" editorial work by selecting novels they truly feel close to can also come with consequences for stories and authors for whom there is an underrepresentation in the editorial role.

Although editors are quick to cite art- and taste-based factors in their selection decisions, lurking behind these statements can also be concerns over market feasibility or fit with the publisher. When deciding to publish a novel, these prongs can sometimes go unstated because they are thought of as "obvious" or "uninterestingly" already baked into the decision. In turn, in decisions not to publish, to openly acknowledge their effects is to come out and declare that one of the primary perks of the job—having relative autonomy in what one chooses to publish—actually comes with limits.

Market feasibility and publisher fit, like perceived artistic ability and personal interests, also often overlap with each other. For one publisher an author's weak sales record, despite strong reviews, may be a prohibitive mark against her book's market feasibility, whereas for another publisher this same scenario can be seen as a good opportunity to take advantage of an irrationality in the way market feasibility is defined by other publishers. Market feasibility, like publisher fit, can also come down to the categories a book falls into, being based on perception of the "hotness," "coldness," or "saturation" of the category (i.e., a broader market-based account), or on a narrower publisher's "fit" with the category: is this book the type of book *we* do? Although often unstated, these heuristics are just as important as the taste-based ones, and are often the concerns for which the limits of an editor's autonomy are reached. Rather than being formally regulated by these concerns, however, as Woody Powell concluded of editors in academic presses, instead of forcing others to regulate them, they *self-regulate* in their selection decisions, working to try not to pitch books that others can't get behind.[18]

If an editor finds herself self-regulating frequently, she'll do one of two things. The more long-term strategy is to seek an editorial job at a different publisher or imprint for which she *need not* self-regulate her decisions, as her sensibilities and tastes better match with the publisher's fit and perceptions of market feasibility. It is for this reason (in addition to the relatively low pay) that editors may frequently change jobs, as part of their compensation is being imbued with the cultural capital of freedom and autonomy in decisions, causing them to seek jobs in which they do not have to regulate themselves.

In the short term, however, as part of a more everyday tactic, the editor will work to get others at the publisher on board with her interests. Editors sometimes creatively convince colleagues and higher-ups that perceived non-fits or market infeasibility are actually something else entirely. It is in this role that editors become, as Rachel Donadio has written, "business people and lobbyists."[19] As cofounder of Simon & Schuster, M. Lincoln Schuster wrote as one of twenty-four points of explanation about the job to young editors, "It is not enough to 'like' or 'dislike' a manuscript, or an idea or a blueprint for a book. You must know and be able to tell convincingly and persuasively why you feel as you do about a submission."[20] Editors rarely if ever expend the capital to try to push manuscripts that others in the house cannot get behind, or that they cannot convince and cajole others to get behind. If they are unsure about a manuscript or proposal, they might ask another editor to take a second look at it rather than entering the editorial meeting (in which projects are discussed) with feelings of uncertainty, or even worse, ultimately having their proposal rejected.

The best way to mitigate against having a proposal rejected is to become a lobbyist before the meeting, and to engage in storytelling about the desired novel around the office as a way to convincingly and persuasively convey enthusiasm for the work in ways that others can get behind. This type of post hoc storytelling is sometimes accomplished through the practice of projecting sales in reverse, or figuring out how many projected copies need to be sold in order to get others on board, and then doing the sales math backward to reach that targeted goal. As an editor explained his process when creating the initial projected profit and loss (P&L) statement for a book, "The key to a P&L is making the numbers work. Even if I've already decided to pitch a book I know that I have to start from the 'back' (bottom of the P&L) because I know what the target should be and what is reasonable and then I fill back in. . . . If the numbers won't work the advance has to be lowered, or I have to really think if I can reasonably argue for a higher total sales figure so [I] look at the author's previous sales figures and different 'comps' and see what might be reasonable. . . . [laughing] You can always make it work. Well, not always, but you can usually make it work."

Much like how this editor works backward to create a reasonable if sunny guess about a manuscript he has chosen to advocate for, "comp titles" are used to signal to others in the house and field which books a new project might be similar to. A good comp might be a recent title of similar topic or format, but not all recent titles of similar topic of format will do. Instead, as a storytelling device comp titles are finely curated lists that exclude all those actually comparable books that do not tell the story one needs to tell, and include only those comparable books that help tell the story.[21] As an editor explained, "Comp titles tell a story, you know, any story really. They're shorthand to tell a story, so the process works backwards. After coming up with a story, comp titles make the story make sense."[22] A different editor likened picking comp titles to the porridge eaten by the three bears in *Goldilocks*. A book that has sold too poorly (i.e., the porridge was too cold) or too well (i.e., the porridge was too hot, and the comparison is not believable) makes a bad comp.[23] Instead, for this editor, "selecting comp titles is an art . . . the porridge has to be just right."[24]

Storytelling about sales is, for editors, another way to convey their *enthusiasm* for a project. As publisher Scott Walker noted of the need to generate collective enthusiasm out of one's own, "An editor must be able to position the book in such a way that other members of the publishing team will share in his or her enthusiasm."[25] Ultimately though, it is an editor's enthusiasm, regardless of which prong of the decision heuristic it is assigned to, that allows her both to do her job of advocating for her work and to try to get her way about what to publish. Often this involves planting the seeds of collective enthusiasm with other editors before the editorial meeting, or the reverse, overtly and demonstrably withholding enthusiasm for projects that are receiving wider "buzz" so that everyone in the house is aware of the lack of enthusiasm for the project from the editor when another publisher later "overpays" for it (in the story that is then told within the house about why it was not taken on).

This power of enthusiasm for editors stands in contrast to how sociologists typically treat the role of emotions in occupations and organizations, in which feelings are most typically a form of labor enacted by those in low-status, service-oriented occupations.[26] Even for those in higher status positions such as managers in white-collar occupations, although they have more freedom to express anger, the managing of emotions is still a regular concern.[27] Yet, for an editor in a publishing house, in which the bestowment or withholding of positive feelings is the primary tool through which she adjudicates on which books her time will be spent, the conveyance of emotions is less a form of labor than a form of capital: granting or withholding enthusiasm for a project is ultimately a tool to get her way.[28] An editor cannot be indiscriminate in the deployment of her enthusiasm—like all forms of capital, its stock can be depleted with use—but, more than anything else, it is the promissory note of enthusiasm from an editor that gets the gears of a publishing house moving toward her interests.

As a result of the power of editorial enthusiasm, editors can sometimes have difficulty explaining their decisions to publish a book or not beyond this language, which does not mean that they in reality are not juggling market- and fit-based concerns with their own sociostructurally derived tastes and preferences. Instead, one or all of these prongs of decision making can at different times be directed into the funnel of editorial enthusiasm or not, and simply just be referred to as "enthusiasm" or "excitement" or "disappointment" on the back end. In this regard, as James Curran notes of editors, "when they say that books select themselves, what they are actually saying is that they choose books within a framework of values they see no need to question."[29]

Yet rather than treating editors as inaccurately narrating how they make decisions, their sometimes inability to discuss their decisions beyond emotional connection is an artifact of the relative freedom of decision making they enjoy within publishing houses.[30] Put another way, for an editor to describe her decision to publish a novel by saying "I just really, really loved it" can both be, for her, an accurate if incomplete portrayal of *how* her decision was made, as well as an accurate description for why the publisher she works for agreed to let her publish it. In these instances, while perceptions of artistic ability, personal tastes, market feasibility, and publisher fit can all contribute to the *generation* of enthusiasm for a project by an editor, they can also be used as available and free-floating signifiers to *explain* her enthusiasm and induce action from others, regardless of where that enthusiasm was truly first derived.

WHY COUNTERPOINT PRESS ACCEPTED *JARRETTSVILLE* AFTER REJECTING IT

Between the first and second submissions of Nixon's post–Civil War story to Counterpoint Press, both the novel and the press changed. Just as *Jarrettsville* was different from *Martha's Version*, Counterpoint was not the same Counterpoint from before; Jack Shoemaker was all that remained. It was these changes—both to the novel and to the context of the situation in which it was placed—that allowed Nixon and Shoemaker's bad match to turn good again.

For *Martha's Version*, the first catalyst for change was the contents of the rejection letters from editors. Although the field of production is oriented around making sense of novels as objects of commerce, editors still serve double duties, and even for books they decline to represent, they still engage in artistic concerns. They do so in these situations not out of pleasure but out of obligation: they are interdependent with literary agents, and in the face of bad matches, their rejections must be explained for them to maintain good relationships. Authors may or may not see their rejection letters, but their agents do, which is why they contain personal notes to agents, a request to keep sending manuscripts, and insight into why the manuscript under question was rejected. These notes both clarify what the editor is looking for in the future and signal that the manuscript was *read* and seriously considered.

All these signaling devices are present in rejection letters to Weil, which in total across all letters contained exactly sixty-five negative and sixty-five positive evaluative statements about Nixon's novel. While there was likely relational massaging present in the *number* of positive statements included (i.e., even in rejection this genre of letter demands the inclusion of good things and bad things), the same is not true for negative statements, and trends can still be deduced from what was plucked out by editors for positive appraisal. As trust and shared sensibilities are important to the relationships between agents and editors, Weil had not randomly selected editors, but instead had sent *Martha's Version* to editors she most thought could share her enthusiasm for the novel. Put another way, an expert in the field had constructed a curated list of editors who she believed were most likely to appreciate the novel. Yet even with this expertly crafted list, as seen in the actual rejection letters for *Martha's Version*, interpretive evaluations were somewhat discordant (see Figure 5.2).

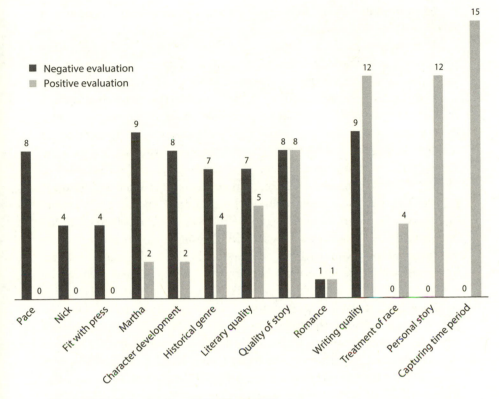

FIGURE 5.2: Rejection Letters for *Martha's Version.*

The most widespread disagreement among acquisition editors centered on the overall "literariness" of the story: editors' opinions diverged on the novel's literary quality, the writing quality, the overall quality of the story, and how successful it was as a work of historical fiction.[31] For some elements there was general positive agreement (Nixon's closeness to the story, capturing of the time period, and treatment of race and racism), and on others there was general negative agreement (the slow pace, the depiction of the main characters, and character development more broadly). While editors' positive and negative evaluative statements were included in their rejections to maintain good relations with Weil, Nixon requested to see them, knowing that they may contain a nugget or two of wisdom that could catalyze her imagination in redrafting the novel. Wanting to keep her author happy despite the disappointment and still believing in the story, Weil obliged. Through Weil, Nixon took the editors' explanations from the field of production back with her into the field of creation, and first alone and then with guidance from her social circle used them to redraft *Martha's Version* into *Jarrettsville*.

With the personal nature of the story firmly in place, in the redrafting process Nixon further developed her treatments of the time period and the role of race and racism in the story. From editors' problems with the pace of the story and the characterizations of Nick and Martha, Nixon realized the mistake she had made. In fact, in a rejection letter she found her solution to unlock what would become *Jarrettsville*: "[T]hough it's not possible to get inside Nick's head," and editor wrote, "it was a letdown to be left with the feeling that he's not much more than your stereotypical cad." As discussed in chapter 2, in *Martha's Version* Nixon had consciously avoided trying to get into Nick's head: "Sometimes men do things, I don't know why," she said. Yet the rejecting editor had been wrong that it was "not possible to get inside Nick's head," as Nixon was a novelist and it was a failure on her part to let the story suffer in favor of avoiding understanding Nick and his motivations. With this realization Nixon went back through her notes and rewrote the manuscript. To get inside Nick's head, Nixon had to figure out who Nick was.

"I was not a learned man. Rumors of knowledge, that's what I had," began Nick's new, first-person section of the novel. His character's complexity emerged through competing tensions: his outsized responsibilities to his family; his perceived inability to live up to his father; an attraction to and repulsion from Martha's forthrightness; and his identities as both a pacifist and a former fighter for the Union in a town that was still divided by the Civil War. In the redrafting of *Martha's Version* to *Jarrettsville*, race relations in post–Civil War Maryland became the linchpin for why Nick left Jarrettsville. While in *Martha's Version* Nick leaving Jarrettsville is just an event that happens to Martha, in the redrafting the reader learns why: Nick leaves out of fear for his life, fear of marrying into the Cairnes family, and fear that Martha's recklessness belied a temperamental similarity to her violent brother. In unlocking Nick, Nixon was able to develop both Nick and Martha as characters, as their complexities and reactions to those complexities required hearing both of their voices. Ultimately it was first through an editor's rejection letter that a story about a woman became a story about two people, and also a story about a town. In the new draft, which thanks to Nixon's social circle was soon to be called *Jarrettsville*, the first eighty-three pages of the novel were told from Martha's first-person perspective, the second eighty-three pages from Nick's first-person perspective, and the final third from the first-person perspectives of other residents in the town, covering the aftermath of the murder and Martha's trial.

While *Martha's Version* was undergoing changes in its path to becoming *Jarrettsville*, Counterpoint Press was also changing. When *Martha's Version* had been submitted, Counterpoint Press, which was founded by Jack Shoemaker and Frank Pearl, was located in Washington, D.C., and was controlled by Perseus Book Group. By the time *Jarrettsville* returned to Counterpoint, the press had been sold to Charlie Winton (founder of the independent distributor Publishers Group West, which still distributes Counterpoint) and save for Shoemaker, the entire staff had changed. As such, not only had *Martha's Version* changed to *Jarrettsville*, but the Counterpoint Press that rejected *Martha's Version* no longer existed. As Shoemaker explained, "I am the only person that's still involved in the idea of Counterpoint or the name of Counterpoint. So [for *Jarrettsville*] there was no difficulty in overcoming that previous situation [of *Angels Go Naked*] with the marketing folks here, or the publicists, or Publishers Group West." Although it's rare for a rejected novel to get a second pass at the same press, it was the social tie of Robert Hass between Shoemaker and Nixon that brought *Jarrettsville* and Counterpoint back together again. As Shoemaker recalls it:

> I was back in California [with Counterpoint], and I had said to Bob Hass, "What ever happened to Cornelia's book?" And he said, "I don't know, I'm going to ask her." And I said, well, if she's worked on it some I'd like to see it again. And then I got a note or a phone call from Wendy [Weil] saying we'd sure like for you to see this. And so I got it and began to read it, and it was riveting because there were these three or four other voices. And it suddenly began to flesh itself out in my mind as a real story. . . . It's a literary book that needed a literary context, and needed a literary publisher.

Shoemaker and Winton had recently hired a new young editor, Adam Krefman, who had previously interned at the publisher McSweeney's. Krefman knew of and admired the work of Nixon's husband, Dean Young, but did not yet know Nixon. Knowing that *Jarrettsville* had been submitted to Shoemaker, he made a point to introduce himself to Nixon at a reading in a bookstore several weeks later. The day after the event he followed up with Shoemaker, asking if he could read the manuscript: "Jack told me that he published [*Angels Go Naked*] and he showed it to me. So I knew that she was published, I knew Jack liked her, and I knew that she was married to Dean Young, whose work I knew and liked." Krefman is adamant that it was not these social ties that caused him to advocate for the publication of

Jarrettsville, while also admitting that his preexisting knowledge of Nixon and her relationships also kept him reading at one point when he had doubts about the manuscript:

> Everything was really strong about it, but, Martha's section, which is the first . . . is so optimistic. . . . But I knew who Cornelia Nixon was and I just gave her that credit in thinking, "oh, this could still be a good story." While having doubts I had forgotten that there was a prologue explaining that there was going to be a murder further down the road, which, blame me as an editor for that, but if I forgot, then an ordinary reader might forget that too and put the book down. But then I got to Nick's part and I thought it was really good. The tension starts to build and I started to really squirm.

When explaining the process through which he was drawn into *Jarrettsville*, Krefman's reliance on his own tastes, interests, and experiences is made clear. Martha's section of the novel worried him because it was "optimistic"; Krefman likely would not have enjoyed *Martha's Version* because it was told entirely from Martha's perspective. Instead, Krefman connected to the first-person narrative of a young man, Nick, and his enthusiasm for the novel grew while reading Nick's section. Just as Nixon did not originally write from Nick's perspective because she did not think she could capture the perspective of a young man, in revision she had managed to capture the attention of another young man, Krefman.

These gendered bonds between individuals and characters were so strong that in developmentally editing the manuscript together, Krefman and Nixon learned that they were reading the same novel differently. According to Nixon, "I'm always tracking Martha, you know, she's partially my mother, and partially me. She's independent. Whereas Adam is, I learned, tracking Nick. For Adam, Nick is the star! That's just so wonderful." Although in *Jarrettsville* Martha and Nick's first-person accounts are afforded equal space, Nixon and Krefman still disagree about which scene is the most emotionally evocative. For Nixon it is when Martha shoots and kills Nick; Martha's clear anguish in committing the violence stays with Nixon. While Krefman agrees with the importance of this scene, for him the most emotionally evocative scene instead centers on Nick's actions, or rather in-actions, when from atop a barn he watches Martha waiting for him below, but cannot bring himself to go through with marrying her. Nixon never much liked this scene when she wrote it, as from her position in the field of creation to have a character watch other characters while in seclusion is to rely on a clichéd staging. Yet Krefman, who was instead deeply emotionally invested in the character of Nick, was not so much concerned with the possibly clichéd staging, and instead reading the scene for the first time brought him to tears. Tethering Nick to his own experiences, Krefman explained his reaction to the scene as if he and Nick were friends:

> [I was most emotional] at the moment he's sitting in the loft of the barn, and Martha is pregnant waiting at the altar at her own house. He's watching everybody walk into the house for his wedding. And he's in a suit, but he can't bring himself to get out of the barn. And he's there for hours and the clock is ticking down, but he can't do it. And then he sees Richard and his own cousin come running out of the house, and Richard wants to kill him. You start to really pull your hair out, you just want to smack him. But you also sympathize with him a little bit. Otherwise it would be too infuriating for me. It's like you want to shake him like you would your best friend, and say, "you're scared, but you *have* to do this."

Krefman, when discussing Nick, describes his character in a multitude of ways: Nick "has good moral intentions" but is also an unrealistic "dreamer." His desire to live a simple life is "admirable," but at other times he is "vile" for having shamed Martha for taking sexual control when in the moment he had not objected. Nick, for Krefman, is complicated—worthy of both empathy and anger. It was ultimately how emotionally evocative Nick was for Krefman that caused him, as a new editor, not only to think that Counterpoint should accept *Jarrettsville* for publication, but also to gently advocate that he should be the editor to shepherd the novel through the production process. In doing so, he used the most penetrating arrow an editor has in his quiver: Krefman adamantly conveyed his own enthusiasm for the work.

Krefman wrote a reader's report on *Jarrettsville* for Shoemaker. His report was infused with enthusiastic language, signaling both his eagerness to take the manuscript on, and the emotional response it evoked in him. These points were made explicitly clear in the first two sentences of Krefman's report: "So, as I mentioned to you yesterday, this book is excellent, and I strongly suggest we publish it. There are some tweaks I suggest (below), but first, I will gush." Krefman goes on to sell Shoemaker on the evocative setting: "It's a complicated story taking place in a very interesting time in US history," in which "the same divisions that led to the war are seething underneath every scene, waiting to boil over." In discussing the "deep-seated racism and abolition of slavery [that] seems to have taken hold only on paper,"

Krefman spends the rest of the paragraph clarifying for Shoemaker that he believes *Jarrettsville* to be a literary book. Rather than being straightforward and commonplace, Krefman argues, the story and its setting are complicated and evocative. After having summarized the major plot points, to further clarify his enthusiasm for the project Krefman returns to emotive language. Nick watching Martha from the barn is "easily the most heartwrenching scene in the book. I was squirming," and Nick's "death is very quick, and so much sadder for it." To make sure his opinion is clear, Krefman ends his report with a short sentence: "This book is really compelling."

Although Krefman was a very young editor when writing his reader report for *Jarrettsville*, the report was, for Shoemaker, further confirmation that the hiring of Krefman had been a good decision, and that Krefman understood the subtleties and nuances of the job. Shoemaker was elated that Krefman already had a feel for the game of being an editor, and knew how and when to advocate for his desires. When commenting later on the effectiveness of Krefman's reader report in guiding his decision to purchase *Jarrettsville*, Shoemaker noted with a wink, "Even though I made the choice [to hand *Jarrettsville* to Adam], I think Adam was an inspired choice. I think I was inspired to make it."

On the wings of Krefman's enthusiasm, the good match that had gone bad between Shoemaker and Nixon over the lack of a paperback edition for *Angels Go Naked* would soon be made good again. Yet Shoemaker, unbeknownst to both Nixon and Krefman at the time, also privately harbored hope that he could further cement the good match with some repair work. As Shoemaker admitted in confidence before *Jarrettsville*'s release, "My hope is that the sales for *Jarrettsville* are strong enough to justify us finally doing *Angels* in paperback." Yet despite Shoemaker's optimism and Krefman's enthusiasm for *Jarrettsville*, their work was only beginning, as Krefman still had concerns about the manuscript, both for himself and for the book's fit at Counterpoint. As a young editor who was good at his job as a lobbyist, however, Krefman had buried his lingering questions beneath his own excited and enthusiastic praise. Once the book was accepted for publication, those concerns could safely be worked out in the process of developmental editing.

INDUSTRY STRUCTURE AND THE POSITION AND DISPOSITION OF PUBLISHERS

OR, HOW SOME OF THE END OF *JARRETTSVILLE*

QUITE LITERALLY BECAME THE BEGINNING

ON MATCHMAKING, AND MAKING A GOOD MATCH BETTER

Adam Krefman had been enthusiastic in his praise for *Jarrettsville*, but a lingering question remained: what kind of novel was it? Nixon had a well-honed reputation as the author of literary fiction, but *Jarrettsville* had a propulsive plot that resulted in a murder and trial, which is more the stuff of popular fiction. How would a reader react when the romantic "optimism" of Martha's opening section was followed by doubt, fear, and violence in Nick's section? Was *Jarrettsville* therefore somewhat of a romance novel in its first third while being something else entirely in the last two-thirds? These questions were high stakes for Krefman, but he was not the only editor who had asked them. As one editor had noted in a rejection letter for the novel, "[I]t seemed to straddle the line between literary and commercial to me. That is, of course, a wonderful area to publish into if the balance is just right." The implication was, for this editor at least, that the balance *was not* just right, although she declined to state to which side the balance was off. Further complicating matters was that, for some editors, the manuscript was clearly a work of literary fiction—perhaps even too literary—whereas for others it was too commercial. As one editor phrased it, *Jarrettsville* "seemed more plot-driven than character-driven," a euphemistic way to say that it was not literary enough.

Whether "literary" or "commercial," *Jarrettsville* was also definitively a work of historical fiction, but again, was it too historical or not historical enough? "While the story remains historically accurate," one editor remarked, "it might not be satisfying or fulfilling enough for a fiction reader."

For a different editor the story "did not seem to soar above its category, the usual realm of historical fiction," whereas for a third it had "captured this period and setting just perfectly, but without any of the self-consciousness I often find in historical novels." Furthermore, was the novel successful because Nixon was a "lovely, lovely writer" as an editor wrote, or was it more appropriate to "worry that the language isn't quite powerful enough to make this novel competitive in the crowded market of Civil War literature," as written by a different editor?

For Cornelia Nixon the question of if *Jarrettsville* was "literary" or "commercial" or "historical" did not make much sense; it was quite obviously, she believed, all of them at once. Although this answer made sense to Nixon from her seat in the field of creation, in the field of production a lack of clarity about what *Jarrettsville* "was" could pose a variety of problems. Likewise, depending on what *Jarrettsville* was deemed to be, through which channels it should be pushed and to which readers it should be marketed and promoted were also up for question.

Apart from the specific case of *Jarrettsville*, a baseline level of discordance over how to make sense of a new manuscript is part of the process all novels go through when moving out of one field and into another. In the field of creation *Jarrettsville* could just be radically itself—a work of art that either "worked" or "didn't work." Yet in the field of production, a clearer category had to be imprinted onto the novel to allow others in the field to be able to make sense of it. Rather than a clear genre assignment being firmly encoded in the text, to some degree the genre had to be assigned. Put another way, figuring out which genre *Jarrettsville* best fit into was partially mandated by the constraints of the text, but it also took insight to derive a category and make it work; *Jarrettsville*'s marketable genre designation created both a challenge and an opportunity.[1] While Adam Krefman saw quite clearly the literary quality of *Jarrettsville*, the novel also, as he explained in his reader report, had him at the edge of his seat at points, engrossed in the plot. In enthusiastically advocating to work on *Jarrettsville*, Krefman had also enlisted himself in figuring out how to explain what *Jarrettsville* was within a semistable set of generic conventions so that it might be successfully weaved through the field of production.

It was both literally and figuratively a sunny day in Northern California's East Bay when Cornelia Nixon drove down to the Counterpoint offices from her condo in the Berkeley Hills. As Nixon would be working with Krefman to develop *Jarrettsville*, Shoemaker wanted to facilitate their reacquaintance over lunch. The Counterpoint offices were just south of the main retail strip on Fourth Street in Berkeley, a former industrial district that throughout the

1990s had gentrified and become a cluster of high-end stores. Although a lumber yard and drop-off and pick-up hub for day laborers still buttressed the main drag, at the time the street's two main retail blocks held two independent bookstores, an Apple Store, coffee shops, boutique toy and clothing stores, the several requisite high-end cafes specializing in brunch, two upscale kitchenware stores, and so on.

This commercial strip was and still is the type of place you would expect to find the offices of a literary or "quality" independent publishing house, and in fact several were located there. On the north end of the strip is Publishers Group West (PGW), the once independent distributor founded by Charlie Winton (owner and CEO of Counterpoint) that *Publishers Weekly* had once credited with saving independent publishing in the United States. The offices of Seal Press, Maple Tree Press, and Avalon Travel are also in the PGW building, adjoining a central courtyard. For sales meetings, the Counterpoint staff would walk together from their offices just south of the Fourth Street retail strip to the PGW offices just north of it.

Yet over lunch that day, Nixon, Shoemaker, and Krefman chatted about industry gossip, old publishing stories, and mutual friends and acquaintances. When independently recounting the lunch, Nixon and Krefman were both certain that they never talked about *Jarrettsville* while eating. The point of the lunch, as facilitated by Shoemaker, was instead for them to get to know each other, and to develop some trust and rapport before they began formally working together. Diving right into intense talk of *Jarrettsville* would not have served those purposes. If Krefman were to edit Nixon's novel, the two of them needed to know and understand each other.

Knowing that Nixon taught in an MFA program and was energized by being around young people, Shoemaker thought that the mid-twenties Krefman was a good match to work with her. Likewise, Krefman's unabashed enthusiasm for *Jarrettsville* made him a good match to work with Nixon. Other factors that made Krefman the right editor, Shoemaker figured, were more ethereal, and came down to sensibility, temperament, and editorial style. As Shoemaker described it,

> Adam's not overbearing. There are some editors that we work with who are a little more tough. . . . If I had a manuscript that I thought was a good non-fiction book written by somebody who didn't write very well but had a great idea, I would want an editor who came in who was tough and demanding; this would not be an occasion where we were trying to be respectful of a literary style. . . . Cornelia Nixon is first a stylist. You're really responding to how beautiful her sentences

are. I think the real editorial trick is to be able to get inside the voice or the mind of the writer and help them do better what they have set out to do. And I think Adam has a kind of innate sense of that.

Once they began working together, Krefman's "innate sense" of Nixon as a stylist was manifest in several ways. Although he would be developmentally editing the novel with her, as Krefman saw it Nixon was "a real pro" and did not need the type of hands-on editing other authors might need: "I didn't want to fiddle with her syntax. . . . I tried to just ask her questions: 'Why did you do this?' or 'Had you thought about doing this or that?'"

In *Jarrettsville* Krefman had picked up on recurring symbolism in Nixon's writing, such as the use of flowers. Yet part of Krefman's "innate sense" of editing was *not* mentioning the symbolism to her. As Krefman described it, "Flowers are mentioned in various scenes early in [Nick and Martha's] relationship, and again when they're making love, and then much later the gun she uses to kill him has engravings of flowers on it. That's a very nice use of symbolism that I picked up on in my first reading. But I never brought it up with Cornelia. When you're talking about symbolism, or the underlying use of symbolism in a novel, if Cornelia didn't notice it but it's in there, I didn't want to point it out to her and have her start revising things to draw it out more or make it more obvious or too much of a good thing." When Nixon was later asked about her use of symbolism with flowers, she was pleased that it had been noted, but perhaps the most important evocation of it, the flowers on the gun Martha used to kill Nick, which evoked the recurring motif of flowers during their courtship, was new to her: "That's right!" she exclaimed, while extolling Krefman's virtues as an editor and reader.

Krefman had also noted symbolism in the opening passage of the novel, when Martha carries a legless Confederate soldier on her back. For Krefman the symbolism was obvious. From her first sentence Nixon was setting her characters in a time and place. The legless veteran was a metaphor for the South, which had been incapacitated by the war, and Martha, in taking the legless man onto her back, represented a major theme of the novel: in the long afterlife of war in patriarchal societies, the loss of men created new opportunities for women to be strong. Like the recurring motif of flowers, Krefman never mentioned to Nixon the clear symbolism he saw in this opening passage. Accomplished fiction writers often unconsciously write with symbolism and do not need to be made aware of it when it is working, Krefman thought, lest they lean into it in revision and overdo it. Yet as was the case with flowers, Nixon had not written the scene of the legless man so that it would expressly serve a symbolic function. While Nixon did not disagree with Krefman's interpretation of the scene upon later hearing of it, while writing it she "just thought it sounded cool, and wanted to show that Martha was a tomboy and could carry this man."

Although Krefman avoided discussion with Nixon of these finer-grained pleasures he took from the novel, he did have an edit in mind for *Jarrettsville*, and it was a major one. Krefman's edit was important enough that before his lunch with her, Shoemaker had contacted Weil to tell her that Counterpoint's contract for *Jarrettsville* was conditioned on Nixon enacting Krefman's suggestion. When recalling their initial lunch meeting, neither Krefman nor Nixon remembers knowing about the behind-the-scenes conversation between Weil and Shoemaker. Instead, they were simply both there to begin to establish a trust so that Krefman was not just a strange young man in his mid-twenties who wanted to dramatically alter Nixon's last decade of work.

After walking back from lunch, standing in front of the Counterpoint offices before saying their goodbyes, Shoemaker introduced the topic of Krefman's major edit. He told Nixon that Krefman had an idea for *Jarrettsville*, and that he supported it and thought it was a good one. Krefman's idea would not take a lot of work from Nixon, but it involved a major reimagining of the structure of the novel: Krefman wanted to take part of the end of *Jarrettsville* and put it at the beginning, starting the novel with witness accounts of the immediate aftermath of Nick's murder, before tracing back through their courtship, and eventually Martha's trial. Why did Krefman want to reorder the telling of *Jarrettsville*, and why did Shoemaker agree strongly enough to put his stamp of support on the idea before it was even shared? To understand Krefman's proposal for changing *Jarrettsville*, one needs to know about more than just the people involved. Instead, to grasp Krefman's edit involves understanding the field of production more broadly, and how different book publishers fit and operate within it.

BALANCING ART AND COMMERCE

Three thousand miles away and decades before the existence of Counterpoint, in its early days Farrar, Straus and Giroux was far from the blue-chip literary imprint of US book publishing. Instead, when John Farrar and Roger Straus first teamed up in 1946, the books they published were a hodgepodge. There was James Branch Campbell's swashbuckler-in-love tale *There Was Two Pirates* (1946), a poetry collection by Owen Dodson (*Powerful Long Ladder*, 1947), the descriptively titled *Why Are You Single?* (Hilda Holland, 1949), William Gardner Smith's critique of Jim Crow through the eyes of African American GIs (*Last of the Conquerors*, 1948), and most importantly for keeping the press in business, Gaylord Hauser's fad diet book *Look Younger, Live Longer* (1950), which argued that toilet seats were too high. In the early days, Farrar brought "literary" works into the house, whereas Straus had, according to former Penguin Group CEO Peter Mayer, a "merchant sensibility" that kept his eye toward profitable books that might make a splash on the market.[2] Some sociologists would predict an inherent tension in this mishmash of literary and commercial books, but the hodgepodge was by design, as clarified in Farrar and Straus's press materials upon launch: "Our list will be a general one, its titles selected with the wish that they will entertain, inform, stimulate. We shall shun neither the realistic nor the romantic."[3]

Over sixty years later the independent Counterpoint Press publishes a similar mélange of works: a literary fiction novel on the effects of the Vietnam War on a small Kentucky town (*Cementville*, 2014), a collection of erotic Indian poetry titled *Love and the Turning Seasons* (2014), and a nearly thousand-page JFK assassination conspiracy theory book (*The Legacy of Secrecy*, 2009/2013). Though Counterpoint is not intentionally modeled on the early division of labor and sensibilities between Farrar and Straus, Charlie Winton and Jack Shoemaker took on similar roles. As described by someone in the field of production with working knowledge of Counterpoint, "Charlie comes from distribution, so he's publishing conspiracy theory books [and titles] that sell really well, while Jack is bringing in, like, obscure and beautiful Buddhist poetry, and couldn't care less how well it sells." This balance of commercial and literary books at Counterpoint, albeit informal, did not cause tension within their offices. Instead, it was a normal and generally unconsidered reality of operations. That Counterpoint had "Jack" books and "Charlie" books didn't make the press act schizophrenically, it made Counterpoint act like Counterpoint, as the contrasting books coexisted harmoniously.

As was the case in the early days of Farrar, Straus and Giroux—publishing both high-minded poetry and advice books about the height of toilet seats—at Counterpoint different books served different purposes. Unlike the taken-for-granted wisdom in much of sociological work about fields of cultural production, for players in book publishing, the primary fear is not of an intermingling of art and commerce, but instead of art and commerce falling *out of balance*. Put another way, what to outsiders may appear as a fundamental and irresolvable tension between art and commerce is for many in the field of production a banal observation that does little to describe the everyday business of producing culture. On the ground and in practice, publishers keep art and commerce in balance through two ways: (1) a balancing of short- and long-term interests, and (2) a balancing of industry and market orientation.

BALANCING SHORT- AND LONG-TERM INTERESTS

Publishing houses generally work to diversify their list between "commercial" books that are hoped to be strong and quick sellers and books with "literary" quality that are hoped to garner longer, if slower, sales. The goal for publishers has historically been to create an equilibrium in sales between their "frontlist" books (the *new* books for that season) and their "backlist" books (the books from previous seasons that are still in print and selling). While some publishers historically have been more backlist or frontlist heavy, for many publishers their backlist might contribute between 30 and 50 percent of sales in any given season.[4] As the relationship between short- and long-term sellers was described by the Publisher at an independent house, "Our goal is to publish hits [i.e., commercial books] so that we can invest in our backlist [i.e., literary books], because we need the backlist to be generating revenue for us when the 'hits' don't hit [i.e., the 'big' commercial books flop, as is inevitable]."

Could-be hits, or "commercial" books, are intended to make a quick splash on best-seller lists by filling unsatiated consumer demand. They can be described in a sentence, and although they are frequently heavily promoted, it's believed they can "sell themselves." Books intended to be hits don't necessarily have to be well written, or believed to hold artistic merit, although they might. Potential hits might include nonfiction books on hot-button issues, celebrity memoirs, cookbooks and children's books by celebrity authors, and new books by famous authors. When projected sales don't meet target goals, a few more "big" books with "hit potential" will be added to the list, part of what John B. Thompson refers to as "extreme publishing."[5]

The upside of "commercial" books are that, if successful, they will generate quick bursts of large revenue. For promotion, marketing, and sales staff, commercial books with hit potential make their jobs easier because their value is easy to describe. The downsides are that, in being of the moment, they may not sell well over the long term, and as potential hits they require large advance expenditures on which they may produce no return. When the hits do hit, however, given the unpredictability of sales in book publishing, their revenue can be used not only to invest in more potential hits, but also to invest in a wide range of "smaller" and more "artistic" books that will hopefully become part of the publisher's backlist.

"Smaller" books are believed to be more "timeless" and "well written," and more often than not are believed to have intrinsic qualities that make them "quality" or "literary." Their pleasures are believed to be more "subtle," "intimate," and "complex," and their worth not possible to describe in a sentence. Smaller books, rather than filling unsatiated demand, have to be "explained" and are hoped to have long lives of slower sales through word of mouth and by being "hand-sold" in bookstores through the recommendations of employees who "love good books." The "timeless" quality of these books means they'll hopefully sell well over time, and keep revenue flowing in even if future seasons' new hits prove to be flops.

The upsides of smaller or more literary books are that the financial investments in them are smaller, many editors are more passionate about working on them, and if they make it to the backlist, they can offer financial stability in an otherwise unpredictable market. In turn, a downside is that while hits might underperform, smaller books, which are harder to describe and not as heavily promoted, are more likely to barely sell at all.[6] By launching literary careers, smaller, literary books also have the potential to offer long-term financial stability. These small bets are "where the major writers of the future usually start," notes Farrar, Straus and Giroux's publisher, Jonathan Galassi.[7] The brass ring for publishing smaller books is widespread classroom adoption, something unlikely with of-the-moment hits, which might lack a timeless quality or literary merit.[8] As described by Talia, an editor at a West Coast publishing house, "If you publish the next *To Kill A Mockingbird*, something school kids are going to be reading for the next fifty years, you can do [i.e., publish] whatever you want for the rest of your life."

The dream of winning this type of literary lottery (i.e., publishing a literary work that is assigned across the country to future generations of students) is rarely realized, although its promise provides a meaningful incentive. In reality, among independent publishers—like Farrar, Straus and Giroux in the mid-twentieth century and Counterpoint today—an active balancing of "commercial" books and "literary" books is a normalized and generally uncontested strategy for staying in business. This requisite feature of working in the field of production was best described by Elizabeth, a colleague of Talia, when explaining the relationship between "big" books and "small" books on her publishing house's list: "Once a year you do your coffee table book about sex or whatever, something you know will sell, and that allows you to publish your 'smaller' books."

While coffee table books about sex may sell in the short term, they are unlikely to have a long life on the backlist, and they also do not help a press build its reputation within the broader field of production. This is unlike publishing more literary books, which in addition to keeping many editors happy and serving as a series of small, long-term investments in the future, also allow presses to maintain a reputation in the field for quality, and to be thought of as favored senders for a review outlet like the *New York Times*. When publishers fall out of this balance, they can be met by others in the field with derision, and be accused of cynicism for trying to minimize risks by working only on low-status schlock. As may have been the case for Cornelia Nixon, while this is a balancing act between art and commerce that may be harder to pull off for an individual novelist, for those in publishing houses that are publishing many books at once it's an unremarkable part of daily life.

EVERY BOOK MUST BE SOLD TWICE: BALANCING INDUSTRY AND MARKET ORIENTATIONS

Historically book publishers have been described as Janus-faced, looking both ways to the fields of creation and reception while guarding the gates between them. Despite this common characterization, the even more obscure Greco-Roman god who best fits as a metaphor for publishers' gaze is the Triple Hecate: the three-headed goddess of crossroads. While players in the field of production spend time looking out to both creation and reception, most regularly their gaze is oriented in a different direction: toward each other and themselves. Although the fields of creation, production, and reception are interdependent, most regularly players in any of them can be found peering into the water of their home field, hoping that their own reflection will be staring back at them. There are fundamental reasons why the field of production maintains such an unflinching interest in itself.[9] The most important is that every book must be sold twice.

The "first" sale of a book, called the "sell-in," usually refers to getting a book "in" to retailers, but is more generally accomplished through selling a book to the field of production itself. The second sale, the "sell through," is to the field of reception; the book sells "through" retailers when it is purchased by readers. To get sell-in for a book means to secure placement in bookstores, and it requires building buzz within the field of production. To diversify risk, all publishers release many new books each season, all of which are at least somewhat unique, and almost all of which will never actually be read by the people who have to decide to stock them or not. As a result the first sale of books into retailers relies heavily on publishers' reputations.

To work in the field of production is to accept that, in the long run, book publishing is a low-margin business. With rampant uncertainty as to which books will return on investment and in a field in which status and social relationships are paramount, the first sale to the industry requires a publishing house to be a known entity, to have a good reputation, and in the case of literary fiction, to be known for taking chances on "quality" or "difficult" books that are believed to be simply too good not to publish.[10] While on one level the balance between commercial and literary books is a balance between short-yet-large and small-yet-steady sales, on another it is a balance between keeping two necessary audiences happy: the industry audience in the field of production whose attention is needed to generate enthusiasm, promotion, and placement, and the consumer audience in the field of reception who, through these pathways, hopefully ultimately *buys* books.

As the importance of publisher reputation was explained by the publicity director of a house with a good reputation for publishing literary fiction alongside more commercial books: "[We] have a really good reputation amongst reviewers [for publishing 'quality' books]. So if we say that we are the most excited about [a particular book] they're going to definitely look at it." For this publicity director, working for a publisher that is a known entity with a good reputation makes her job easier. Her phone calls are returned and book review editors take seriously her enthusiasm and claims of quality for the titles she promotes. While on the one hand her employer could not stay in business exclusively publishing books that appeal to the high literary sensibilities of the field, they would run similar risk by wholly forsaking their peers and adopting a "cynical" strategy of publishing only books with schlock value. This was, at one point, what happened to Simon & Schuster, which after being purchased by the multi-industry conglomerate Gulf and Western in 1975 was derisively referred to as "Simon & Shoe Store" for their purported singular focus on commercially oriented books at the expense of more artistic and literary works.[11]

At an independent publishing house, the balance of art and commercial books is informal, yet when unbalanced, it can threaten a publisher's long-term viability. If oriented too closely to the industry and literary books, a press may never see the large returns that allow for freedom and experimentation. Without sufficient orientation to the industry and too much of an orientation to commercial books, a press may end up chasing hits that never come—and quickly go out of business. In what would seem paradoxical if not for a diversified and harmonious publishing strategy, a long-time publisher recalled how for his independent press having a surprise hit was almost ruinous: "That was the worst thing that ever happened to us. It was hard for people to go back to normal and a lot [of them] ended up quitting. If you have a hit it can change your thinking, and you take bigger risks, and then you wake up and if you don't have your hit each year you're out of business. You become dependent on them. It's like any casino game where your luck eventually runs out."

Because every book has to be sold twice, by balancing industry and market orientations in their publishing schedules, independent publishers not only balance short- and long-term interests, but also keep themselves from becoming hit-dependent. While most sociologists, following the theory of Bourdieu, bifurcate the literary field into artistically and commercially driven poles, it is at the organizational level within the field of production in which art and commerce are harmonized as a requisite feature of being in the business of promoting and selling books.[12]

Yet in the past forty years larger publishing firms, knowing that a balance between artistic and commercial books is necessary for long-term success, have formally and physically separated them. This separation, rather than signaling a tension between artistic and commercial concerns, further cements their interdependency and the smoothness with which they may be kept in harmony within the large publishers.

THE CASE OF THE BIG GUYS: OPEN SYSTEMS AND BEING BOTH BIG AND SMALL, FAST AND SLOW

The first wave of conglomeration in US book publishing occurred between the late 1960s and early 1980s.[13] In this twenty-year period, multi-industry conglomerates purchased publishing houses with dreams of media convergence and to diversify their portfolios. They also laid off editors to streamline operations, and in the process, some firms centralized decision making and control over which books were published. Due in large part to these changes, the era immediately preceding this one (the 1950s and early 1960s) has been rewritten as a golden age of US book publishing in which literary passion ruled decision making and publishing houses operated independently of commercial concern. Although this is an apocryphal account of what had actually gone on at publishers such as Farrar and Straus in that era, the narrative functioned to argue that the *balancing* between artistic and commercial concerns had fallen out of equilibrium under conglomerate control. The first wave of conglomeration in book publishing was relatively short-lived, however, as large multi-industry conglomerates learned that book publishing was a low-margin business, with profits in a "good year" often between 1 and 4 percent.[14] In assessing the profits and losses of their publishing ventures, for these conglomerates, the old industry adage rang true: the best way to make a small fortune in book publishing is to start with a large one.

During the second wave of conglomeration, from the 1980s through today, multi-industry conglomerates sold off their book publishing ventures, which were then purchased by conglomerate businesses whose core ventures remained in book publishing.[15] It is in this second wave that the informal balancing between artistic and commercial concerns that had long existed in independent houses was structurally formalized and solidified in the large conglomerates as well. In the second wave, like the first, large firms again purchased many independent publishers, but unlike during the first wave, decision making about what to publish remained almost entirely decentralized and autonomous, and entirely so for books without blockbuster-sized advances. This "open system" or "federal" model of organization allowed different, mostly autonomous publishing imprints within conglomerates to build specialized identities, and both physically and symbolically separated artistic and commercial books into nonoverlapping concerns.[16] For example, Penguin Random House controls about 250 separate imprints that specialize their foci and operate almost entirely independently of each other when selecting which books to publish: Sentinel publishes commercial nonfiction for conservative audiences, Spiegel & Grau focuses on breaking new literary authors, Grosset & Dunlap publishes licensed children's books (e.g., *The Care Bears*), and Schocken publishes fiction and nonfiction on Jewish-themed interests. While for the most part the ins and outs of different imprints' specialized identities are unknown in the field of reception, in the first "sale" to the industry itself an imprint's identity clarifies what its new books "are" and where they fit in the wider field.

The autonomy granted to individual imprints offers three advantages for the large conglomerates. First, imprints can rely on the benefits of size while still maintaining focus and expertise across what is collectively a wide array of market niches. Second, this multi-imprint model preserves a diversity of decision making about what to publish, which allows the big conglomerates to stumble onto new trends rather than just sucking the life-blood from old ones.[17] Third, by having multiple imprints conglomerates can essentially pool the risk of working in book publishing: many different imprints concurrently do many different things, with none of them guaranteed to know what readers will be looking for in the next few months, let alone years. Thus, while an imprint can, and often still will, balance between more literary and more commercial books within its niche, at the conglomerate level there is a second type of balancing that allows for the preservation of a system-wide equilibrium even as individual imprints may occasionally fall in and out of balance.

Given this arrangement, on the editorial side the imprints of large conglomerates can be small and slow, as they know that a few bad seasons or missed bets won't bankrupt them. In contrast, on the marketing and publicity side, conglomerate publishers can at the same time be large and fast, directing the gasoline of financial resources and industry clout onto those books and imprints that unexpectedly ignite. In this way, by being multitudinous, small, and slow on the editorial side and monolithic, large, and fast on the promotion and publicity side, large publishers are even *more equipped* to let the hits come, and to avoid making editorial decisions with only financial considerations in mind. In this model the balancing of art and commerce barely takes any work at all, as it is fully formalized and deeply embedded within the organizational structure of the system.

THE CASE OF THE LITTLE GUYS: BALANCING ART, COMMERCE, AND SPECIALIZED IDENTITIES

Non-conglomerate (or "independent") publishing houses like Counterpoint Press don't have the advantages possessed by the large conglomerates. In what is for everyone a low-margin business, independent presses are smaller and leaner, and arguably more efficient. They operate with fewer bureaucratic levels, sometimes contract out tasks like copyediting and cover design, and contract out their distribution to independent distributors, or to larger, conglomerate publishers. Independent publishers also do not have the capital—or often the desire—to offer large authorial advances, and they rarely if ever involve themselves in bidding wars, or "auctions," for new manuscripts. As independent presses' bets are smaller, more often than not their wins and losses are also smaller.

While conglomerate presses mitigate against the inherent uncertainty of selling culture by pooling risk across multiple imprints and putting the full force of their weight behind hits (to launch them into the stratosphere), independent presses mitigate against uncertainty in two other ways. First, independent presses can develop highly curated and specialized identities for doing one thing particularly well, and, second, they can maintain generalist lists that span genres and categories while hunting for pockets of space between, in front of, or beneath the lists of conglomerate publishers. In the case of specialized identities, rather than publishing some artistic books and some commercial books, the specialized publishing niche is just what it is, and the most commercially viable books are essentially the same thing as the best artistic representations within that niche. In the case of generalist lists, the goal is to reach equilibrium between fast and slow sellers, albeit on a smaller scale than the conglomerates.

For independent publishers that create and rely on specialized identities, they hope their reputations are known across all three fields and that at least those in the fields of creation, production, and reception who are positioned to be interested in them know what they do and who they are. Independent presses with specialized identities may focus on feminist literature (Seal Press), politically left (Haymarket Books, Seven Stories Press) or right leaning (Regnery) books, or art and design (Taschen).[18] For other specialized independent presses, the niche is the publisher and the publisher is the niche. The ideal case in point is McSweeney's, an independent nonprofit publisher founded by the name-economy author Dave Eggers. An editor who did not work at McSweeney's described how the press both fostered and relied upon its niche identity:

> For them each book isn't just the book, it's an art object. It's this bespoke piece of art that you want to display after you read. A McSweeney's book means something to people. There are fans of the publisher, not just whichever author they happen to be publishing. They do direct sales and have a subscription business. They have somewhere around one thousand people who pay $100 for the next ten books that McSweeney's puts out regardless of what they are. And when people sign up, McSweeney's only maybe has the next four books scheduled, but there's a thousand people or whatever who like and trust McSweeney's enough to want to have whatever they decide to do. So if McSweeney's publishes a book it's actually impossible for them to sell less than one thousand copies of it, because people have already purchased it before even knowing what it is.

For McSweeney's, in developing a specialized identity to the point that readers are willing to pay in advance for their titles, a niche identity keeps them in business, and also allows them to take risks, as the worst flop McSweeney's publishes is still guaranteed to generate sales through their subscription business. McSweeney's is also able to leverage their clear identity in the field of production: they don't rent booth space at BookExpo America— although they are there—because booksellers will stock McSweeney's titles simply for being McSweeney's titles. They're also able to stay lean thanks to a steady stream of interns who started as fans. Due to both Eggers's status as a name-economy author and McSweeney's nonprofit work, others in the field are also willing to do favors for them that they wouldn't do for conglomerate presses.

While sociologists have highlighted how maintaining a clear, strong identity helps connect producers and consumers—a story that fits quite well with McSweeney's, if not most publishers—too strong of an identity can at the same time pose challenges for publishers. As explained by a McSweeney's employee, "Our identity is shaped pretty naturally and organically through the things that we want to do, but at the same time that means we get people writing for us. We get a bunch of submissions in which people are writing like Dave [Eggers], or imitating [David] Foster Wallace or [George] Saunders because that's what we 'do,' but we already do that and we don't need someone to write like Dave [Eggers] because Dave writes like Dave better than someone else can. That's a challenge."

While independent presses with curated and specialized identities like McSweeney's can face the problem of authors writing too much "for" them, other independent presses that do not possess such specialized identities do not face this challenge. To compete against the large conglomerates, these presses must use other tools. Such is the case for more generalist independent publishers (which still maintain a broad literary focus) such as Graywolf Press, Grove Atlantic, Melville House, Milkweed Editions, Overlook, and Counterpoint. At Counterpoint, like different imprints at a conglomerate publisher albeit on a much smaller scale, "Jack" books and "Charlie" books served different purposes. Jack books catered to the backlist and Counterpoint's literary reputation (i.e., the art side of a balanced publishing strategy), and Charlie books contributed more purposefully to the seasonal bottom line (i.e., the commerce side of a balanced publishing strategy). As an editor familiar with Counterpoint's operation described it, "I think Jack's been in the business long enough to know that if you're doing exactly what you want in the right way that it's a break even business at best. He's been in it for a while, and he's not hunting for the next best seller. He just wants to publish things that he likes, whereas I think Charlie is more sales oriented and I think he wants to hit a home run, because those are the books that he likes."

At the time Jack books were those like *Jarrettsville* for which the value had to be explained and sold, and Charlie books were those for which there may already be a native audience: the memoir of a former NFL player about his health challenges after retirement, and a work of genre fiction that had already been optioned by a major film studio by an author who wanted the literary imprimatur of publishing with a literary publisher. Importantly, both Winton and Shoemaker were seeking the types of books they respectively *liked*; in both doing what they wanted to do, they balanced the publishing aims of Counterpoint.

While some niche-oriented independent publishers expressed criticism over Counterpoint's more generalist "old-school" strategy (the belief was that over the long term Counterpoint simply could not compete being a micro-mirror of a generalist major publisher), other niche and generalist independent publishers saw Counterpoint engaging in strategies that carved out subtler spaces in the market from conglomerate publishers. As described by a different editor who was familiar with the press, "Counterpoint basically exists as a corrective against the majors' abandonment of midlist authors. We have all of these wonderful writers who, for whatever reason, their first or second novels only sold five thousand copies so they're 'failures,' which allows Counterpoint to come in and resurrect the careers of really talented writers that fell victim to not meeting expectations that were probably too high to begin with. Five thousand copies is a nice title for them, but you sell three, or four, or five thousand copies for FSG and you're a 'failure.'"

Thus, working with definitions of "success" and "failure" that differ from conglomerate publishers is another strategy used by independent publishers to thrive. Sometimes this is achieved by picking up talented writers who have underperformed by conglomerate standards, for which Counterpoint's smaller advances become more attractive, and for which smaller expectations are more likely to be met. With smaller bets, losses are less likely to be catastrophic, and by the same token, winning is also redefined. As described by an editor at another independent press, the success or failure of a book has as much or more to do with expectations as it does with outcomes: "[A book is] only a dud if you think it's going to sell well and it doesn't. It's not a dud if you don't think it's going to sell well and then it doesn't sell well. This is why you have to pick a margin on a book, if the advance isn't too high and you don't print way too many [copies] you're not going to lose money on a book that doesn't sell well. Maybe you'll lose time, but if it sells three thousand and you print four thousand you've made money on that. And you didn't spend a lot of money on the advance or sending them on tour and doing all these ads or whatever—so that's not a problem."

While smaller losses allow more generalist independent presses to operate, that these smaller losses are often paired with smaller hits and that they offer smaller advances pose their own set of challenges when competing against conglomerates. Thus, generalist *and* specialist independent presses legitimize their validity—and, they would argue, their necessity—in the field of production through two other ways. First, they are willing to take on titles and authors who are ignored or rejected by conglomerate publishers, and, second, they are willing to spend more time working with authors on perfecting their manuscripts—an argument for dedication, enthusiasm, and care over the dollar amount of the advance. As the argument goes, independent presses offer time and attention in lieu of money. Yet even this, in reality, has more to do with where an author is "slotted" on a publisher's list.

A "frontlist" author at an independent press gets no more attention than a frontlist author at a conglomerate, but if that same frontlist author at an independent were at a conglomerate, she would likely instead be a "midlist" author and get far less attention, whereas a midlist author at an independent would get no attention at all at a conglomerate, as her book would not be published.

As a result, generalist independent publishers are correct when they claim to give more attention to authors than they would otherwise receive, but they also differentiate themselves through a willingness to bestow attention on projects that may *need* a lot of attention. Put another way, sometimes independent publishers are spending more time on books not because they "care more," but because the books they are able to attract simply *take more time*. As explained by an editor at an independent press: "All the books that come to us have been, almost all, have been rejected by other places. It's not for no reason—sometimes they just need a new paint job or some personal care. So that's the only way we're able to get great books—they might be slightly irregular, but with really special and unique things in them that just need to be unearthed."

For editors at conglomerate imprints, the ideal manuscript is one that—with the help of a literary agent who has already performed her double duties—is ready to be published without editorial lifting. Editors at independent presses much more rarely find themselves in possession of these gems, as instead of digging through submissions in search of diamonds, they're digging through submissions in search of diamonds in the rough. As a result, editors at independent presses spend more time and care working with authors not necessarily because they want to, but because they have to. This is not to suggest that editors at independent presses are any more or less capable or dedicated than their counterparts at conglomerates. Instead, and particularly for generalist independent press, it is a matter of specialization: to be an editor at an independent press is akin to being a talented groomer who specializes in the beautification of what are sometimes shaggy dogs.

HOW THE END OF *JARRETTSVILLE* QUITE LITERALLY BECAME THE BEGINNING

Although Adam Krefman was incredibly enthusiastic about *Jarrettsville*, he still saw in it a shaggy dog quality that had also been identified by the editors at conglomerate presses who had rejected it. The novel contained exceptional promise, Krefman thought, but there was *something* about it that did not quite work right. It was not just Krefman's position and disposition that caused him to advocate for the publishing of *Jarrettsville* when others did not, but instead it was the position and disposition of Counterpoint Press, too, that made it a novel worth pursuing.[19]

Krefman, as an editor at Counterpoint, was not scared off by Nixon's weak sales for her two previous novels. Instead, from Counterpoint's perspective, Nixon was the author of two well-reviewed novels, and her strong reviews and weak sales were in some ways what made her an author whom Counterpoint would and should want to work with. To Counterpoint, Nixon was a talented writer who had been slipping through the cracks in the transition from the field of production to reception. Because of this slippage she would likely not get another chance to connect with readers through a conglomerate press, despite her established gifts as a writer. If Counterpoint could keep their advance to Nixon low and their sales expectations in check, Nixon was actually exactly the type of author they were looking for: an accomplished writer who would not require a large financial risk and whose work could pay off in a big or small way in the end. And so Shoemaker contacted Weil and they negotiated a $6,000 advance for Nixon. As long as Counterpoint did not overprint the novel, they could sell five thousand or so copies and have a win by the scaled down standards of an independent publisher.

Yet although Nixon was precisely the type of author that a press like Counterpoint would and should be interested in, within the press, and from Krefman in particular, there were still concerns about the novel itself. As Krefman had phrased it, the first third of *Jarrettsville* was very "optimistic," and not the type of story that a casual reader expected to descend into a murder and a trial. In support of Krefman's summary, the first third, told from Martha's viewpoint, covered her courtship with Nick. Despite major familial differences, they fell in love, wrote each other love letters, and stole time together in fields of flowers. As one of the rejecting editors wrote in response to the opening third of the manuscript: "It was the love story itself that bothered me . . . the writing seemed overwrought, over-romantic, unlike Nixon's style when she was relating the courtroom scenes."

Krefman, even more pointedly, had some of the same concerns while reading Martha's section: "At one point while reading I wrongly thought [*Jarrettsville*] was a paperback Danielle Steel kind of thing, and I got really nervous that it was not culturally the right fit [for Counterpoint and myself]. . . . The big editorial question was how to keep the reader interested past Martha's very romantic section, which is only one voice in the narrative." If the first third of *Jarrettsville* could be confused for a romance novel, it was not the type of book that Counterpoint could take on. While categorical overlap between historical, literary, and commercial fiction can be managed and overcome, the categorical distinctions between literary and romance fiction are impregnable. At all times and places this need not be true—one of Nixon's early inspirations, D. H. Lawrence, wrote love stories while maintaining his literary bona fides, albeit as a male author—but in the field of production as it currently stood, a work of literary fiction that first reads like a romance novel is a problem, just as a romance novel that ends in murder is a problem. Counterpoint didn't know how to market and promote romance fiction, nor did they have any interest in doing so. Instead, for Counterpoint to be a generalist firm while maintaining a reputation for "quality" in the field of production, publishing romance fiction, or even something that could be confused for romance fiction, would be general anathema. There are presses that specialize in romance fiction and make money and produce "good work" while doing so, but Counterpoint was not one of them. Likewise, Nixon's reputation as a well-reviewed literary novelist was also incompatible with producing work that could be confused for romance.

Over time, in dialogue with her social circle in the field of creation and her literary agent, and in response to editors in the field of production, before arriving to Krefman *Jarrettsville* had already been made more "literary." Nixon had gone from a single first-person narrative to multiple first-person narratives, deepening the characters by exposing their motivations, and more centrally focusing on the subtext of the setting, which was infused with post-slavery racism and post–Civil War hostilities. To fit with Counterpoint though, Nixon would have to take yet another step in a more literary direction. As Krefman explained his intervention:

> To Jack I suggested that because the novel is broken into thirds, with the third part being peripheral accounts of the aftermath of Nick's murder and Martha's trial, something we could do was bring in about four or five of those peripheral characters and move them to the front of the novel. That way you get about twenty-five pages of tension from just after the murder. You get this sense that something went terribly wrong. You don't really have the details and you don't know exactly what happened, but you're drawn in, and then when you get the love story you already suspect that Martha has killed him, or at least played a part in his killing. By retelling the story out of linear order you add a really dark element to this very moving and romantic courtship recounted by Martha. It turns the optimism of their romance into a strength and makes it more heartfelt and tragic because you know it isn't going to end well.

For Krefman and Counterpoint, rearranging *Jarrettsville* into a nonlinear narrative that begins *in medias res* was a way to use the plot-driven facets of the novel to its literary advantage. Rather than leaving the full weight of *Jarrettsville*'s literary justification on Nixon's prose, the quality of her writing could be further buttressed by introducing even more complexity in form. Nixon, who had already infused more complexity in *Jarrettsville* when revising it from *Martha's Version* into multiple narratives, thought that Krefman's suggestion was "wonderful." It was, "brilliant, I'll never be able to thank him enough," she said, eyes gleaming.

As one of *Jarrettsville*'s rejecting editors had noted, the novel "seemed to straddle the line between literary and commercial," which is "a wonderful area to publish into if the balance is just right." Krefman's suggestion, and Nixon's resulting excitement about it, was a creative editorial act to get that balancing right. As a result Krefman, like Wendy Weil, rather than simply being a gatekeeper into the field of production, became yet another silent partner in the creation of *Jarrettsville*. Nixon was an author who fit the position and disposition of Counterpoint Press, but it took Krefman to rework *Jarrettsville* into a Counterpoint book. In the duality between a publisher's reputation and the work it publishes, *Jarrettsville* became the rare type of book that all at once could balance artistic and financial concerns at an independent generalist imprint like Counterpoint. It had a commercial story that was told in a literary style, and was written by a well-reviewed novelist for whom sales had remained elusive. Although the diamond in the novel had taken some work to unearth, after years of things being wrong with *Jarrettsville*, they suddenly appeared to be going right. Yet how right they'd continue to go, at least for a little while, was still unknown, even to Krefman or Nixon.

STORYTELLING AND MYTHMAKING

OR, HOW A ONE-SENTENCE EMAIL NEARLY

DOUBLED A PRINT RUN

SOWING A WEB OF COLLECTIVE BELIEF

It did not take Nixon long to enact Krefman's suggestion of moving part of the end of *Jarrettsville* to the beginning. Based on Krefman's suggestion, in its reformulation the story begins with witness accounts from immediately after Martha's murder of Nick, traces back to Martha's section of them first falling in love, moves to Nick's section covering the dissolution of their relationship up to the moment of his death, and then closes with Martha's trial. After this major structural change, only smaller developmental edits and copyediting remained.

Copy editors, in their formal occupational role, are paid to maintain stylistic and grammatical accuracy, not to have opinions. Yet copy editors also come in different types, and there is an often unacknowledged subtlety to the work they do. To copyedit *Jarrettsville*, Krefman contacted Mikayla Butchart, an editor at another publisher who also occasionally moonlighted as a copy editor and illustrator. Just as Shoemaker had selected Krefman to work on *Jarrettsville* for his "innate" sense of working with a literary author, Krefman selected Butchart for her "innate" sense of editing a literary writer: "She does really thorough work, and in a way where if I tell her not to mess with a writer's writing, she'll honor that. Some copy editors are so literal that they edit all the poetry out of the language . . . but Mikayla is a copy editor who I totally trust, the kind of copy editor I would trust to make the right judgments."

Krefman's selection of Butchart, while partially based on her sensibilities as a copy editor, were also based on a second consideration. *Jarrettsville* still had a long way to travel through the field of production before being pitched into the field of reception, and it was unlikely that anyone, save for the copy editor, would be fully reading the novel from start to finish until that transition. For Krefman then, his trust of Butchart was not only as a copy editor of a certain sensitivity, but also as a *reader* of *Jarrettsville*, and one whose day job as an editor made her opinions about the novel additionally useful. Butchart and Krefman had worked together before, and in their emails Butchart quickly became a sounding board for Krefman's broader interpretive and evaluative questions about Nixon's novel.[1]

> From: Adam Krefman
> To: Mikayla Butchart
> Subject: Re: Available to copyedit?
>
> . . . Off-the-record question: did the first 4 chapters at the beginning make sense? i.e., the ones before Martha's big chapter? Those used to be in the back, next to all the others, but I told Cornelia we ought to move them up, to give Martha's chapter more darkness and tension. I'm curious to hear your thoughts on the actual narrative, writing, etc. . . .

> From: Mikayla Butchart
> To: Adam Krefman
> Subject: Re: Available to copyedit?
>
> . . . As for your off-the-record question about the organization of the manuscript, a resounding yes! I think the large Martha and Nick chapters are far more engrossing for the demise of their relationship being laid out at the beginning of the novel. I found the whole story very moving, surprisingly so, and I'm usually really tough. That response probably wouldn't have been the case if the book had been arranged chronologically—romantic tension is usually not enough to keep me interested in a story (especially with the main characters being so charming and beautiful and all). Moving the timeline around makes it much more than a romance/tragedy and lends it a dimension that readers might not recognize until halfway through, had the story been arranged as the author intended. . . .

For most editors, as for most people, there is a fair degree of uncertainty in private evaluation and interpretation; evaluation often unfolds in *processes* of interaction and social influence. Using "off-the-record" colloquially to signal talk that was not part of Butchart's formal role as the copy editor, Krefman was able to check in with a mostly uninvested third party about her evaluation of the novel and the decisions he had made in reshaping it.

Though Krefman had already received the support of Shoemaker and Nixon in his editorial suggestion, receiving further confirmation from Butchart was enough to assuage the rest of his doubts. From Butchart's next email, the following day, Krefman had two more of his private evaluations confirmed:

From: Mikayla Butchart
To: Adam Krefman
Subject: Re: Available to copyedit?

. . . All in all, and more off the record, I found her story compelling and well-constructed and unexpectedly moving, as I've mentioned. . . . You can tell her that the copy editor cried twice. . . . She does an excellent job of vocalizing for a range of different characters, and I found her writing eloquent and engaging.

What is your feeling about the last paragraph of the novel, the one in her own words? It reads almost like an author's epilogue, which I assume it kind of is, though it seems to straddle this gray place between fact and fiction. Perhaps it would be best broken out, part of the backmatter preceding the genealogy and map, instead of where it is currently located. . . . Anyway, I didn't make any comments of the sort in the manuscript, and only offer up these observations for you to do with them what you will.

For Krefman this email bore two gifts beyond the returned and copyedited manuscript that came with it. First, as an editor herself, Butchart had offered an editorial suggestion, and in the final draft of *Jarrettsville* Cornelia Nixon's first-person narrative did appear as an epilogue. Second, both as a managing editor and as a reader, Butchart corroborated the enthusiasm Krefman felt for *Jarrettsville*, noting that she had twice been drawn to tears by the novel while ostensibly copyediting it. From Butchart, Krefman now knew that the emotional reaction he drew from *Jarrettsville* was not entirely idiosyncratic.

Beyond the "artistic" side of an editor's double duties (i.e., evaluating manuscripts and working with authors to improve them), a good editor must also be a good salesperson. Once the "art-based" work is done, an editor must then use his own enthusiasm as a tool to generate positive appraisal for the novels he works on. In most cases, the actual book will not be read by the people to whom an editor needs to pass on his enthusiasm. Instead, the editor becomes a storyteller in his own right, building webs of collective belief around his most favored books. The editor's initial enthusiasm must be strong, and clearly stated for others, as it will need to pass down through a circuit of senders and receivers as a manuscript works its way through the field of production and toward reception. A different editor explains the importance of this type of advocacy work through the language of "infecting" others with enthusiasm:

> Being enthusiastic is the most important thing, even better if it's real, because if you can say "I really love this book" or "We really love this book" and mean it then it gets it closer to the top of people's lists. So I have to be really enthusiastic and infect the copy editor and the cover designer with that enthusiasm to get their best work out of them, and infect our marketing staff with enthusiasm so they can infect the sales team who can infect [bookstore] buyers who can then infect readers. And meanwhile you've got other people working to infect the bloggers and reviewers, you know, really letting them know how enthusiastic you are about this title. So you want that enthusiasm to build through people, not dissipate, which is what happens if you just like something instead of really loving it.

For Krefman, "the copy editor cried twice" was an important anecdote to circulate around the office, as that she was so emotionally engrossed in the story while ostensibly correcting dangling modifiers lent further credibility to his enthusiasm. The story was a useful, albeit small, signal to send about *Jarrettsville* within the Counterpoint offices as Krefman started to coordinate people around the object of his affection.

But it was a different email from a different sender that would chart *Jarrettsville* onto a new course at Counterpoint. About a month after Butchart's message, Charlie Winton, the CEO and publisher of Counterpoint, received his own email about *Jarrettsville*. Its brevity belied its importance. Amounting to a signal sentence, the email read: "About halfway through *Jarrettsville*, and really enjoying it so far." This was the first significant step in raising *Jarrettsville*'s profile from a book that would be published to a book that would be collectively pushed in its path to the field of reception. But why and how, and who was this email from?

ON MIDLISTS AND LEADS: TO SINK, SWIM, OR BE CARRIED

A key division within publishers' "frontlist" books is between "lead" and "midlist" titles. The "list" is a publisher's catalog, or the (physical or electronic) seasonal promotional pamphlet that publishers use in their coordination with retailers. As one would expect, a publisher's "backlist" books (i.e., books from previous seasons) appear at the back of their catalog, while new midlist books appear in the middle and lead titles appear at the front.[2] To be a lead or on the midlist, however, is about much more than where a book appears in a pamphlet.

The positioning of books in a publisher's catalog is archaeological evidence as to which titles in any given season have won the battle for enthusiasm inside the house. Sometimes this is based on true, unforced belief, and sometimes the lead titles come preordained, be it through their name-economy authorship or through a publisher chasing the tail of an outsized advance. To be a lead title is to be treated differently by being bestowed with the gifts of money, time, and resources that enthusiasm affords. "Midlist" titles, as Paul Hirsch put it, are the "understudies": in the cases where lead titles cannot perform the sales duties expected of them, publishers hope the midlist books will take their place.[3] Put another way, as a matter of belief and investment, lead titles will be carried to the shores of the field of reception, whereas midlist titles will be dutifully placed into its waters and left to sink or swim on their own.

In many ways, the web of collective belief that forms around lead titles is intended to be self-fulfilling. The goal is to shower them with resources such that as they pass through the field of production, they will continue to be showered with more. At Counterpoint, compared to most other publishers, lead titles less frequently arrive into the house already anointed as such, and instead emerge in the publication process. Because Counterpoint is partially in the business of reclaiming the careers of talented writers who had failed to sell as midlist authors at conglomerates, there is more room for a conglomerate's failed midlist author to become a lead author. Furthermore, because Counterpoint does not offer large advances, no promissory notes about who will be taking the lead position have been granted before the decision is made. Most importantly, Charlie Winton, who had made his career in distribution as founder of Publishers Group West before purchasing Counterpoint, was particularly attuned to the first of the two sales that every book goes through: the selling to the field of production itself.

Winton's background in distribution causes him to be circumspect in his decision making for lead titles. The lead title position is an important one, as being anointed a lead title helps get distributors committed and on board in pushing a book out to the field of reception. For that reason, rather than anointing lead titles and leaving it fully up to the Counterpoint publicity and marketing staff to infect others with enthusiasm, finding out where the enthusiasm of others was more naturally forming could clarify decisions in picking leads. The logic of this was that if midlist titles are to sink or swim on their own, if Counterpoint could wait to get some early feedback on their strongest swimmers, they could better target them for additional carrying. As an employee at Counterpoint described the strategy, "In Charlie's vision, the way that [sales] projections take place is that they're a very fluid and organic and subjective matter. Obviously in anybody's mind it is. But what we're doing here is betting that one book it going to stand up and take the lead in any given month. You have to either designate that book and force it to be the lead title of the month, lead fiction and lead nonfiction, or you can wait and discover which book steps up and becomes the lead."

To wait and discover which book becomes the lead ultimately means to stave off a decision and to incorporate new information from distributors and the like into the decision as it is accumulated; it means trying to ride waves of collective enthusiasm rather than always trying to create them. The upside of this approach is that rather than getting stuck in a commitment trap early in the production process, the web of collective belief can start to spread naturally as the production process unfolds. The downside is a different kind of risk: a press can find itself with time ticking down and no lead titles that have emerged. Luckily for Counterpoint, the enthusiasm for *Jarrettsville* had started to build early in the production cycle.

COVERS, PHOTOS, SYNOPSES, AND BLURBS

The goal of advertising, as seen in its Latin root, *ad vertere*, is to make people turn toward something. In this broad definition, the "packaging" of books—from their formats to their covers, back-cover synopses, blurbs, and author photos—is all advertising. As what is more traditionally thought of as advertising—television, radio, print, and online campaigns—is practically nonexistent for non-name-economy authors, the "packaging" of books is the primary place in which publishers can tell their self-defined story about a new novel. Far from a recent trend, the practice of including attractive cover art and "blurbs" from name-economy friends about a book's exceptionality is almost one hundred years old, first emerging in the United States around the 1920s.

Book covers, like movie posters, primarily rely on two devices: tropes and trends. Tropes on book covers are intended to convey to intended audiences that the book in question is a piece of culture that has been made for them. They can rely on clichés and standardized generic conventions in imagery or typeface not because designers lack creativity, but because these things are instantaneous visual cues for the category into which a book falls. Trends (e.g., "hand-drawn" typeface, very large typeface, white text on black backgrounds, minimalist and "clean" cover design) are tropes that may jump categories and are more prone to falling in and out of fashion. As noted by Tom Dyckhoff, this type of "design shorthand" makes bookstores "almost color-coded to make selection easier."[4]

A book cover, in addition to capturing the eye and conveying a category, should ideally capture the core essence of a book. This can be metaphoric or lightly suggestive and broad, but a good book cover nonetheless should represent what is contained within. For two reasons, however, capturing the essence of a book through a cover design is no small feat. First, rather than actually reading the books for which they will be designing covers, cover designers receive a "brief," which often contains a synopsis of the story, its category, the intended audience, any available art that has already been sourced, the covers from the author's previous books, and competing titles in the category so that the cover of the book in question can be somewhat differentiated. Second, even if a cover designer had the time to actually read the book, what a book "is" may not always be clear. Consider, for instance, how, using the following prompt, one might convey what *Jarrettsville* is in a noncluttered, visually arresting way: *Jarrettsville* is a literary *and* commercial *and* historical work of fiction that is based on a Civil War–adjacent true story that is infused with the lingering tensions of the war and racism, while also tracing how romantic love has devolved into murder and a trial, all while being deeply rooted in a sense of place.

The cover designer for *Jarrettsville*, Gerilyn Attebery, had previously been the design manager at an imprint run by Jack Shoemaker. Attebery had a good relationship with the Counterpoint staff, and found work with them to be easier because she had previously sat at the opposite side of the table from cover designers. Whereas left to her own devices a cover designer might orient toward the *design* in "cover design," a publisher is more oriented toward the *cover*, and having served in both roles, Attebery understood this. Cover designers, like agents, editors, and copy editors, are also typecast to some degree, and are "matched" to certain types of books and not others. At Counterpoint, Attebery had been typecast as the designer for their more "commercial" literary books.

Included in the cover designer's brief for *Jarrettsville* was Krefman's synopsis of the story, assorted historical maps of the area, and a photo of Martha Jane Cairnes. Though the photo could convey some historicity and the true-life aspect of the story, it didn't convey the murder at the core of the novel. Just using the photo of Martha could also risk alienating male readers, who, like Krefman, might enjoy the novel if they could be induced to

FIGURE 7.1: *Jarrettsville* Covers. Images courtesy of Counterpoint Press.

read it. As such, Attebery needed to incorporate the photo of Martha while still having the cover appeal to both male and female readers, and while also working within the conventions and constraints of cover design. In the first round Attebery provided Counterpoint with five covers (see Figure 7.1).

Knowing that Counterpoint thought of her as the designer for their more "commercial" titles, she knew she had to provide them with at least one cover that was, in her words, "bright" and "literal" rather than "staid" and "historical" or "literary." The goal was to find not an entirely "commercial" cover, but one that was harmoniously both "commercial" and "literary." Based on her own tastes she preferred the second, third, and fourth covers that she had presented to Counterpoint, already knowing that they would be interpreted as too "historical" or "literary" without being sufficiently "commercial": "I started with getting the photo of the woman, and loving it, and a bunch of historical maps. The maps I felt were really beautiful but everything has maps on it these days, and they also had talked about using those for the end papers, which is a beautiful idea. So I abandoned the maps and decided to try her [i.e., the picture of Martha] out. I started off with these three [covers 2, 3, and 4] . . . which I loved. I love the boldness of the colors and the type. I just absolutely love these three covers." Despite her own personal preference for these covers, Attebery drafted and placed first in the packet another cover (number 1), which was less overtly historical and a bit more commercial:

> The first three are my favorites, but I had a feeling they were going to pick [cover 1], I knew that they would pick it because it probably is a little more commercial. . . . The typography [on cover 3 conveys historicity but] probably wasn't going to be legible enough for them, but I thought I'd try it out anyway. For [cover 1] . . . I thought I'd try bright color, with the [background] photo establishing a sense of place, and the gun, I knew there was a gun in the story. . . . I wouldn't have done a *photo* of a gun. It needed to be something interesting to look at and a photo of a gun would have never worked with this. If I hadn't found this gun, which is ornate and makes it interesting, I would have left the gun idea and gone somewhere else. This cover [cover 5] I like but don't love, but I figured I'd give them another one because [covers 2, 3, and 4] are so similar.

Having sat at both sides of the table, Attebery knew that Counterpoint would prefer the first cover; it satisfied design elements that made it "good work" even if it was not her personal preference. When looking at cover 1, designers believe that the eye starts at the top left, then from left to right traces the barrel of the gun. The eye then loops back down through the photo of Martha, is brought back to the left again by the curvature of the crops, and then heads back to the right across Nixon's name. This is a "Z pattern" or "reverse S pattern" layout, which is one of a few common layouts in advertising and, by extension, book cover design.

In addition to satisfying these design elements, cover 1 also did the "cover" work in cover design. It satisfied the demand of attracting both male and female readers, as in the trope-based shorthand of cover design, for women there was an ethereal Martha, and for men there was a gun. Although this characterization is based in broad generalization, the point of book covers often is broad generalization. As the recurring "problem" with *Jarrettsville* had always been balancing its commercial and literary aspirations, the cover too had to balance these aspirations, and as the designer predicted, cover 1 in her packet was quickly deemed a favorite among Counterpoint staff. Although the cover was perhaps a bit more commercial than Krefman or even its creator preferred, the Counterpoint staff agreed that it incorporated some commercial elements without being "frivolous" and still maintained a literary and historical tone.

In the next round of covers, the only changes made were to the topography of the background image, which had not evoked the rolling hills of the setting; it provided a sense of place, but not the right place. Attebery provided four more options of the same cover with different topographical backgrounds for Nixon and Krefman to choose from. Though these other backgrounds lost some of the "reverse S pattern" from the curvature of the crops in the original image, the new cover now better represented a sense of place for where exactly the story was set.

For Nixon's author photo, Counterpoint wanted to hire a local photographer. Nixon, on the other hand, wanted her author photo to be taken by Marion Ettlinger, who first rose to prominence in the early 1980s when *Esquire* hired her to shoot portraits of American writers. She is almost entirely unknown in the field of reception, and only sometimes known in the field of production, but with her name comes a host of meaning for a particular segment of authors in the field of creation. As one knowledgeable publisher described it, an author photo by Ettlinger signals that "the marketing department for the publisher is serious about this book, or that [the author] is famous," whereas for another an Ettlinger photo was simply "vanity that the author wants . . . [and] money [that] might be better spent on other more beneficial things in marketing."

Yet to authors, having a photo from Ettlinger is a status symbol, and a symbolic representation of where the author belongs in the field of creation. As described by Lee Siegel in the *New York Times*, "To be 'Ettlingered' means to have imparted to you an aura of distinction and renown."[5] Given Cornelia Nixon's reputation in the field of creation, as an accomplished literary writer who had won awards despite elusive sales, being photographed by Ettlinger was, for her, an important mark of accomplishment. In recounting her decision to be photographed by Ettlinger, Nixon recalled how frequently her name had come up among authors: "I mentioned needing an author photo, and [a fellow author] said 'Oh, get Marion Ettlinger. Then everybody will know they have to pay attention to you.' And the day before Vendela [Vida] had also told me that it was Marion Ettlinger who took her photo. And thinking about it, I started looking at the books on my shelf, and oh my God, like half of the recently published books on my shelf had an Ettlinger photo . . . she's very good, but it's also a fashion, and she's got the buzz."

For Shoemaker, however, who took a long-term view on celebrity author photographers, a photo by Ettlinger was not worth the financial expenditure: "There is one of those [i.e., a trendy photographer among authors] every five years. It used to be Tom Victor, then it was Jerry Bauer, and now it's Marion Ettlinger. Somebody that everyone gets their picture taken with. Usually it's whoever Knopf is using at that particular time. . . . We don't believe in the $2,000 author photograph." Simply put, for Counterpoint an Ettlinger photo was an unnecessary expense. In the first sale to the field of production, in the absolute best-case scenario it would be marginally useful at signaling *Jarrettsville*'s literary qualities, but the imprimatur of Counterpoint should already do that work. Likewise, for readers in the field of reception, an Ettlinger photo would be entirely meaningless. Yet, for Nixon, who had been working on *Jarrettsville* for almost a decade, the signal of an Ettlinger photo to her peers in the field of creation was important and worth the expense, and she opted to pay out of pocket for one. For those who cared to look and knew how to read the signal, Nixon's Ettlinger photo meant that she was still a literary author despite her half step into commercial fiction with *Jarrettsville*.

The balancing between literary and commercial concerns continued with other elements of *Jarrettsville*'s packaging and cover design. Krefman, who had been trained in McSweeney's culture of books as art objects, advocated for *Jarrettsville* to be published in paper-over-board (i.e., a jacketless hardcover). Winton, on the other hand, with his background in distribution and his eye toward the preferences of retailers, thought that *Jarrettsville* might be best served as a paperback original (i.e., a "PBO"; a paperback without a hardcover edition preceding it). Krefman surreptitiously listed *Jarrettsville* as a "POB" (a made-up initialism for paper-over-board) on the seasonal scheduling list, under the pretense that it might slip under the radar as a typo for "PBO." His "typo" was ultimately corrected when it was noticed in an editorial meeting.[6]

While Krefman's preference for paper-over-board was based more on sensibility than market consideration, there were upsides and downsides to publishing *Jarrettsville* first as a hardcover edition before then releasing the paperback. On the upside, a hardcover edition would be more "literary," meaning Nixon would prefer it, and the belief was also that reviewers would take a hardcover more seriously. A hardcover would also mean that *Jarrettsville* would get two chances in the field of reception, with the profit margins being larger on the hardcover edition as well.[7] The downsides were that for non-name-economy authors, hardcovers don't sell well (particularly when eBooks are released simultaneously and are much cheaper); if the hardcover failed, the paperback would never be released; retailers prefer paperbacks because they take up less shelf space and move more quickly (i.e., readers prefer paperbacks); and to publish in paperback would mean that *Jarrettsville*'s marketing campaign would be timed with a format that readers and retailers preferred.

In practice, however, as Counterpoint debated the format, none of these opposing constituent factors were really what was being debated. Instead, everyone more or less agreed that there was a more abstract question at the heart of the matter: was it acceptable these days for literary novels to be published as PBOs? If yes, then there was little debate. In Europe, the paperback original is much more typical for literary books. In the United States by the mid-2000s, Morgan Entrekin at Grove Atlantic and others had also slowly begun to publish their non-name-economy literary authors in paperback, and in 1999 the short story collection *Interpreter of Maladies* by Jhumpa Lahiri was published as a PBO and went on to win the Pulitzer Prize. On the other hand, what European publishers were doing in Europe may not have been particularly relevant to those in the United States, *Interpreter of Maladies* was perhaps more of an anecdote than a trend, and that some other literary imprints were experimenting with the practice was a data point providing a subject of discussion rather than a decisive answer.

This same discussion—what was acceptable for a "literary" book—re-emerged during talk of the blurbs to be put on *Jarrettsville*. Blurbs, first emerging in the nineteenth century, are quoted snippets of praise for a book and, like all other elements of cover design, are simply advertising. While in subsequent editions of books blurbs may come from reviews of the first edition, on first editions, printed before reviewers have seen the book, "advance praise" comes from name-economy friends and allies of the author in the field of creation.

There are two metrics by which the quality of blurbs is evaluated: the fame of the "blurber" and the effusiveness of the praise. A blurb that is not effusive in its praise is not a good blurb, or put more cynically, a blurb that does not overpromise on quality is not a good one. In turn, as the praise is over the top, it should come from a name-economy author whose "judgment" is seen as valuable and worthy of consideration. Like all other elements of cover design, however, the best blurbs should speak to people in the fields of production *and* reception. Some blurbs might carry weight among readers but be meaningless among producers. Such is the case with an effusive blurb from Gary Shteyngart, whose name is recognized, and perhaps trusted, by literary fiction readers. Among those in the field of production, on the other hand, it is well known that Shteyngart is willing to blurb almost anything and is quite open about never having read most of the books he blurbs. The reverse logic is true for Ayelet Waldman, who is perhaps less famous among readers than Shteyngart, but among some in the field of production is known for declining requests to blurb. As a result, her name carries a bit more weight. Waldman, a friend of Nixon's, agreed to blurb *Jarrettsville*.

Having fun with the conventions of blurbs and their demand for effusiveness, Waldman provided Krefman two options, one for fun that was clearly unusable and the other sincere:

1. "This is a fucking AWESOME book."
2. "A haunting and powerful evocation of a neglected moment in the American story. Nixon is a writer of unusual gifts; her prose rises to the level of poetry, flawlessly capturing the authentic, earthy flavor of a blood-soaked land."

Counterpoint also solicited blurbs from other name-economy authors who were friends with Nixon. These included the former Poet Laureate for the United States (and Pulitzer Prize winner) Robert Hass ("A terrifically gifted storyteller and a wonderful and surprising writer"), and author and co-founder of the nonprofit organization 826 Valencia, Vendela Vida ("I happily follow Cornelia Nixon's exquisite prose wherever it takes me. Her writing is witty, honest, and profound"). Counterpoint also opted to include as a blurb Michiko Kakutani's praise for Nixon in her *New York Times* review for Nixon's first novel, *Now You See It* ("Nixon has a thoroughly original voice, a voice that moves fluently from the poetic to the visceral, from the absurd to the mundane. . . . [She is] wonderfully talented").

With blurbs in hand, the next question for Counterpoint was similar to the question of publishing *Jarrettsville* as a hardcover or PBO: was it currently acceptable for a literary work to have a blurb on the front cover? In the quest for harmonious balancing between the literary and commercial intentions for *Jarrettsville*, if a literary work could include a blurb on the front cover, it was in everyone's best interest to include it. If, however, it were to appear gauche and unliterary, it might hurt the chances of receiving a major review. In the field of production, the norm against blurbs on the front cover of literary titles, rather than being a fixed rule, had emerged over time as a late twentieth-century affectation. By way of example, in 1925 the cover of the first US edition of Ernest Hemingway's *In Our Time* had six blurbs on it, which occupied over 70 percent of the total space of the cover.

For Counterpoint the front cover blurb was really a two-part question: (1) Could they put a blurb on the front cover of *Jarrettsville* and have its packaging still read as "Literary," and (2) if they could, which blurb should it be? On the first question, they decided in the affirmative. As for the second question, both of Nixon's previous novels had been reviewed by the *New York Times*, and there was a reasonable chance that the *Times* would also review *Jarrettsville*. This eliminated the Kakutani blurb from consideration on the front cover, as the *Times* might not look fondly on it. This left the blurbs by Waldman, Hass, or Vida. Ultimately, Counterpoint decided to use Waldman's blurb, as it was expressly about *Jarrettsville* rather than just Nixon's more general gifts as an author, and they figured that if they were to put a blurb on the front cover of a literary novel, its contents must clarify that the book was in fact a literary one. As Waldman's blurb was on the longer side, Counterpoint truncated it to read "Haunting and powerful . . . flawlessly capturing the authentic, earthy flavor of a blood-soaked land." In this form the blurb clarified that despite the cover image of a woman and a gun, *Jarrettsville* was about much more. Among the staff at Counterpoint there were jokes about the "earthy flavor of a blood-soaked land"— like a zombie flirting with vegetarianism, someone quipped—but the quote got the point across, and was chalked up to poetic license.

The synopsis on the back of a book, like the cover and blurbs, also serves two audiences: a producer audience that needs to know how to make sense of a novel without reading it, and a consumer audience, for which the synopsis is an *amuse-bouche* to whet their appetites. Although synopses are believed to be necessary, even those who write them can sometimes find them unpalatable, particularly in the case of literary novels. As an editor unaffiliated with Counterpoint described writing synopses, "There's moments when it feels very silly, like it cheapens the book because you are using these very crude superficial tags to instigate enthusiasm for this thing that is not concrete. [A novel's] beauty is often difficult to describe. And for an editor to be able to sum up even what happens in a book, let alone why you should read it, in 150 words for a jacket copy seems really sad and reductive but also a necessary part of the game."

Within those few words of a synopsis are the competing imperatives of pitching to the "first sale" audience in the field of production and the "second sale" audience in the field of reception. For the producer audience the plot is key, or a "just the facts, ma'am" approach as one Counterpoint employee described it. For consumers, rather than just the facts, a synopsis should be evocative and make them want to read more. As Krefman described the process of revising the synopsis for *Jarrettsville*, "we had written copy that was geared more towards [industry] sales people and we had to gear it towards the average buyer."

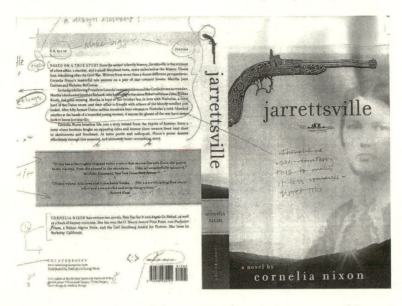

FIGURE 7.2: The Final *Jarrettsville* Cover in Process. Image courtesy of Counterpoint Press.

As had been the case with every element of *Jarrettsville*'s packaging, the balancing of the synopsis was not just in simultaneously pitching it to an industry and consumer audience, but also about how to get the balancing between its commercial and literary qualities just right. Once again, any possible miscategorization of *Jarrettsville* as a romance novel had to be mitigated. As seen in Figure 7.2, on the first mock-up of the cover that circulated around Counterpoint, a staff member had circled a passage from the synopsis and written the note, "I thought we were rewriting this to make it less romance-novel like," which was later crossed out. Did describing Martha as a "beautiful young woman," Richard as a "hothead," and Martha and Nick as "star-crossed lovers" in an "affair" make *Jarrettsville* sound like a romance novel? Someone had thought so and removed this terminology by the time the mock-up cover returned to Krefman.

Unsure about these changes, Krefman took the revised mock-up to Shoemaker: "I showed Jack and said, 'What do you think of these edits?' And he said, 'We're not cutting [those things].' And I asked 'what if it sounds like a romance novel?' And Jack said, 'Well, this is the story.' I think he's right. And there *is* a romance aspect to it. I don't think it's something to pretend isn't in there. You maybe don't want to lead with it, but if you just pretend it's not there, a reader gets to Martha's section and is blindsided by it." Following this conversation Shoemaker and Krefman reinserted the descriptors, both to more accurately represent the story and to pitch the synopsis more to readers and less to the industry.[8]

Throughout the cover design process, inclusive of art, format, blurbs, and synopsis, the goal was to balance competing categorical imperatives and present them in a harmonious fashion. Sociologists regularly find market benefits in producers presenting reviewers and consumers with clearly categorized products and services. Most often analyses begin after categorical decisions have already been made. As a result, the relationship between objects and their eventual categories can inadvertently be treated as givens, or as "natural" pairings that came preordained in the objects themselves. Yet as in the case of *Jarrettsville*'s packaging, sometimes categorical labels have to first be figured out. To get to clear categories is an iterative process between text and context, as categories have to be massaged, brokered, avoided, highlighted, or balanced.

While clear categorization is a nice target, creating clarity is made more difficult by the "two sales" model under which the field of production operates, as there are competing audiences with competing demands. In turn, *Jarrettsville* itself, throughout its writing and production, had always straddled categories. This is not unexpected from a literary author who consciously wrote a novel with its potential commercial appeal in mind. Likewise, word of mouth is also important for both placement and sales, and to clearly and singularly categorize *Jarrettsville* as either commercial or literary would be misleading, and would ultimately amount to a broken promise. As such, like the actual text of *Jarrettsville*, its packaging took balancing, and a balancing between literary and commercial appeal that had to be just right. These were the issues on the minds of the Counterpoint staff as they packed up their cultural wares for a presales meeting with their distributor, Publishers Group West.

PERFECTING THE PITCH

It was an unusually chilly morning when the Counterpoint staff walked down Fourth Street over to the offices of Publishers Group West. Just four months earlier, Krefman had made this same walk with Shoemaker and Nixon, but since then a lot about *Jarrettsville* had changed. As interest in *Jarrettsville* had grown, Krefman had begun to lose control over the decision making around the novel. As a result of this growing enthusiasm at Counterpoint, *Jarrettsville* had slowly been working its way up the fall list, and by the time the staff were making their morning walk, it was set to be the lead fiction title for October.

At PGW, Krefman and the rest of the Counterpoint editors would be pitching their titles to reps who manage different retail accounts (e.g., Barnes & Noble, Amazon), wholesale accounts (e.g., Ingram, Baker & Taylor), or regions (e.g., Canada, or "the field," meaning independent bookstores). Just as marketing and distribution staff understand the enthusiasm cues in the sequencing and space dedicated to books in a publisher's catalog, they too sequence their projections in presales meetings so that "smaller" accounts (e.g., Books-A-Million, a Southern regional chain) can be reactive to larger accounts (e.g., Barnes & Noble). It would be the job of the reps to secure placement (i.e., copies, and hopefully many) through these various channels, so that if a book "sold through" to demanding readers, there would be actual copies available for them that had been "sold in." Just as what *Jarrettsville* was in the field of creation had been converted by Weil and Krefman for the field of production, starting with the PGW meeting, the language used to discuss *Jarrettsville* again transitioned for the field of reception. For a young editor such as Krefman, whose pitching at that point had mostly been done in editorial meetings, this pitch was nerve-wracking.

The PGW conference room is large, with a door on each end, a long wall of windows, and a fourth long wall covered by the requisite overstuffed shelves of books. Assembled mostly at the southeast corner of the room, Counterpoint staff would take turns pitching the books they had been working on, and the reps would respond by asking questions that, in the process, worked to translate the meanings of projects into a language that would make sense in their impending field transitions.

First, there was direct category talk, oriented toward both production and reception. Category talk, unlike genre talk, is expressly oriented toward the shelving categories of bookstores, and the goal is to get books shelved in the categories that at the time are believed to be the strongest sellers. This is most clearly seen for nonfiction, which in bookstores tends to be more segregated into discrete categories than fiction (e.g., there's a nonfiction section for travel, but not a fiction section for travelogue). For literary fiction, in which bookstores do not shelve according to discrete categories (e.g., historical-literary, commercial-literary), category talk mostly takes the form of signaling belief in a manuscript's commercial appeal, which can sometimes be the same thing as literary quality. For *Jarrettsville*, Charlie Winton made Counterpoint's intentions clear in his introduction of the list to the PGW staff, before the pitching had even begun: "We have three fiction titles we're really excited about, and it's really a diverse group. . . . They're really well written, and they've certainly also all got really strong commercial elements; *Jarrettsville* in particular has a very strong commercial element."

Direct category talk is supplemented by two forms of indirect category talk: comp talk (the category talk for the field of production) and cover talk (the category talk for the field of reception). Comp talk refers to comparable titles, and comps work as shorthand among producers to both set the category a book falls into and roughly suggest a publisher's sales expectations. While some books might be incredibly similar in content, if they have sold too poorly or too well they do not make for good comps. By way of example, saying a children's book is "like *Harry Potter*" or a nonfiction book is "like Malcolm Gladwell" would provide a descriptor of a book's contents among authors or readers, but in the field of production to make such a comparison would be amateurish, signaling unrealistic sales expectations.

Instead, as far as sales, awards, and reviews go, a good comp is a *reasonable* yet very optimistic expectation. More generally within the field of production the public citation of figures (e.g., size of an author's advance, informal relaying of print run, sales expectations) doubles as a promotional device, and should normally be revised down by about 30 percent or so to arrive at the true figure. By this logic, rather than a good comp title being a realistic sales expectation, it should overpromise a bit, but not so much as to be unbelievable. That comp talk only rarely ends up accurately reflecting how many copies a book will sell ultimately does not matter though, as it is a form of talk that is only for insiders who know how to decipher it, and readers can live freely without even knowing that comp talk exists at all. For those in the field of production who know the rules of comp talk, however, it is generally understood that comps are a device to convey a publisher's hopes and commitments, and are not to be mistaken for true expectations or promises.

More expressly oriented toward the field of reception is cover talk, a second indirect form of category talk. While cover talk may also be aimed toward producers (and sometimes, to the chagrin of publishers, authors must also have their say), by the time of a sales meeting cover talk is expressly oriented toward readers and attracting perceived market niches. Cover talk at this stage is mostly marketers and distributors working to make the job of intended readers easier. Whether this is a "dumbing down" of book covers or a clarifying of them for readers is a matter of perspective.

Although these are the three common topics of conversation about books in sales meetings, all books are not afforded equal time in discussion. Instead, the amount of time spent discussing a book in the sales meeting, just like a book's placement in a publisher's catalog, is a tell of sorts about if that book will be left to sink or swim on its own, or if it will be carried. *Jarrettsville*'s quickly rising importance to Counterpoint was once again made

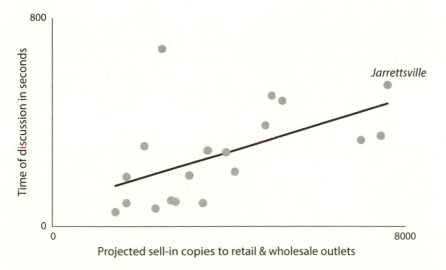

FIGURE 7.3: Discussion Time (Net Time of Pitch) by Estimated Number of Copies Placed.

clear in the presales meeting, not only by it receiving special mention at the start of the meeting, but also by reference to it throughout, as well as the time spent on it for focused and dedicated talk. If anything, Winton's special notation of *Jarrettsville* before the meeting started was to clarify to anyone in the room who might be unaware that it would be appropriate to spend extra time on the discussion of *Jarrettsville*.

While publishers' lists are implicitly broken out into a binary "frontlist" and "midlist" distinction, as seen in Figure 7.3, talk time in the sales meeting could be broken out between the three "lead" titles for the season (i.e., one for each month) and the midlist books, but there was also clear variation *within* these categories, suggesting that not even all "lead" titles or "midlist" titles are created the same.[9] Overall however, there was a clear and linear relationship between the amount of discussion time dedicated to books and their projected sell-in to retailers and wholesalers, which for PGW and Counterpoint in that season amounted to about fourteen copies per dedicated second of talk.

Despite this linear correlation between a book's placement and the amount of time spent talking about it, it would be a mistake to think of the relationship as a causal one in either direction. Instead, talk time and placement are both the effects of socially generated enthusiasm, and the web of collective belief in the *process* of production and promotion that is built around some titles and not others. This does not mean that hits in the field of reception are forced upon readers or even predictable, but there are certainly coordinated efforts among producers to guess the hits in advance so as to be ready for them when and if they emerge.

HOW A ONE-SENTENCE EMAIL NEARLY DOUBLED A PRINT RUN

By itself the one sentence email Winton received, "About halfway through *Jarrettsville*, and really enjoying it so far," increased the print run for the novel by one thousand copies, while also setting the wheels in motion for larger changes. Importantly, an email such as this can be a catalyst for larger change only under the right organizational conditions. In this instance, that Counterpoint did not anoint lead titles and waited for them to emerge, set the stage for a single email to eventually turn into a rolling snowball of enthusiasm. Equally important was the sender of the email: *who was it* who was halfway through *Jarrettsville* and enjoying it so far? The sender of the email was the VP of sales at PGW, Kim Wylie, who had sent it in advance of Counterpoint's presales meeting, for which she was also in the room. Enthusiasm from Wylie could move the needle because with her on board it would not be up to the Counterpoint staff alone to spread the seeds of enthusiasm required for *Jarrettsville* to be successful. A Counterpoint editor described the importance of Wylie coming on board in the "first sale" of *Jarrettsville*, the sell-in into bookstores:

> Kim's voice is very important because all of the national accounts sales go across her desk, and her employees sell [into] all the major [bookstore] accounts. . . . She's way up there in the sales apparatus, so when she speaks other reps listen. And at that table if you can get her [or a few of the other reps] to say something, the other field reps will all listen. There's nothing like a rep being enthusiastic [about a book] in front of other reps. It's much more impactful than if I'm enthusiastic because they expect I'm going to be enthusiastic. I'm paid to be enthusiastic. I'm not going to present [to them] a title that I don't believe in, or publish a book that I don't believe in, but every day of the week they are selling books that they don't believe in, or that they don't have enough information to know whether they believe in it or not. If Kim is enthusiastic it means a lot more to them.

By the time of the presales meeting with Publishers Group West, mostly due to an email, there was general awareness among Counterpoint and PGW staff that *Jarrettsville* had been rising into a lead position. This was further clarified by Winton at the start of the meeting when he stated that "*Jarrettsville* in particular has a very strong commercial element," which was reinforced by Wylie, who immediately chimed in with agreement about this characterization. Krefman, as the editor, presented the plot and background of the novel using the same enthusiasm-laden language about emotional effect that he had used in his initial reader report to Shoemaker. Further cementing Counterpoint's enthusiasm for *Jarrettsville*, Winton then took the reins of the pitch, discussing *Jarrettsville*'s promise as a work not only of literary quality, but also with commercial appeal. In *Jarrettsville*'s corner was that it was a true story based on the author's family history—a point in its favor that had even been agreed upon by otherwise discordant editors who had rejected the novel. Counterpoint also had a picture of Martha on the cover, and historical maps and *New York Times* coverage of Martha's trial as front and back matter. Nixon, Winton told everyone, had also been well reviewed by Kakutani for a previous novel. Due to *Jarrettsville*'s privileged position on Counterpoint's list, a lot of time was dedicated in the room to cover talk and comp talk, with both discussions aimed at clarifying the quickly expanding niche *Jarrettsville* was hoped to best fit into.

The two main topics of cover talk were how to clarify that *Jarrettsville* took place around the time of the Civil War, and how to balance attracting both men and women readers. While looking at the cover, one of the reps noted, "It looks more Western than Civil War, she [i.e., Martha] looks a little like Annie Oakley." The first raised solution to this problem was to replace the design element under the title with crossed Union and Confederate flags. This was dismissed as too literal and déclassé for a novel like *Jarrettsville*, which Counterpoint hoped would both attract readers and receive literary awards and artistic recognition. Shoemaker instead suggested that rather than simply putting "a novel" under the title to signal the book as a work of fiction, on *Jarrettsville*'s cover they could put "a Civil War novel" or "a novel of the Civil War" to better signal the time period.

Also remarked on by the reps was the balancing of the image of Martha and the image of the gun. As a rep suggested, "The gun's not interesting to the women readers, there's just 'too much gun' for women." To the group, Krefman noted that Nixon had approved of the gun on the cover, and that it was historically accurate; the same make and a similar model to the one used in the story, and with the ornate carvings on it like the gun described in the story (a happy accident; the cover designer did not know these details and picked the gun because it looked old and the carvings made it look more interesting). Winton suggested that the gun might attract male readers who wouldn't pick up a novel with only a picture of Martha on the cover, whereas women may not pick up a novel with only a picture of a gun; he thought the two balanced each other out. Shoemaker too worried that just a picture of Martha on the cover would mislead readers into thinking *Jarrettsville* was a romance novel: "I hope we don't miss the point that this is first and foremost a murder story and that she gets off is inexplicable. This is not a love story with a happy ending." For Shoemaker, who had advocated for the more flowery descriptors on the back-cover synopsis, using the front cover to make clear that *Jarrettsville* was not a romance novel remained important.

Whereas cover talk for *Jarrettsville* was oriented toward readers, comp talk, as it should be, stayed oriented toward the field of production. Possible comp titles for *Jarrettsville* that were discussed were other literary novels that took place at the conclusion of the Civil War, such as Spring Warren's *Turpentine* (published by Grove Atlantic in 2007) and Delia Falconer's *The Lost Thoughts of Soldiers* (published by Soft Skull in 2006). Yet neither novel had sold enough copies to be a good comp. Also discussed, and ultimately settled on, was E. L. Doctorow's *The March* (published by Random House in 2005). It had sold too well to be a perfect comp, but it was at least a reasonable if extremely ambitious expectation. Likewise, the open secret in the room was that for Winton, a private but unusable comp for *Jarrettsville* was Charles Frazier's *Cold Mountain*, a love story set during the Civil War that had sold upward of three million copies and that Winton, with Morgan Entrekin at Grove Atlantic, had "made happen" while running Publishers Group West. *Cold Mountain*, though, like the works of Malcolm Gladwell and *Harry Potter*, was too successful to be a comp for public consumption. Instead, mention of it occurred only in hushed tones and preceded by caveats by both Winton and others at Counterpoint and PGW (e.g., "I don't mean to jinx this, but . . ." and "not to get too excited but there's a chance that . . .").

With Counterpoint's growing enthusiasm for *Jarrettsville* both reflected and confirmed by the sales meeting at PGW, the pieces were beginning to fall in place for wider interest in the novel. An externally validating email and the initial response by field reps in the presales meeting made clear that Krefman's enthusiasm was not idiosyncratic, and that *Jarrettsville* might be able to do some of its own swimming, which meant for Counterpoint that it was worth pushing and carrying. The burgeoning interest in *Jarrettsville* also clarified many of the discussions that the Counterpoint staff had been having about the best way to package and promote the novel. If PGW was already getting behind *Jarrettsville*, the more commercial cover option—

which was still believed to signal commercial, literary, and historical appeal at once—could be selected without much further conversation. This was also true for publishing in PBO rather than hardcover, as positive word of mouth within the field of production could serve as a counterweight against the status penalty of the format, if any such penalty still existed. This also held true for placing a blurb on the front cover and what language would be used in the back-cover synopsis. If Counterpoint had a potential hit on their hands, they could lean into it, rather than be circumspect by trying to balance potentially irrelevant demands.

For Krefman it was both elating and a bit unmooring to have his enthusiasm for *Jarrettsville* be so quickly and widely shared by others. As he would later remark, "after the email from Kim I started to lose control [over *Jarrettsville*] a bit." His feelings about this, as they must be, were complicated. Given Counterpoint's strategy of waiting and letting lead titles present themselves, for Krefman to not lose control over how *Jarrettsville* was packaged and discussed would have meant that others did not share his enthusiasm for the novel, and were not spending focused time on it. As it is part of Krefman's job to infect others with enthusiasm for the projects he works on, to lose control a bit meant that he had actually done his job well. Krefman had not only brought in a manuscript that was a good match for Counterpoint, but in the process of working on it had made it into an even better fit for the press, and as a result of raising its profile, he had to let it go. Rather than feeling regret, as a young editor Krefman was making sense of the two sides of his work: when things were working correctly the same enthusiasm that tethered him to projects also pulled them out of his hands. Krefman recognized this peculiar feature of his work: "This is the program that Counterpoint is running. It's rehabilitating writers who are great but don't have an audience, and taking their work and turning it into a sellable thing by putting it in paperback and getting PGW to get behind it. And it works. I mean, we'll see if it works. I think *Jarrettsville* is the ultimate case study for that."

While *Jarrettsville* was certainly a case study in Counterpoint's strategy, it still remained to be seen if it would be a case study in success or failure. Either way, as had been the case with Wendy Weil before him, Krefman's active involvement with reworking and shepherding *Jarrettsville* was now complete. The archival effects of his enthusiasm—in memos and synopsis— would still be useful, but leveraging the enthusiasm of both Counterpoint and PGW into the wider field was not his job. Transitioning *Jarrettsville* from the field of production to reception would instead take the coordination of retailers and review outlets, a field transition populated by an entirely new set of actors. If Counterpoint was successful in this second field transition for *Jarrettsville* did not mean that readers would necessarily come, but it would mean that through reviewers they might at least be invited to share in the enthusiasm, and through retailers there might be a party waiting for them should they choose to arrive.

PART IV

FROM PRODUCTION TO RECEPTION

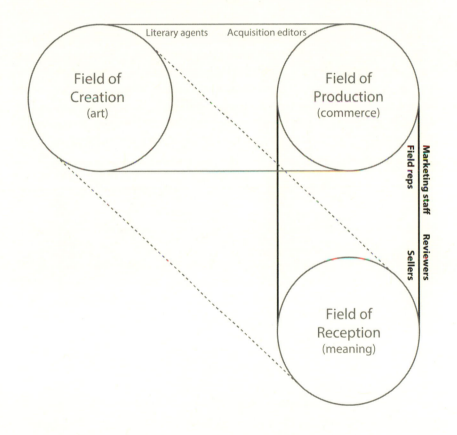

RETAILERS AND REVIEWERS

OR, HOW BEING PLACED ON THE FRONT TABLE

COULD HAVE TANKED *JARRETTSVILLE*

MAKING THE PITCH

Early on a Thursday morning, Abbye Simkowitz, Counterpoint's publicity director, was running through practice pitches to review outlets with a new employee. She listened intently as the new recruit, sitting at Simkowitz's desk, picked up the phone and simulated the pitching of *Jarrettsville*. As Simkowitz listened she nodded with encouragement. "That's great, really great," she said. "The first part especially, really great enthusiasm, they know right away how excited you are [about *Jarrettsville*]." Despite the encouraging words, the practice pitch was too long, and Simkowitz's encouraging nodding trailed off toward its end. "One note would be that you're talking about the book too much, going into too much detail about the plot, so let's do it again but this time cut your description of the book in half." The new employee understood the request and tried again, although she later admitted to finding some humor in having talked too much about a book while pitching it.

Later, the Counterpoint staff would meet with Cornelia Nixon, working to coordinate her book tour around her teaching schedule, and mining her for any preexisting promotional contacts. The plan was described to Nixon by Winton this way:

> If you want to be excited, the table is set for this to possibly be significantly successful. . . . Right now, the [PGW] reps are really pushing it, and we're targeting some review outlets. . . . But again, they're all just bricks in the wall, each of them are little things that you build up. Each thing isn't really anything individually. There are other smaller pieces in the puzzle: if we get a starred review from *Publishers Weekly*, or *Library Journal*, which is going to help us with our print review coverage, and with the placement which the reps are already

fostering. And then maybe we can get [the promotional campaign] Discover [Great] New Writers at Barnes [& Noble], or "co-op" at Borders. Those are a couple of pretty big blocks in the wall. And we do the great indie events, we can get [the American Booksellers Association promotional program] IndieBound, we get some good blurbs, we get some critical attention, and build that up into a major human interest story around Baltimore and Maryland. And obviously if we get a rave review from the *New York Times* things can keep going from there. That's a brick that, with all those other bricks, we can go to Terry Gross [at NPR] and say, "So this is one of the more interesting novels that is being published this season and there is this back story that is unique." And all of that can just keep building, eventually, into winning some awards and you just go from there. . . . So sorry to say all that, I don't want to get you too excited. There's a lot of moving parts, but you know, if you *want* to know, I'm saying we might really have a chance.

Nixon, after the meeting, was elated: "In my career before never have I received this level of attention. It's just so different, I don't want to go back!" The "back" to which Nixon was referring was the midlist. Despite her excitement about the attention, she was worried about a potential *New York Times* review. She was not worried about whether or not she would receive one, but rather, if she did, which day of the week it would run. She hoped for a weekday review rather than one in the larger, more widely read Sunday section. Simkowitz, whose job it would be to pitch the *New York Times*, agreed, albeit for different reasons, that sometimes a lesser-read weekday review can be better than a review in the Sunday *New York Times Book Review*.

With promotion staff such as Simkowitz working hard to secure reviews in highly visible and prestigious outlets, other Counterpoint and PGW staff could focus on converting production-side enthusiasm for *Jarrettsville* into shelf space at retailers. As Winton would later phrase it, to successfully sell a novel twice, meaning to "sell-in" to bookstores and then "sell-through" to readers, "the stars have to align" across the fields of production and reception. If Counterpoint and PGW could drum up enough propulsive enthusiasm in the field of production, that enthusiasm might spillover into the field of reception. In trying to ignite these flames of cross-field enthusiasm, however, why was it a mistake to share too many details about the story with review outlets, and how many was too many? In turn, if the general purpose of reviews is to generate awareness and sales, why would both Nixon and

Simkowitz prefer a less widely read review? To understand these questions, one must first understand how novels are transitioned from production to reception, and how the first sale of a novel must be successful in order to create the opportunity for success in the second sale.

BOOKEXPO AMERICA AND FIELD CONFIGURATION

BookExpo America (BEA) is an annual trade conference for publishers to coordinate with booksellers in May or early June, in advance of the important fall/winter publishing season. In a perfect world for publishers and booksellers, BEA would provide a keyhole into the field of reception. It is, effectively, the primary venue through which publishers clarify to the field of production, and those at its reception-facing boarders, exactly which titles they will be promoting. Booksellers, the primary audience to whom publishers pitch at the BEA floor show, play a large role in facilitating that field transition.

How space is apportioned within a publisher's booth at BEA is intended to correlate with which books they want to talk about most; books that take up a lot of space are, without fail, those being most pushed into the field of reception. Space and its use also clarifies for the field a publisher's transitive intentions for their different offerings that season. While some books may have their covers displayed as posters (i.e., vertical space), it is the three-dimensional space afforded to stacks of copies of the same book that sends the strongest signal of a publisher's enthusiasm and support. These stacks are "advanced reading copies" (called ARCs) or "galleys" that are given away as significant promotional devices. The presence of ARCs for a book is a promissory note for retailers that if they stock it in large quantity, the publisher will work to drive readers into the stores so that it will sell-through. Yet ARCs at BEA are not just to give away, as they are also meant for show, arranged in stacks or wheels from the floor or in high columns on tables. A publisher's strongest show of force is to have its author buried among stacks of her ARCs. Hopefully, as she dutifully signs away each copy, she is also taking her time chatting so others can see how long of a line has formed for her: "Just remember to go slowly," an overwhelmed debut author for a major conglomerate remembers being told by her publisher's staff before making her grand entrance into the field at BEA.

Although nominally ARCs at BEA are meant to be given away to retailers, in practice they are given away to any and all attendees, and even publishers leave the convention with bags of each other's books. As explained by a Counterpoint employee, "When you commit to doing ARCs the presales distribution is broader, the awareness is more widespread, so it's not just for media and the bookstore reps, *it's for the industry*." This point was clarified by a speaker on the trade floor in the official opening announcements at the Northern California Independent Booksellers Association, one of eight regional BEA sub-conferences: "Some of these people you'll know, others you won't, and we're hoping you'll take the opportunity to get to know each other. . . . There will be plenty of time for everyone to get books. If there are any books here . . . that you would like, please feel free to collect them, trade books with each other as much as you'd like. We have enough books for everyone here to take home. And with that, let's let the locusts descend!"[1]

A scattershot approach to ARC distribution is normative, and reflects a concerted effort to foment wider awareness in the field of production. For agents, authors, and employees at other publishers, ARCs are a reminder of the publisher that gave them away. In addition to promoting the book in question, an ARC comes with the easily decodable message that says "remember who we are, because this is what we do." Because building industry buzz is an imperfect science, ARCs double as promotion for a book *and* a publisher. It is for this reason—beyond just the financial cost of creating ARCs—that their existence is so important in conveying enthusiasm: to create and distribute ARCs is to clearly state that, at least temporarily, the book is the publisher and the publisher is the book.

Rather than a mere gathering in which publishers and retailers coordinate, BEA is for the field of production in the United States a "field-configuring event."[2] In formal panels and in hallways, focal issues concerning the wider field are clarified, revised, and refined, and status hierarchies are confirmed and reconfirmed. The "core" of the conference, made up of the physical clustering of the large conglomerate publishers into roughly the same area, moves around the convention floor from year to year. Yet if discount sellers were ever to become confused about their status, at BEA they would have the annual reminder of being tucked away in the corners, always far away from wherever the roaming "core" of conglomerates are in any given year.

Power hierarchies between publishers are also clarified through booth space, which may operate along the lines of sheer size, but can also operate relationally. Historically, one has been able to know if a publisher is ascendant or receding as the size of its booth at BEA grows or shrinks. By 2009, however, these standards were changing. While walking the convention floor that year a representative from a major conglomerate publisher passed the booth for Quirk Books, an independent publisher from Philadelphia.

Several months before Quirk had released the surprise blockbuster *Pride and Prejudice and Zombies*, which would go on to spend almost a full year on the *New York Times* best-seller list. Quirk was there not only to promote a forthcoming "Deluxe Edition" of *Zombies* (and their follow-up *Sense and Sensibility and Sea Monsters*), but also to more generally announce their arrival as a player in the field.

Remarking on the size of the Quirk booth, the representative from the conglomerate publisher pointed over to it and sardonically whispered "well look at them." With this comment she was suggesting two things. First, she was signaling that she thought it might be Quirk's one year in the sun at BEA; many before Quirk have had a surprise best-seller, announced themselves as major players, and then slowly receded as future hits never came. Second, and more cuttingly, she was suggesting that Quirk was actually conveying the reverse message from what they intended. By announcing themselves as newly arrived players via an outsized BEA booth, Quirk had inadvertently reconfirmed its status as a non-core player. By 2009, core players were decreasing their booth space, or forgoing booths all together and avoiding the rabble on the convention floor by holding closed-door meetings on another level of the Javits Center. As a result, the use of booth size had begun to take on a parabolic function, and Quirk had built out space to announce its arrival precisely when those already inside the party had retreated to a VIP section. Was Quirk announcing its arrival as a publisher of note, or was its announcement out of touch and clunky, ultimately reconfirming its own peripheral status? That this was all occurring at an event in which the *purpose* is ostensibly to loudly promote and publicize one's wares clarifies the multifaceted uses of BEA as well as the status games played within it.

FROM FIELD REPS TO BOOK SELLERS

Although by 2015 eBooks accounted for about 30 percent of all book sales, for the vast majority of authors and publishers making it into a wide variety of brick-and-mortar bookstores is still a book's best chance at a broad readership. Field reps, the people responsible for getting books into retailers, inhabit one of the two reception-facing wings of production (the other being publicity staff). They are the honeybees of the field as they travel from bookstore to bookstore trying to pollinate seeds of enthusiasm for the books they represent. As one of two pathways through which the boundaries between production and reception are mediated, the relationship between field reps and buyers at retail outlets (who pick which books will be stocked) is akin to the relationship between agents and editors who mediate the boundaries between creation and production. For that reason, once again, these field-transitioning players navigate the interconnected problems of oversupply and fundamental uncertainty in a familiar way: they rely on interpersonal relationships and trust, webs of collective belief, and received wisdom and "horse sense" about how the field at the receiving end of the transition might in fact receive things. Because no bookstore buyer will ever be able to read and evaluate all of the books she stocks, the signals sent through publishers' catalogs and in conversations with field reps are of the utmost importance.

When opening a publisher's catalog, a buyer can be sure that even if she is not able to read each book, those at the front with double-page spreads have won out in the season's battle for collective enthusiasm at the publisher.[3] She may not know why or what it means for her particular bookstore (e.g., the "type" of store she's selling in and the readers it attracts), but that is why a field rep is there to guide her through the catalog. Nonetheless, the catalog alone can be a powerful, sometimes too powerful, signal. As explained by a field rep, with a bit of exasperation, "I have accounts stop at a book because it has a double-page spread [in the catalog], and even for books that they probably should not carry at all, they'll take copies of it because of the double-page spread." For this field rep, to see the buyer rely solely on the catalog is a personal affront. What is more regularly a relational exchange of mutual dependence and consideration now reduces the field rep to a courier.

A different field rep explains the reverse scenario, in which the catalog itself is reduced to an afterthought due to the primacy and mutual dependence of the relational exchange between parties: "I have accounts that, over the years, we've gotten to know each other well enough that, I know what they want and I can help point them. Like Jerry at Yellowtail Books, when I visit him he doesn't even open the catalog. He just leaves it closed on his lap and we sit down and we talk about books." These stories are worth sharing because they are, in opposite directions, exceptions to the rule. In the typical exchange, an interpretation of the catalog and the interaction between the field rep and buyer are both important.

Catalogs, just like agents' descriptions and editors' reader reports, are influential because they are "secondary texts" that translate novels into the logic of their new fields.[4] Yet field reps are influential and important, just like the conversational exchanges between agents and editors are important, because they are interactive and can go off-script. If one were to hypothesize about the ultimate primacy of catalogs versus field reps, the best indicator might be to identify the one for which publishers are least likely to cut financial corners. By this metric, the field rep holds primacy over the catalog, as publishers have increasingly transitioned to using the online catalog service Edelweiss, which saves on printing and distribution costs, but can make the signaling function of the catalog less effective. In light of this cost cutting, luckily, field reps are still there. As explained by Counterpoint's publicity director, "It's simply part of the process . . . that the reps have only so much time, [and] book sellers have only so much time to consider new lists. And that they're going to weight things, their presentations or their listing based on how the books are weighted by the distributor or by the publisher. So if you go in and say, 'this is my lead novel' they're going to be thinking in terms of five or ten copies, but if you go in and say 'this novel by Cornelia Nixon' they're going to be thinking two or three copies." In conversation field reps can also provide background, reminding buyers about publishers and contextualizing what they are doing.

As explained by a regional field rep when discussing her practice of always naming the publisher or editor when opening a catalog, "For Counterpoint, or Tin House, Milkweed, Grove, McSweeney's, they have a reputation for literary fiction that [bookstore] buyers respond to. When I used to work at [a large publisher] some of their imprints don't have a reputation for literary fiction, so it was important to say who the editor was. . . . So Counterpoint has a reputation for American literary fiction, but also Jack [Shoemaker]'s name carries a lot of weight. . . . So for Counterpoint you say 'a lead title from Counterpoint, and Jack just loves it' and they get it immediately because this book makes sense to them coming from Counterpoint."

Although a field rep's loyalty in the transaction is almost always to the publisher or distributor she works for (just as an agent's loyalty is almost always to her author), trading favors also cements the exchanges as unavoidably relational ones. It is in these moments of shifting loyalties and going off script that bonds are strengthened and future transactions are made smoother and easier. By way of example, while a field rep might be under direction to push a book particularly hard, she also has discretion in what she does, as she knows things about her accounts that the publisher or distributor does not. Because unsold books can be returned—a practice developed to keep bookstores in business during the Great Depression—it is in the interest of neither the publisher nor the field rep to saddle a bookstore with copies of an unsellable book. In these instances, a field rep may say to a buyer something like "I'm supposed to really be pushing this but I don't think it will work for your audience," just as in reverse a buyer may say to a field rep "I can take on a few extra copies if it will help you."

This type of favor trading most regularly occurs with independent book-stores, which make up a small albeit important channel into the field of re-ception. While books are sold through a wide variety of channels (e.g., the library market, gift shops, and boutique stores that stock a few books), the retail market for books primarily flows through three channels: indepen-dent bookstores, chain bookstores and "big box" retailers, and Amazon. In transitioning books from production to reception, a publisher must navi-gate these three channels in dramatically different ways.

INDEPENDENT BOOKSTORES AND BRICK-AND-MORTAR CHAINS: FROM COOPERATION TO CO-OP

After decades of retrenchment, independent bookstores have recently been bouncing back. The number of member stores of the American Booksellers Association increased by about 30 percent from 2009 to 2015, and their per-store sales on average increased about 8 to 10 percent.[5] Rather than being an unmitigated success story, however, this return of the independent book-store is instead the result of changes in the resource space for brick-and-mortar bookselling due to the demise of Borders in 2011. It also reflects the reactive move by some independent bookstores to give up their generalist aspirations for niche specializations.[6]

Although life for the owner of an independent bookstore is not easy, softening the blow is that independent bookstores are in several ways the sacred retailers for many in the fields of production and reception. In the field of reception, independent bookstores, more so than other types of in-dependent retailers, are the go-to symbol of the vitality of neighborhoods and local community. When David Kidd Booksellers, the last generalist bookstore in Nashville, closed its doors in 2010, local author Adam Ross referred to the loss as "a civic tragedy," and the Nashville Public Library, community leaders, and local activists started to coordinate to open a new independent bookstore in the city. Two years later, when name-economy author Ann Patchett and Karen Hayes (with a background in distribution and sales from Ingram and Random House) opened Parnassus Books in Nashville, it was the subject of national news.

For the field of production, independent bookstores also occupy a larger amount of symbolic real estate than their collective sales would suggest. Only about 10 percent of books sold in the United States are sold through independent bookstores, yet they remain the favorite (if not favored) trad-ing partner of publishers in the field of production. Publishers prefer them for several reasons. First, there is a collective belief that independent book-stores, unlike Amazon or chains, *care* about books: they too, like publishing staff, have accepted lower wages to "work on what they love," trading immediate economic capital for the cultural capital of privileging "art." Put another way, publishers favor independent bookstores for their perceived *enthusiasm* about books, and independent bookstores, the story goes, like publishers, use their enthusiasm as a form of capital to influence readers to share in their affections.

This is most often articulated through the language of "handselling," the practice through which independent bookstore workers are trusted allies of their customers, and use their own enthusiasm to "sell-through" books that otherwise may not have a chance. Handselling can occur interactionally between employees and customers, or visually through denoting some books over others as "employee picks." Diana, an independent bookstore buyer, explains this process and the special status it brings to independent bookstores for publishers:

> I fell in love with this book that [had been published by a small press and would not seem to have wide sales potential]. And I started handselling it and I sold 96 hardcovers, which was [the most copies sold] for any single [retail] location in the United States. And when the paperback came out I sold about 145 paperbacks. So I'm standing in the store one day and this delivery person's walking through . . . carrying this huge vase of purple orchids, and [he's talking to the staff], and when I get closer [I hear him say] "Who is Diana?" And I said, "I am." And [the publisher had] sent me this giant vase of purple orchids just for that book that had decent sales across the country and then this giant blip in our [book]store. And we do this all the time. Every single independent [book]store has stories like that.

In one sense, publishers prefer trading with independent booksellers because publishers cannot control what happens in the field of reception, and they see their fate tied to chance. Through this lens, due to their enthusiastic handselling, independent bookstores (more so than chains and Amazon) diversify the possibilities of chance, which allows publishers to hold out hope for surprise hits.[7] It is this belief in enthusiasm and handselling that causes publishers to argue that independent bookstores, more than other retailers, can *make hits* where they otherwise would not exist. Yet despite some general truth in this characterization, it elides other reasons why publishers prefer independent booksellers.

Rather than publishers having a preference for independent bookstores merely due to their propensity to shine the light of random chance on surprise books, publishers have historically preferred working with independent bookstores because they cooperate with each other in coordinating the possibility for chance to occur. Often lurking in the background of day-to-day business between publishers and independent booksellers is a micro-transactional relationship of gift exchange. Contra a story of random chance, independent booksellers can also be *reactive* to publishers' own enthusiasm, and can sometimes exchange the favor of orienting their enthusiasm and attention to a publisher's interests. One publisher explained this phenomenon through the example of the American Booksellers Association's IndieBound promotional program, the Indie Next List, which promotes upcoming releases to independent bookstores:

> The way IndieBound works . . . is that there's got to be a nomination that comes from a bookseller. But in reality the nomination really has to come from three or four booksellers, not just one. So if we want an IndieBound nomination we have to prime the pump, make sure that the field reps are saying, "Hey look, I really love this book, and I'd like you to really read it and give it serious consideration for an . . . IndieBound nomination." Whether she [i.e., the bookseller] reads it, whether she likes it, whether she's motivated to do that, those are all the things that we can't control. But generally it's okay to push for it because we're not doing that once a month. We're only doing that a few times a year. . . . So hopefully if we seed with seven or eight or ten people, and to the degree that you've got three people that are independent of our little gamesmanship that's going on, that's just all for the good. So if you have a few people that you've gotten on board with you, then you can get what you want. Generally the way it works is that a nomination from Prairie Lights, or Elliott Bay, or Politics and Prose are going to carry a little bit more weight than the bookstore in [Scranton, PA], so maintaining good relationships with them in particular is very important.

Within this theory of gamesmanship is a hierarchy of independent bookstores. Some focal independent bookstores drive the decisions of both IndieBound itself and, ostensibly, the decisions of other independent bookstores through IndieBound. Though the list of which bookstores are the important ones for the wider diffusion of enthusiasm varies based on both publisher and location, almost always included are Prairie Lights (Iowa City), Elliott Bay (Seattle), Politics and Prose (Washington, DC), Tattered Cover (Denver), and Powell's (Portland, OR).[8] Publishers, for their part, do not have to directly pay independent bookstores for these coordination efforts. This is not because payment would be illegitimate or illegal, but because this system of "pump priming" is ultimately mutually beneficial. Rather than direct payment, publishers maintain good relationships with focal independent bookstores through favors and hidden monies. This is done most concretely by delivering name-economy authors to focal independent bookstores for readings and signings, while also hiding other forms of financial compensation to ostensibly cover the cost of snacks, beverages, flyers, and newsletters for those events.

In exchange, independent bookstores will sometimes let publishers do some of their prescreening when deciding which books to order (i.e., they will predominantly select from publishers' "lead" titles rather than picking books by other criteria). They also may gift to publishers desirable placements in their stores (on front display tables or endcaps), or give those books that publishers are most enthusiastic about an extra look when selecting employee picks within the store. It is ultimately a system of mutually beneficial gift exchange between publishers and independent booksellers, as both parties would prefer readers to take interest in the books that are well stocked and available.[9] For chain stores like Barnes & Noble (and formerly Borders and Waldenbooks), this type of cooperation is formalized and rationalized as "co-op," and the gifts given to publishers by independent sellers through mutual interest are instead bought and sold.

At chain retailers, rather than front table space and endcap displays being awarded through genuine enthusiasm or cooperative gift exchange, these prime locations are sold through co-op programs. In advance of publishing cycles, publishers submit titles for co-op, and from those submissions the chains select which publishers will have the privilege to pay for high traffic space within their stores. The arrangement is such not because independent retailers are generous and chain retailers are nefarious, but because independent retailers are diffuse and small and chain retailers are centralized and large. Put another way, chain stores put a formal price on cooperation because they can, whereas independent stores cannot. This is part of a more general pattern in which chain retailers are less favored trading partners (at least in sentiment, if not fealty) for publishers because chain retailers are large enough to *demand things* from them.

Although she is generally unknown in the fields of creation or reception, Sessalee Hensley, who is responsible for selecting literary fiction for all of the more than six hundred Barnes & Noble stores in the United States, can and does have the power to make demands on publishers. In publishers' marketing and distribution meetings "Sessalee will like this" or "Sessalee won't like this" is a common refrain, and it is not an entirely irregular occurrence for cover designers to be sent back to their drawing boards after Hensley's disapproval. Due to her power as a circuit breaker (or maker) into the field of reception, publishers sometimes lament in hushed tones that Hensley may be the most powerful decision maker for literary fiction in the United States. This does not mean that Hensley is unreactive to publishers' preferences as expressed through enthusiasm—"You can't downplay a publisher's enthusiasm, but make the eye contact and figure out if it's real," she once remarked—but unlike the buyers for independent bookstores, publishers are regularly forced to react to *her* preferences, and also in some ways cater to them.[10] For this reason publishers that enter co-op arrangements with chain stores still often prefer "cooperation" with independent retailers—to say nothing of the arrangements required of them from Amazon, which is closer to outright coercion.

AMAZON: SOMETHING OLD, SOMETHING NEW

For many reasons, those in the field of production are often fans of Amazon, until they are not. Unlike independent and chain bookstores, Amazon pays up front for its books and, because its stock is not limited by shelf space, does not return unsold books. As a result it is through Amazon that much of publishers' backlists remain accessible to consumers as impulse purchases. Amazon, like the brick-and-mortar chain stores before it, has also brought in readers from locales that were previously underserved by independent bookstores. And while Amazon was not the first adopter of eBook technology, it has gone on to dominate that market and has done more than anyone to improve its viability as a format through which to sell books.

Critiques of Amazon generally fall into two classes: (1) old critiques that have been made for at least the past hundred years about any and all dominant book retailers, and (2) new critiques that are particular to Amazon. These two classes of critique also map neatly onto two different strategies adopted by Amazon, with the former pertaining to *how they mediate* between the fields of production and reception, and the latter pertaining to their *attempts to disintermediate* the rest of the field of production from the fields of creation and reception, as if they were just inefficient middlemen (see Figure 8.1). As cooperation between publishers and independents evolved into co-op with retail chains, co-op with Amazon is an even less consensual arrangement than before. At Amazon, rather than opting in to an in-store promotion as with chain brick-and-mortar stores, to sell one's books on the website is effectively to have already entered a co-op agreement. Amazon's mandatory version of co-op is to hang onto a proportion

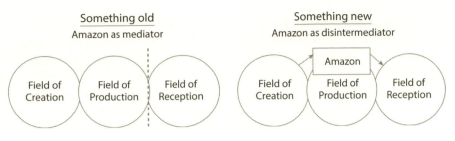

FIGURE 8.1: The Two Classes of Amazon Critiques.

of revenue made by all publishers from their sales on the website and to require publishers to put that money back into Amazon as advertising purchases in the next calendar year. Put another way, to sell books on Amazon means to agree to the company's double dipping; they take their cut of a book sale, and also siphon off from the publisher's cut of the sale by mandating future advertising on Amazon. How cost-effective this mandated advertising and promotion on Amazon is for publishers is only irregularly discussed because, by agreeing to sell on Amazon, publishers ultimately have no choice over the matter anyway.

Yet many critiques of Amazon as a mediator between the fields of production and reception in the early twenty-first century vary little from those expressed about department stores in the first half of twentieth century, and chain stores in the late twentieth century. When people claim that Amazon "does not care" about books, they often point out that despite between 40 and 50 percent of the retail book market flowing through Amazon, only about 7 percent of its annual revenue even comes from books. Yet, this was also the case in the early 1950s when an estimated 40 to 60 percent of books purchased in the United States were sold through department stores, despite books making up a very small proportion of their total revenue. For department stores, books were a device to draw in customers who might make larger retail purchases, and to offer legitimacy and high-mindedness to broader retail aspirations.[11]

Amazon, like department and chain stores before them, also treat publishers' most treasured books as loss leaders. Margaret Mitchell's 1936 novel *Gone with the Wind*, for instance, is credited as the first major blockbuster to pull the US book market out of the Great Depression. Despite a listed price of $3 on the novel, using a loss-leader strategy to draw in customers, department stores competed with each other over who could offer the novel at the lowest price. In New York City, betting markets emerged over how low the price would go; *Gone with the Wind* had been discounted by

70 percent and was being sold for 89 cents. Publishers fought back against this loss-leader strategy by setting "price floors" under which their books could not be sold, legally winning the right do so first in 1908 in *Bobbs-Merrill Co. v. Straus*, and again with *Gone with the Wind* in the mid-1930s. Department stores responded to these price floors by returning tens of thousands of copies of *Gone with the Wind* unsold: rather than honor the $3 price, Macy's alone returned thirty-six thousand copies and cancelled an order for another ten thousand.[12]

In effect, this story is of little difference from the early 2010s, when Amazon took losses selling eBooks at $9.99 in order to draw consumers into the site (where they might make broader retail purchases) and into their Amazon Kindle ecosystem; the $9.99 price point was 62 percent lower than the average suggested retail price for a new work of hardcover fiction. Publishers responded by developing what they termed an "agency pricing model," which is just a different turn of phrase for setting price floors below which retailers could not sell their eBooks.[13] Amazon, in turn, responded to the adoption of the agency pricing model by becoming more aggressive in its next round of negotiations with publishers, and effectively removing the publisher Hachette Livre's titles from the site until new terms could be met. As evidenced by this comparison, some of the present-day critiques of Amazon as an unfair mediator between the fields of production and reception are in fact "old" critiques that had been leveraged against department stores and other previously dominant retailers in decades past, even following the same moves and countermoves that had played out almost a hundred years prior.

Yet there is a second class of critiques of Amazon that are new. These critiques focus on Amazon's efforts to entirely *disintermediate* the rest of the field of production from its position between the fields of creation and reception. While in the early 2010s Amazon flirted with becoming a traditional publisher (i.e., signing name-economy authors to large advances and developing different imprints), more efficacious has been its cultivation of authors in the field of creation who were previously denied entrance into the field of production. Nominally referred to as "self-publishing," to publish one's work through Amazon can more accurately be described as having one's work pass through an *uninvested* publisher in the field of production rather than an *invested* one.

"Traditional" publishers in the field of production make bets and take risks: they *invest* time, money, and resources into individual books. Put another way, invested publishers incur measurable fixed costs on each manuscript they publish. Due to their investment in certain books, they must also be *exclusive*, or refuse to invest in other books. As a result, many would-be novelists who have not found safe passageway into the field of production are excluded from traditional publishers' model of *invested exclusivity*. In contrast to traditional publishers, Amazon, through its self-publishing ventures, takes an *uninvested* publishing strategy. Due to its lack of investment on any individual title, Amazon can instead be *inclusive* in allowing entry to anyone. In lieu of making bets and taking risks, Amazon lets all who come enter, and rather than investing time and resources (e.g., developmental editing, copyediting, packaging, cover design, promotion) into its authors' works, it gives authors the option to pay out of pocket for these services. The uninvested publishing strategy works for Amazon because it has at or near zero fixed costs on any individual manuscript it publishes, while also claiming 30 percent of the revenue of each sale, in addition to charging authors 15 cents per megabyte for the data transfer of each sale; by point of comparison, on a typical US cell phone plan one megabyte of data transfer costs the user about nine-tenths of one cent.[14] This is to suggest not that one publishing strategy is objectively better than the other—both have their upsides and downsides—but merely that two diametrically opposed publishing systems exist: *invested exclusivity* and *uninvested inclusivity*.

As a result of this, Amazon, as a newer player in the field of production, sometimes works to disintermediate all other players. In place of agents, editors, cover designers, marketing and publicity staff, and so on, there is just Amazon standing between the fields of creation and reception. Amazon's audience for these services, authors in the field of creation who mostly have otherwise been excluded from the field of production, provide an army of foot soldiers to extol the superiorities of Amazon's model of uninvested inclusivity. And for many of them, who now have broad access to readers, it *is* a better model.

While one strategy taken on by Amazon is to disintermediate other players in the field of production by working around them, Amazon also attacks them more directly. This is primarily done in two ways. First, Amazon launched what was internally referred to as "Project Gazelle." It placed book publishers into one of three categories based on their dependence on Amazon revenue streams, and those most dependent on Amazon (mostly small and independent publishers) were then targeted for increased co-op fees and lower revenue splits. Amazon's founder, Jeff Bezos, clarified the meaning of the project's name when joking that "Amazon should approach these small publishers the way a cheetah would approach a sickly gazelle," picking them off first and weakening the overall herd of publishers before targeting the rest.[15]

Second, through active investment in cultivating a seamless and vibrant used book market, Amazon is able to generate capital from the only category of books that does not generate revenue for traditional book publishers. By selling used books on its own site, Amazon cannibalizes about one-sixth of its potential sales of new books, yet when factoring in Amazon's 15 percent cut (plus closing and transaction fees) taken from its "affiliate" used book program, it was estimated in 2006 that by selling used books Amazon had increased its overall revenue by $66 million while costing publishers $45 million.[16] Because Amazon controls about 30 percent of all physical book sales, by selling used books on its site, it effectively converts about 5 percent of overall sales away from new books (in which revenue is shared with publishers) to used books (in which revenues are not). By weakening publishers' revenue streams from print books, Amazon also gently pushes publisher preference toward eBooks, a market for which there are not used books and of which Amazon controls about 70 percent.

Last, if only indirectly, Amazon disintermediates the rest of the field of production from the field of reception by weakening the role of non-Amazon-controlled boundary spanners that traverse these fields. By dominating bookselling, Amazon weakens the channels to reception that traditional publishers hold through their relationships with brick-and-mortar sellers, and through the cultivation of amateur book reviews, they also weaken the role of professional book reviews, the second channel through which traditional publishers have access to the field of reception. As professional book reviewing has been on the decline, user-generated book reviews have been on the rise, and Amazon owns all of the major outlets. In addition to hosting user-generated reviews on its own website, in 2008 and 2013 Amazon purchased the two major competing social media sites for amateur book reviews, Shelfari and Goodreads. Put another way, to the degree that Amazon can dominate retailing and reviewing, it can also weaken the two major pathways through which traditional publishers have sent their books downstream to readers.

Overall, for independent bookstores, chain retailers, and Amazon, book publishers have different relationships and hold different sympathies. Across all three channels, there are field reps and buyers that help pitch products out of the field of production and into the field of reception. From a production-side perspective, what most distinguishes one trading partner from another is the degree to which it can force publishers to *do things* for it. Independent bookstores, symbolically and financially attractive to publishers, are favored trading partners. Big box chain bookstores, on the other hand, were villains until the arrival of Amazon and since then have become allies of sorts. In turn, some of what Amazon does—its strategies in mediation—is quite old and familiar to the field of production. And finally, some of what Amazon does—its strategies of disintermediation—is for the rest of the field of production quite concerning, if not sometimes terrifying.

PUBLICITY STAFF, REVIEWERS, AND AUTHOR OMERTÀ

The second major pathway from production to reception occurs through the relationships between publicity directors and review outlets. As is the case in all field-transitioning relationships, the exchanges between publicity directors and review outlets are based on shared knowledge and trust. As is also the case in earlier field transitions from creation to production, the reliance on interpersonal relationships is a way to help manage the twinned problems of oversupply and fundamental uncertainty over quality.

With regard to an oversupply of books to review, the *New York Times* states that it receives between 750 and 1,000 submissions per week, and on average will publish about 800 book reviews per year, or about 1 to 2 percent of submissions. The first winnowing strategy engaged in by the *Times* is to eliminate from consideration all how-to, self-help, self-published, diet, and financial books. This brings the number of submissions to about 6,000 per year. Getting from 6,000 to 800 is like the feverish nightmare described by a literary agent earlier in this book—to have to pick the "good" books from an entire bookstore of coverless volumes. It is not feasible for the *Times* to hire enough "preview editors" to actually fully read each of the 6,000 submissions, and so metrics of evaluation that go beyond the content of the books themselves are crucial. As is also the case with bookstore buyers, the *Times* uses the reputations of publishers as a device to reduce oversupply and uncertainty. As *Times* book review editor Barry Gewen has acknowledged, submissions "from major publishing houses—Knopf, Random House, and Farrar, Straus and Giroux, for example—may be given more time compared to those from, say, a small university press."[17]

The second device used by review outlets like the *Times* is relationships with publishing houses' publicity staff. As a publicist for a publisher who had first worked in New York but now works on the West Coast explained, "I couldn't do my job here if I hadn't fostered those connections [while working in New York]. . . . [I'm going to New York to] cultivate a relationship, and then also for outlets that I already have a pretty established relationship, I'm just trying to maintain it. . . . [It's important to meet with review outlets face-to-face because people] really want to schmooze, they want to talk a little bit more."

In addition to fostering and maintaining an interpersonal relationship, much like the work of field reps with book sellers, it is important for a publicity director both to understand and know the needs of the review outlet, and to *translate* a publisher's understanding of its own seasonal catalog to reviewers by explaining books in a language that matters to them. Abbye Simkowitz, publicity manager at Counterpoint, described the contents of her pitch to major outlets like the *Times*, in the context of *Jarrettsville*:

> I will definitely tell them *Jarrettsville* is our lead novel for the fall season, because you want to establish what your priorities are for them. Especially if Counterpoint holds count with these reviewers, which it does, communicating to them what we consider some of our best books of the season is something that will go somewhere with them and something that they're interested in knowing. So I say, "this is our lead novel of the season, the editors are just completely in love with it, they think it's brilliant. She has an amazing track record. She's gotten extremely well praised in the past and she's an incredible writer." And then I tell them it's based on a true story, which is a great hook, describe a little bit of the plot and maybe say that it's told in different perspectives. Then I'd say she has been influenced by Virginia Woolf or someone like that, some sort of a comp[arison].

As this is a new field transition that requires conversion to a new set of expectations and normative understandings, Simkowitz's pitch of *Jarrettsville* to a review outlet translates the book's meaning quite differently from how Krefman pushed *Jarrettsville* in his reader report. The language of enthusiasm is present in both, but while Krefman focused on the specifics of the characters and plot and the emotive reactions they drew from him, Simkowitz relies almost exclusively on extra-textual factors in explaining *Jarrettsville*'s quality. For Simkowitz, the story itself and how it is structured is not much more than an afterthought, emphasizing instead that it's Counterpoint's lead title, that the editors "love it" (i.e., this work has real literary merit; it is not a cash grab), and that Nixon has been well reviewed in the past.

Given Simkowitz's position between the fields of production and reception, there are two reasons why she doesn't much discuss textual factors in her pitch, or why she thinks that when pitching a review outlet it can be amateurish for the description of the book's contents to go on for too long. Most importantly, she has not read *Jarrettsville* in its entirety, nor likely will the review editor to whom she's pitching. In turn, should the novel be forwarded on for review, it is the job of the reviewer, not Simkowitz or the editor who assigns reviews, to ultimately decide what *Jarrettsville* is "actually about." While everyone pitching the *Times* can and will say their books are great, it's better to focus on objective statements that cannot be said for all books: the privileged placement of a book on the publisher's list, and that the author has already been well reviewed. Put another way, Simkowitz's job is to paint a picture of where *Jarrettsville* is located in a seasonal landscape, whereas it is the job of the assigned reviewer to paint a picture of its contents in detail. Translating from one to the other is part of how books transition from production to reception.

Review editors' selection of reviewers is more often than not another matching process. Ideal would be a reviewer who has written a book of the same genre or type so that she can better understand the space the author is writing in, and make sense of the work's successes and failures in relation to other books in that space. In a way, the reviewer should be structurally similar to the author without actually being interpersonally close to her in an observable way (e.g., a shared agent or publisher) so as to avoid the impression of impropriety; a good reviewer should be "informed but not entrenched," as the *Times'* public editor has stated.[18] Yet for book reviewing in particular this network-based avoidance of conflicts of interest regularly fails not because of reviewers' interpersonal relations, but because of who book reviewers typically are and where their allegiances typically lie.

In sociology, the work of professional reviewers and their relationships to producers and consumers is typically treated in one of two fashions. The first, as inspired by Paul Hirsch, asks how publishers try to co-opt intermediaries (such as reviewers).[19] The second, as inspired by Pierre Bourdieu, asks how reviewers consecrate some objects as "art," and maintain their legitimacy as having the right to define quality within the community of reviewers.[20] Putting these two strands together, the question is whether reviewers are allegiant to producers, allegiant to consumers, or maintaining their reputations among other reviewers. Yet the majority of book reviewers are categorically dissimilar from reviewers for nearly every other cultural product (e.g., film, music, television, restaurants, dance, fine art, and so on). For these other cultural products, professional reviewers are almost entirely critics by trade—not creators of similar objects themselves. But for books, the vast majority of reviewers are also *practitioners* of the art they are reviewing and write reviews only as a sideline activity.[21] While there are, to be sure, some full-time, professional book critics, most professional published book reviews are written by book authors. As a result, for the tripartite cultural fields of books, to ask if book reviewers are allegiant to producers or consumers risks misinterpreting who book reviewers are and where they spend the majority of their time. They are, at the end of the day, authors first, and their allegiances lie to the field of creation.

It is for this reason that when compared to other cultural criticism, sharply negative book reviews are rare. Rather than being a recent phenomenon, the platitudinous book review has extended even as far back as the "golden age" of publishing in the 1950s and 1960s. As Elizabeth Hardwick wrote in *Harper's* in 1959:

> Sweet, bland commendations fall everywhere upon the scene; a universal, if somewhat lobotomized, accommodation reigns. A book is born into a puddle of treacle; the brine of hostile criticism is only a memory. Everyone is found to have "filled a need," and is to be "thanked" for something and to be excused for "minor faults in an otherwise excellent work." "A thoroughly mature artist" appears many times a week and often daily; many are the bringers of those "messages the Free World will ignore at its peril." The condition of popular reviewing has become so listless, the effect of its agreeable judgments so enervating to the general reading public that the sly publishers of Lolita have tried to stimulate sales by quoting bad reviews along with, to be sure, the usual, repetitive good ones.[22]

As Barry Gewen of the *Times* has noted, when reviewing, "You have to have a hard heart. One can't afford to think a person has spent ten years of her life and I'm spending 30 minutes to throw it away."[23] Yet, because most reviewers are also authors (who spend most of their time in a field almost exclusively populated with authors), hardness of heart is nearly impossible for them and they are not only sympathetic to the years of life being thrown away in the thirty minutes, but also knowingly empathetic. It is for this reason that an informal code of *author omertà* often exists between authors and their reviewers.

Omertà, a masculinist Southern Italian code of honor most frequently associated with the Sicilian Mafia, is an oath of silence that demands that its adherents not report on others' malfeasances to outside parties. In this same way, author omertà demands that regardless of one's true feelings about a book, extremely negative evaluations are to remain private within the "families" of the field of reception. Essentially, to report the mediocrity or worse of published novels is to break the code of silence.[24] Although the code is not universally adhered to, a well-reviewed author and occasional book reviewer for a major outlet explained the phenomenon: "I think [hav-

ing published a book and been reviewed] gives you a certain respect for
the work at hand. It's not easy to write a book and it's not easy to get a
book published and so as long as the author has good intentions, which
they almost always do, in my review I honor those good intentions. Also
other writers may review *me* one day. So as I see it there's no point in being
needlessly critical or uselessly dismissive." For this reviewer, faint praise is
the public face of harsh criticism. Other author-reviewers, to maintain the
code, expressly avoid reviewing books for which they cannot offer praise.
As another author-reviewer explained it, he would turn down a review opportunity before "assassinating" a book's author in print:

> I don't think I'd ever do an assassination review . . . I just don't see any
> point in that. It would be better to just, if you don't think you're going
> to do a positive review or at least one that is illuminating in some way
> on some aspect of the book or some aspect of contemporary litera-
> ture, I would just turn down a review. . . . There are lots of different
> types of books and lots of different sensibilities and just because a
> book doesn't adhere to my taste doesn't mean it's not good. . . . From
> being an author, in my world I'm seeing all sorts of different stuff that
> people want to write, and I'm trying to help them no matter what it
> is they're trying to write, even if it's not something I personally like
> or do well.

Deeply entrenched in the code of author omertà is that generous reviewing
is a favor reserved by authors for their non-name-economy peers. The belief is that to publicly and strongly criticize the work of non-name-economy
authors is to steer readers away from books they would not likely read anyway. A negative review, then, is a needless act of symbolic violence that,
according to another author-reviewer, "doesn't make a difference except
on the author's psyche."

Further evidence of the code's existence between authors is its observable absence in reviews written by full-time book critics. Only here will you
find a book dismissed in review as "an odious self-portrait of the artist as a
young jackass: petulant, pompous, obsessive, selfish and overwhelmingly
self-absorbed," as Michiko Kakutani wrote of Jonathan Franzen's memoir
The Discomfort Zone in 2006. Perhaps most symbolically telling of the code
was the *New York Times*' two reviews of J. K. Rowling's *The Casual Vacancy*
in 2012. In the end of September of that year Kakutani harshly panned the
book, using her affection for Rowling's *Harry Potter* novels as a bludgeon
with which to pummel *Vacancy*. Yet a month later, the *Times* published

a second review for *The Casual Vacancy*, this time by the fiction author Amanda Foreman. Foreman was much more complimentary than was Kakutani, and in suggesting that the book was too long and unfocused, she blamed Rowling's editor for failing to perform "a thoughtful edit."[25] From one author to another, the minor sins of *The Casual Vacancy* were clearly someone else's.

None of this is to suggest that among authors the code of omertà is upheld at all times. Yet recognizing exactly when and where the code is most regularly broken further corroborates its general existence. Sharply critical and negative book reviews of non-name-economy authors most regularly appear in *Publishers Weekly* and *Kirkus*, the latter of which has been referred to as "reliably cantankerous" in its reviews.[26] The more frequent appearance of negative reviews in these outlets further confirms the broader existence of author omertà, because they differ from every other outlet in two meaningful ways: (1) they are trade journals for the field of production rather than reception, and even more important, (2) unlike almost all other review outlets, reviewers for these publications are written anonymously. Put another way, to criticize an author's work in the pages of *Publishers Weekly* or *Kirkus* is the authorial equivalent of breaking omertà from within the safety of the witness protection program.[27]

HOW BEING PLACED ON THE FRONT TABLE COULD HAVE TANKED *JARRETTSVILLE*

When the Counterpoint staff arrived at BEA, they came with *Jarrettsville* in tow. They had printed about 850 ARCs of the novel, the only book they'd be giving away that season. At BEA, in an announcement to the field of production, Counterpoint had made itself and *Jarrettsville* temporarily synonymous. In the days and weeks following the convention, the first discussions and reviews of *Jarrettsville* started to appear online. It looked like Counterpoint was already achieving some success in growing awareness for *Jarrettsville* in its "first sale," and it was still four months out from the novel's official release.

Building on the push for *Jarrettsville* at BEA, at a later sales meeting at PGW for Counterpoint's fall list, Charlie Winton doubled down on his earlier enthusiasm for the novel. To the field reps assembled in the room he declared, "*Jarrettsville* is a great book, and it's a big title for us, so sell mightily!" Sell mightily they did. Reports from the field reps, who were working to pollinate seeds of enthusiasm for *Jarrettsville* at their various accounts, started to trickle back in a few weeks later. The enthusiasm they had passed

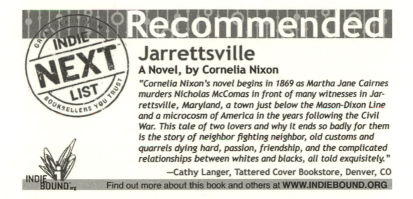

Recommended

Jarrettsville
A Novel, by Cornelia Nixon

"Cornelia Nixon's novel begins in 1869 as Martha Jane Cairnes murders Nicholas McComas in front of many witnesses in Jarrettsville, Maryland, a town just below the Mason-Dixon Line and a microcosm of America in the years following the Civil War. This tale of two lovers and why it ends so badly for them is the story of neighbor fighting neighbor, old customs and quarrels dying hard, passion, friendship, and the complicated relationships between whites and blacks, all told exquisitely."

—Cathy Langer, Tattered Cover Bookstore, Denver, CO

Find out more about this book and others at **WWW.INDIEBOUND.ORG**

FIGURE 8.2: *Jarrettsville* Receives Praise on the Indie Next List.

on for *Jarrettsville* was being reciprocated. Reports also came back that retailers were grateful for the novel being released as a paperback original; it allowed them to take on more copies, or for some, to take on any copies at all. Through field reps, the threads of Krefman's initial enthusiasm for *Jarrettsville* had woven across Counterpoint and through the PGW staff, and were now diffusing out into a broader web of collective belief that could position *Jarrettsville* to truly be successful if everything fell perfectly into place.

Counterpoint had also crafted a letter and sent it to buyers at some of the focal independent bookstores with which it had friendly relations. Counterpoint could not control if these buyers would share in their enthusiasm for *Jarrettsville* and nominate it for special recognition—other publishers were also advocating for their lead fiction titles in similar ways—but to not try was to already have failed. For *Jarrettsville* these efforts were successful, and the novel appeared as a recommended title on the Indie Next List (see Figure 8.2), as well as on *Publishers Weekly*'s Indie Top 20 list of titles to watch for in the coming publishing season. Counterpoint had also nominated *Jarrettsville* for co-op at Borders, and again at this they were successful. Running through the month of October, *Jarrettsville* would be on front table display at all Borders stores across the United States, and then placed "cover-out" when moved back to the shelves.

As part of the co-op agreement, Borders required Counterpoint to supply them with 3,500 copies of the novel—about a third of the total stock—so that they could replenish copies if it sold quickly while in co-op. With a stronger than expected buy-in from Barnes & Noble, library sales, and the independents as well, this did not leave much stock in reserve at PGW and

Ingram, about 700 to 800 copies total not in active distribution. Winton described the 3,500 copies held by Borders as "a lot of copies. Without an incredible [*New York*] *Times* review they probably won't be able to sell even a third of that. But once you're in the stores you're halfway there, and you're hoping that maybe lightning is going to strike. But the problem is there's no middle ground. You're either going to sell 600 or 3,500 through [Borders]. There's nothing in between, and no way to know which one it will be."

Further complicating matters was that just in advance of *Jarrettsville*'s release Borders changed its merchandising policy, and raised the minimum level of stock for cooperative promotion from 3,500 copies to 4,200 copies. This meant that almost all of the *Jarrettsville* stock that was being held back for restocking across channels instead was rerouted into Borders' warehouses. The change to Borders' policy put Counterpoint into a bit of a commitment trap with the retailer, as if the novel sold too quickly at outlets that weren't Borders, the retailers in which readers were congregating would not be able to fulfill demand, the doomsday scenario for any publisher.

Although the stock at Borders was a real concern at the press, if Counterpoint couldn't get publicity for *Jarrettsville* through well-placed reviews and speaking engagements for Nixon, the problem likely would not matter anyway. Simkowitz, however, *was* having success in pitching *Jarrettsville* to review outlets. She told them the novel was Counterpoint's lead fiction title for the season, that the editors loved it, that Nixon had been well reviewed before, and that it was based on a true story from the author's family history. From Simkowitz's work in advance of its release, *Jarrettsville* received a glowing review in *Kirkus*, a first for Nixon in that outlet, and also received a more measured review in *Publishers Weekly*. Good reviews in these two outlets, with their anonymous reviewers, were good signs. Along with the positive online chatter from BEA, the enthusiasm of the field reps, and the strong buy-in from retailers, enthusiasm begot more enthusiasm, and with each successive win Counterpoint could build upon the last.

On the eve of *Jarrettsville*'s release, while Nixon was preparing for the first stop on her book tour at the Southern Festival of Books in Nashville, she received word from Counterpoint that the *New York Times* had requested a high-resolution author photo. This was not a guarantee that the *Times* would run a *Jarrettsville* review, but signaled it was very likely. Nixon, to her delight, had the photo by Ettlinger handy. The photographer credit beneath the photo would mean nothing to readers of the *Times* at large, but other authors from the field of creation would notice.

For Nixon, to know that she was very likely to receive a *Times* review for *Jarrettsville* was both elating and nerve-wracking. It would make her three-for-three in receiving *Times* reviews in her career as a fiction writer. "Fingers crossed for a weekday!" she said excitedly, and with a broad smile. From Simkowitz's perspective as a publicist, there were positives to reviews in both the Sunday *Book Review* and the Thursday edition. In favor of Sunday, Simkowitz figured, people are reading the Sunday *Book Review* looking for the next book they will buy; it's a captured audience of people in the market for new books. Thursday reviews were also good though, as there are fewer of them, so those who are casually browsing the *Times*' website are more likely to come across the review as the first or second item in the Books section—a less motivated market, but perhaps also a broader one. For Nixon the number of readers, or who they were, had nothing to do with her preference; instead, her preference for a Thursday review came from a belief that reviews on that day were more likely to be done by "real pros," people who knew of Nixon's literary reputation and would really understand her intentions when reviewing the book. A Sunday review could be written by anyone, with any number of unpredictable opinions about *Jarrettsville*. While as an author Nixon wanted to attract readers, ultimately her capital in the field of creation was symbolic and cultural; she was the writer of quality literary fiction. For Nixon then, the marginal chance at a broader readership from a Sunday review was not worth the marginal chance of drawing as a reviewer a "wild card" who could hurt the literary reputation she had spent decades to establish.

The ideal reviewer for *Jarrettsville* would be a novelist who also wrote literary fiction and, even better, had also written historical literary fiction. Better yet, the ideal reviewer would be a writer of literary historical fiction about the Civil War who traversed the divide to popular fiction, and who did not have a competing book that had recently been or was soon to be released. This ideal reviewer should not have an interpersonal relationship with Nixon, but would otherwise structurally overlap with her in the field of creation; he would be informed but not entrenched. He'd be Charles Frazier, or Nick Taylor, who reviewed *Jarrettsville* in the *Rumpus*. For authors and publishers, reviews are like playing Russian roulette—somewhere in the cylinder is a negative review, so they hope it is fired out of a low-circulation, low-stakes chamber rather than the alternative. But for Nixon, Counterpoint, and *Jarrettsville*, by far the most negative review the book would receive had been loaded into the most damaging chamber possible.

When the *New York Times* review first appeared online, word passed quickly through the Counterpoint staff that had worked on *Jarrettsville*. The review's contents weren't much discussed, and instead, to answer the question of what the reviewer had written, one staff member just stared blankly and elliptically answered the question by responding to a different one: "A historian," she said. To say that an academic historian, even one of the Civil War, had reviewed a work of historical fiction was to say enough. "He's never written a book, never been reviewed," someone else said in disappointment. Rather than begrudging the reviewer his opinion, their regret was that a historian had been tasked to review a work of fiction, and that he had not himself yet published a book. Much of the reviewer's criticism, as might be predicted coming from a historian, was concerned with historical inaccuracies. Yet for special condemnation he closed his review with discussion of the scene of Martha and Nick having a romantic encounter—the scene Nixon had "left" for D. H. Lawrence by consciously "overwriting" it in a Romanticist style to match the time period, figuring that he had gotten to it first. As the reviewer summarized the scene, and ended his review of *Jarrettsville*, "That kiss left me gasping for breath—and not in a good way. While badly rendered history, like a forged painting, may pass undetected for only a little while, writing like that is timeless."[28]

Later, other reviewers, all fiction authors and none who knew Nixon personally, privately referred to the *Times* review as "mean-spirited," "petty," and "entirely unnecessary." Like the Counterpoint staff, these reviewers did not begrudge the reviewer his opinion, but instead begrudged his lack of commitment to the omertà code, if he had even been aware of it at all. When the code is broken, a deeply critical review of a non-name-economy author stands out even more, giving the impression that the panned book is demonstrably worse than all the other novels that, due to the code, have been ritualistically graced with faint praise. Some of the Counterpoint staff, out of both optimism and reputational self-interest, wondered if the *Times* had placed its *Jarrettsville* review toward the back of the *Sunday Book Review* so as to do both them and Nixon the favor of burying it a bit. According to Winton, the *Times* review not only kept Counterpoint from building more buzz for *Jarrettsville*, but also punctured the balloon of buzz that had been steadily filling since Krefman first offered up his enthusiasm:

> Books are a whole process of building buzz, and as most people can only imagine, it's not something that you can control. It's kind of amorphous, and it's also really fragile. So you start to build some momentum for something and in order for you to continue to build that momentum you need the bloggers and the *New York Times* and all of those things to be harmonized, where everything is essentially reinforcing one another towards a positive end. And what happened with the *Times* was that that little organism of buzz was really punc-

tured, just in that moment, because that's the national book review, so when that happens all the buzz that's been building up just deflates and seeps right out. So the question becomes, a positive review there, how much might it have helped? Probably given the level of distribution [we achieved], it probably would have been very positive for sales, certainly for Amazon, Barnes & Noble, and the library business. The other thing that happens with something like the *New York Times* is that it's a tastemaker so an endorsement there usually means we do an email blast and reconnect with other pending opportunities that may be on the fence as to whether they're going to review the book or not. So it allows us to keep the momentum going in a forward manner, and that's what's disheartening about it. It's just sort of ironic and slightly disheartening for us that basically, over the last two years we've had pretty close to twenty, or maybe more, full reviews in the *New York Times* and we really only had two negative reviews, and the two negative reviews we've had were on both of our lead fiction titles for the fall seasons, which are the books which we had the best distribution on.

Despite being panned in the *Times*, *Jarrettsville* was still selling briskly. Normally this would be good news, but the problem was that it was selling briskly at every outlet—chain, independent, Amazon—*except* Borders, which fifteen months later would file for bankruptcy.[29] By the end of the Borders co-op promotion, of the 4,200 copies of *Jarrettsville* they held, they had sold only several hundred, fewer than a quarter of what had been sold at Barnes & Noble in the same period. By late November *Jarrettsville* had sold out at Amazon and through some of the independents, but all of Counterpoint's reserve stock was still tied up at Borders. As Winton described it several months later, after the Christmas season had passed:

By the end of October [Borders] had already cut a return of 1,000 copies. So then we were in no-man's-land where we knew we were getting 1,000 copies back from Borders, but that doesn't happen instantly. We got 150 back and then later the other 850. And several hundred of those books came back damaged; they had stickers on them so we had to throw them away. And then they returned another 1,500 copies. So after November we've basically just been cycling through [restocking other sellers] on Borders returns for the past two months. But it was really November and early December when we were out of stock. And so I never reprinted. . . . There were times when I thought of doing a 500-copy reprint to fulfill those [orders] but that would take five weeks and by the time we get them we don't need them because within a week of fulfilling them we could have the Borders returns there. And it wasn't really the 3,500 [copies that Borders initially wanted for co-op], it was really the 700 [additional copies]. If they just hadn't taken the last 700 books they would have probably lasted for that interim period before Borders figured out that they really couldn't sell them, and that would have carried us over until the Borders returns came back. So what happened is that we had books that were coming back, so we knew we didn't need to remanufacture, but at the same time we didn't have the continuity of distribution. We didn't have stock where people were buying. They come in and leave empty-handed or with another book. And that was really a drag. . . . There were many aspects of the publishing of [*Jarrettsville*] that were very satisfying and there were also a few aspects of publishing it that really related to Borders and the *New York Times* that were very frustrating.

Despite the ups and downs, Winton and Counterpoint had successfully navigated *Jarrettsville* from the field of production to reception. Yet beyond broad brushstrokes, publishers don't know much about what happens to books after they do or do not sell through to readers. Here's what Counterpoint did know: Nixon's author tour had been successful, and in no small part due to the personal and true nature of the story, she had been warmly received across a wide range of media opportunities. Her best turnouts were in the South and Mid-Atlantic. For her appearance on the author-interview and live broadcast variety show Thacker Mountain Radio in Oxford, Mississippi, hundreds had turned out, and the crowd there cheered during Nixon's reading when a character referred to Nick as a "Yankee bastard." Someone even let out a rebel yell at the end of her reading.

More generally, readers in the South and Mid-Atlantic seemed to be taking particular interest in the book, which Counterpoint could observe through sales tracking (see Figure 8.3). *Jarrettsville* sold most strongly in the South-Atlantic region, measured both by the percentage of overall sales and by per capita sales.[30] *Jarrettsville* also sold well in the Mountain region, whose readers are known by reputation for liking historical fiction. Also on the positive side of the ledger was the Pacific region, where both Nixon and Counterpoint were located. Although what regular readers had to say about *Jarrettsville* was observable on sites like Amazon or Goodreads, these reviews were treated as anecdotes rather than data points—nice to see when positive, dismissed when negative.

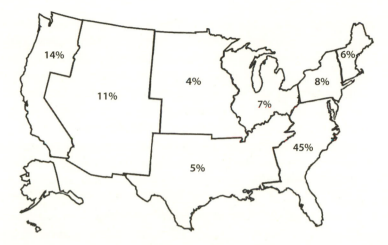

FIGURE 8.3: Percentage of Overall US *Jarrettsville* Sales by Region.

More important to Counterpoint was that despite being panned in the *Times*, *Jarrettsville* would soon again be noted by *Publishers Weekly* as a summer recommendation for book groups. A year later the book won the Michael Shaara Prize for Excellence in Civil War Fiction as awarded by the Civil War Institute at Gettysburg College. "And without a single scene set during the Civil War!" Nixon exclaimed. It was particularly an honor because Michael Shaara's own *Killer Angels*, which had won the 1975 Pulitzer Prize, had been an inspiration to Nixon for *Jarrettsville*. The cash prize for the award nearly matched Nixon's advance for *Jarrettsville*. Even more importantly to both Nixon and Counterpoint, however, the award they felt, given by the Civil War Institute, was a needed counterweight to the *Times* review by a Civil War historian who had panned the book, which Nixon in particular was still smarting over.

Overall *Jarrettsville* had sold well enough, but without being a runaway success. It had also garnered mostly positive reviews and won a minor literary award: again good, but not a runaway success. What Counterpoint knew about *Jarrettsville*'s life in the field of reception was that publishing the novel had not been a mistake, but at the same time it had not been a hit, which could have made up the difference for future publishing mistakes, which are in every publisher's future.

What Counterpoint didn't know about *Jarrettsville*'s new life in a new field was everything else about its reception. Did readers like the novel? What, if anything, did it mean to them? As part of a field transition, just as Counterpoint couldn't know what readers were doing with *Jarrettsville*, those who read it couldn't know what had been done with *Jarrettsville* in prior fields. In the field of reception readers wouldn't know about Nixon's research process, or how the book received its name. They wouldn't know that Weil had taken on Nixon as a client so that she would write *Jarretts-ville*, that the writing of it took years longer than Nixon had promised, that a rejection letter had reshaped the text, or that the novel was ultimately published on the back of Krefman's enthusiasm for it, and that his sugges-tion would restructure it yet again. Readers wouldn't know that the copy editor had cried twice, that Kim Wylie's endorsement had begun to inflate the balloon of buzz for the novel, that Krefman had struggled with losing control, and that *Jarrettsville*'s publisher was still lamenting what could have been had the co-op with Borders worked out and the negative review for *Jarrettsville* been published anywhere except the *Times*. For readers in the field of reception *Jarrettsville* was just a novel, and mostly an unknown one until they began to read it.

PART V
THE FIELD OF RECEPTION

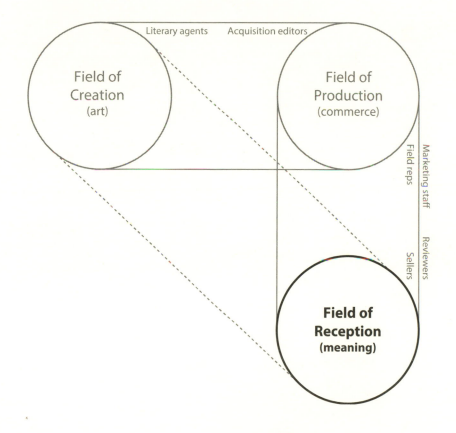

READING LIFE INTO NOVELS

OR, WHY A MISANTHROPIC THUG MAY

NOT BE ALL BAD

THINK AND LET THINK

How can readers, let alone professional readers, draw many divergent meanings from the same novel? In his review of *Jarrettsville* in the *Washington Post*, Robert Goolrick, a memoirist from Virginia, asserted that the novel was primarily about race, and its crowning achievement was the nuance with which Nixon gave historical context to the still-unanswered problems of racism in the United States. For Goolrick, racism "infuses every important action" in *Jarrettsville*: "In the slanderous and racially charged atmosphere of the just-post–Civil War years, there is not a single human exchange that does not pass through a filter of distrust and rage" he wrote in review, and "no moment of [the characters'] lives is safe from the venom of racial hatred."[1] Goolrick would, at a later date, remark about his understanding of *Jarrettsville*: "Racism in Obama's America is an extremely, extremely delicate and important subject. And I was glad that under the guise of writing what would essentially be a romantic novel about the post–Civil War, she also addressed the issue which was very current and very important. . . . It's clear, it's obvious . . . the book is about [racism]."

For the anonymous reviewer in *Publishers Weekly*, it was not obvious that *Jarrettsville* was about racism, or even what *Jarrettsville* was about at all. The *Publishers Weekly* reviewer felt that Nixon's decision to (re)write from the perspectives of multiple narrators "renders unclear what kind of story the author is trying to tell." Both Goolrick and the *Publishers Weekly* reviewer did, however, agree that the final third of the book—the trial of Martha Cairnes—faltered. *Publishers Weekly* wrote that "the riveting beginning [is] sabotaged by the restrained conclusion," and Goolrick agreed that "the final third of the book doesn't live up to the passion of the earlier sections."[2] Yet unlike these two reviewers, the anonymous reviewer at *Kirkus* (2009) thought the trial was "epic." The *Kirkus* reviewer did not have any uncertainty about what kind of story *Jarrettsville* was supposed to be. Unlike Goolrick, who understood the novel as a meditation on the interpersonal effects of structural racism, the reviewer at *Kirkus* appreciated *Jarrettsville* as a "thrilling and cathartic" work of "imaginative, well-crafted historical fiction [that] meditates on morality and the complexity of motivation."[3] Was *Jarrettsville* worth reading because of its treatment of racism in America, or because it transcended time and place in its examination of humankind's internal struggles with morality and action?

When Civil War historical fiction novelist Nick Taylor reviewed *Jarrettsville* for the online literary magazine *The Rumpus*, he took a middle-ground position between complimenting Nixon's treatment of social structure and character: "Nixon weaves together a tapestry of events and psychology to explain how an ordinary girl comes to kill her lover, and how she is acquitted by a jury of her peers."[4] For Taylor, there were two crowning achievements of *Jarrettsville*. The first was the pace of the story ("patience reminiscent of Tolstoy") and quality of prose ("never mind the plot; you might read *Jarrettsville* just for the prose"). The second was how accurately Nixon captured the subtleties of the people, weather, and sensations of the Mid-Atlantic region. According to Taylor, Nixon's descriptions could come only from a writer who really knew and had spent time in the region, which Nixon had.

While the overall quality and accuracy of Nixon's writing were what was most admirable about *Jarrettsville* for Taylor, for the Civil War historian Adam Goodheart writing in the *New York Times*, these two factors were *Jarrettsville*'s weakest characteristics: "Nixon fumbles repeatedly when it comes to the finer details of history that, woven together, form a credible fabric of the past," Goodheart wrote, noting also that he found the quality of writing "timeless" in its badness.[5] Equally problematic to Goodheart was the dialect used by the African American characters in the novel, which he found "cringe-producing," although "the white characters . . . are[n't] much better." For Goodheart, Nixon's decisions to write the love story in a Romanticist style to match the time period and her inclusion of Tim's linguistic code-switching did not come across so much as literary decisions as they did maudlin and even offensive prose. While for Goolrick *Jarrettsville* was an indictment of racism, for Goodheart the novel itself may just have been racist.

As *Jarrettsville* transitioned from the field of production to reception, what it was, and if it was successful in being so, were once again active questions. Just as was the case in *Jarrettsville*'s first field transition, discordance in how to make sense of the novel emerged as it underwent another. As was the case in editors' rejection letters, reviewers, in making sense of a novel that had come from one field and was heading into another, drew vastly different meanings out of *Jarrettsville*. Was the novel primarily about racism, as a reviewer who took a keen interest in present-day racism in "Obama's America" thought, or was it about the complexities of morality and motivation? Was its potential destroyed by historical inaccuracies as understood by a historian, or was its potential soaring due to historical and geographic accuracies as understood by a fellow writer of literary Civil War historical fiction? To what degree had reviewers imprinted their own lives, interests, and expertise onto their understandings of the novel? Well beyond the purviews of Nixon and Counterpoint, in the field of reception everyday readers would also make their own personalized, and even local, sense of the text. Relatively untethered by the text itself, readers, like reviewers, attributed a wide range of meanings to *Jarrettsville*.

How to make sense of Richard, Martha's brother, was one such cleavage between readers. According to Taylor in *The Rumpus*, Richard is "misanthropic," and in the *Kirkus* review he is described as a "Confederate thug." While writing, Nixon was afraid of how her family would react to her portrayal of Richard, which is incredibly unsympathetic. For many readers the text itself seemed to support these concerns. In *Jarrettsville*, Richard is a rapist, and a co-conspirator of John Wilkes Booth. After raping Sophie, a freed slave of his family who is described as looking "more child than woman," he publicly beats Nick nearly to death to shift the blame for his act of sexual violence. He then beats Tim, his victim's brother, for having embarrassed him by having silently left the farm with his family in reaction to Sophie's rape. Richard is so villainous that some readers considered him more caricature than character; he just embodied evil, they thought. Yet despite finding Richard's actions no less deplorable, some readers sympathized with him, and some even empathized with him. How, and why?

READING LIFE INTO NOVELS

To read one's life into a novel means to make sense of it using the tools that one possesses. More than just the ability to read, what is taken out of a novel is conditioned on what readers bring into it. To their reading experiences readers bring a complex web of prior experiences: their preferences and tastes, the other things they've read, their demographic backgrounds and experiences, and so on. As a result, for different readers the same novel can effectively be different novels: some readers loved *Jarrettsville* whereas others did not, just as for some it was about love and loss whereas for others it was about fear and violence.[6]

Yet for readers to be entirely unconstrained in the meaning they make out of novels would be to suggest that when it comes to making sense and meaning of things, the things themselves may as well not exist; they are the blank slates on which readers imprint themselves. Although these days nobody actually believes this, due to the split of the studies of creation and production from reception, the possibilities of textual constraints in reception processes is left mostly unobservable.[7] As Wendy Griswold has argued, "Sociologists should rediscover that forgotten soul, *the author*, who has been deconstructed into oblivion. . . . [T]here is no reason why authors, with their intentions, experiences, sociological characteristics, and 'horizons' of understanding, cannot be treated in parallel fashion to readers: as agents who interact with texts, working to encode meanings."[8]

Likewise, for the French sociologist Robert Escarpit, literary success is conditioned on "a convergence of intentions between author and readers"; literary acclaim for Escarpit is the result of interpretive harmonizing across fields.[9] In contrast, for literary theorist Alberto Manguel it is precisely the dialogue between authors' intentions and readers' interpretations in which the act of reading comes alive, as it is readers' ability to read beyond authors' intentions that allows for an exchange of ideas to take place.[10] Ralph Ellison took a similarly dialogic stance when responding to a letter from a high school student about symbolism in his work: "Readers often infer that there is symbolism in my work, which I do not intend. My reaction is sometimes annoyance. It is sometimes humorous. It is sometimes even pleasant, indicating that the reader's mind has collaborated in a creative way with what I have written."[11]

To understand why a character in a novel is seen by some as a misanthropic thug and by others as something else requires three steps. First, as in the dominant framework in the study of cultural reception, it must be established that readers are relatively unconstrained by an author's intentions for a text. Second, both readers' evaluations of and interpretive meanings for texts should be, to at least some degree, conditioned on their demographic backgrounds, experiences, and previously derived preferences; that is, variation in evaluation and interpretation comes from somewhere. Third, these evaluations and interpretive meanings should be flexible: evaluations and interpretations are not inborn and affixed to readers just as they are not static and inborn in texts. Instead, as the quality and meanings of novels are subjective affairs, evaluations and interpretations of them should be malleable as based on new information or experiences; if they were not, readers would never have diverged in their interpretations and evaluations at all. Although novels surface for readers in the field of reception as complete and finished products, they are instead imperfect hodgepodges of experiences, chance encounters, enacted suggestions, demands, enthusiastic support, doubt, and compromises within and across fields and their transitions. This is also true for readers, who are themselves not complete and finished products, and in their evaluations and interpretations undergo similar social-structural processes and changes.

GETTING OUT WHAT NIXON WAS PUTTING IN, OR NOT

Cornelia Nixon had not only influences and inspirations for *Jarrettsville*, but intentions as well. Though she deliberately left open some interpretive questions in the story, she also wrote *Jarrettsville* for it to be read, and desired to convey to readers the story as she intended to tell it. Readers, for their part, also had their own interpretations of the text and in some ways read it as Nixon had intended, and in other ways did not. To begin to understand the puzzle of where authors' intentions and readers' interpretations overlap and diverge, before the release of *Jarrettsville* Nixon recorded her privately stated intentions for readers' interpretations across thirty-seven different dimensions; readers then recorded their actual interpretations along the same dimensions after having read the novel. Overall, readers diverged from Nixon's privately stated intentions for the text on thirty-three of thirty-seven interpretive dimensions, and across all dimensions on average diverged from Nixon by twenty points on a hundred-point scale.[12]

On average, readers found Martha to be much more of a traditionally feminine character than Nixon had intended, and found Richard much more responsible for the dissolution of Martha and Nick's relationship than Nixon had intended (see Figure 9.1). Divergence from Nixon's intentions was also present in the role of economic class in the story, for which readers read in a class difference between Martha and Nick's families that Nixon had not intended. More generally, whereas Nixon had intended for the structural conditions of racism and the Civil War to be the two primary factors in the dissolution of Martha and Nick's relationship, for readers there was a wider mélange of personal characteristics and structural factors that led to their demise.

With regard to characters, Martha was read as being less responsible and other characters as more responsible than Nixon had intended. Despite readers not finding Martha as responsible for what happened as Nixon had intended, they did find her less justified in her actions, chiefly, murdering Nick. Nick leaving Jarrettsville was also viewed more harshly than Nixon had intended. Although Nixon had tried to insert some levity into the text, readers did not find much, feeling the story to be much less funny than Nixon had intended. Readers also diverged from Nixon about the accuracy

FIGURE 9.1: Readers' Divergence from Nixon's Intentions.
Note: *N* = 202. Reported at means across readers on a 100-point scale. Nixon's intentions in brackets.

of describing different scenes as the climactic moments. Just as readers thought it more accurate to characterize *Jarrettsville* as a work of romance fiction than Nixon had intended, they found scenes of Martha and Nick falling in love together to be more climactic than Nixon had intended. Particularly, they read Nick's beating—which Nixon fully had not intended to be the climax of the novel; for her it was clearly either Nick's murder or Martha's trial—as much more climactic than Nixon had written it.

Although readers were relatively unconstrained by Nixon's intentions, what Nixon "put into" the novel was not entirely unrelated to what readers "drew out" of it. On four interpretive dimensions, readers read *Jarrettsville* with no statistically significant difference from Nixon's intentions: (1) how sympathetic a character Martha was, (2) how traditionally masculine a character Nick was, (3) the likelihood of Tim and Martha having had an off-page sexual relationship, and (4) the accuracy of the broader characterization of *Jarrettsville* as a "love story." Likewise, when relaxing the standard of the relationship between intention and interpretation from a hundred-point scale to a yes/no dichotomy (i.e., greater or less than fifty on the scale), readers' interpretations aligned with Nixon's intentions on twenty-nine out of thirty-four dimensions. Put another way, readers were not constrained by Nixon's intentions for *Jarrettsville* while making their own interpretations of it, but at the same time, in making meaning they were neither entirely without guideposts nor left alone to figure it out for themselves. Through this lens, readers were free to make their own meanings of *Jarrettsville* while at the same time Nixon's intentions tended to pitch them in general interpretive directions.

LIKING *JARRETTSVILLE*, OR NOT

Overall, readers generally liked *Jarrettsville*, rating it on average seventy-five on a hundred-point scale. Readers who had been born or lived in the South appraised *Jarrettsville* seven points more favorably than others.[13] Regional culture as expressed through literary preferences is still quite common, and is driven not only by natives of the region but also by "cowbirds," transplants to a region who learn about their new environs by engaging with local literatures.[14] This is true among the *Jarrettsville* readers, as both natives of and transplants to the South liked the book more than those outside the South.

Readers' education and income levels were not related to how much or little they liked the novel. This may have been because readers were omnivorous in their tastes (i.e., liking many different things), as their preferences for eleven different fiction genres were also unrelated to their incomes or education, save for romance fiction, which was less preferred by those with advanced degrees than those without.[15] Readers' incomes and education levels were also unrelated to the frequency with which they read for pleasure, with the average respondent reading about two books for pleasure per month. The readers of *Jarrettsville* who were surveyed were members of what Griswold calls the "reading class"; they had higher incomes and more years of education (over half had an advanced degree) than does the general population, both of which correlate with reading for pleasure. As a result, any education- and income-related sorting for *Jarrettsville* or reading for pleasure more generally may have already occurred through selecting into reading books as a regular leisure activity.[16]

Readers' like or dislike of *Jarrettsville* was more clearly, however, related to their preferences for different genres of fiction. Of the eleven fiction genres presented to them, on average respondents liked four, and with each additional genre of fiction they liked their enjoyment of *Jarrettsville* increased by about three and a half points on a hundred-point scale. More specifically, readers who expressed a like for genres of fiction that had been discussed in relationship to *Jarrettsville* in the field of production liked the novel more. Such was the case, on a hundred-point scale, for fans of historical fiction and romance fiction (each eleven points more for liking *Jarrettsville* over non-fans of these genres), as well as popular fiction and mystery novels (each eight points more).

How did reading toward or away from Nixon's intentions affect readers' like or dislike of *Jarrettsville*? Should readers in the field of reception be completely untethered from Nixon's encoded meanings in the field of creation, the closeness or distance from which they read to Nixon's intentions for the text should be unrelated to their like or dislike of the novel. This was not the case. The more readers' interpretations aligned with Nixon's intentions regarding the genre designations for *Jarrettsville*, the more they liked it. Put another way, if readers read the book fully literary and historical while shading over to popular fiction with some romance elements thrown in, which was how Nixon intended for the novel to be read, they enjoyed it more. In turn, the more readers' interpretations of the novel cohered with Nixon's intentions across the more textually specific interpretive dimensions of it (i.e., climatic scenes, responsibilities and sympathies for different characters, and so on) the more they liked it (see Figure 9.2).[17] As argued by the French sociologist Robert Escarpit in the late 1950s, for *Jarrettsville* to be deemed a success for readers seemed to at least partially be conditioned on a convergence of intentions and interpretations between them and its author.

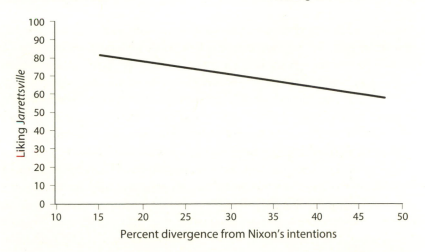

FIGURE 9.2: The Relationship between Liking *Jarrettsville* and Interpreting the Novel along Nixon's Intentions.

WHAT *JARRETTSVILLE* MEANT, OR NOT

Although part of liking *Jarrettsville* was reading it more closely to Nixon's intentions, rather than being merely dependent on Nixon to make meaning out of the novel, readers also brought their own backgrounds into their reading experiences while making sense of it. Older readers found the story to be both more true to life and faster paced than did younger readers. As readers' age increased, they were also more sympathetic to the character of Martha's mother, Mary Ann; each year of increased age correlated with a 0.36-point increase in sympathy for Mary Ann on a 100-point scale.

A second major divergence in interpretation occurred between Southern and non-Southern readers. For readers who had been born or lived in the South, Nick was interpreted as much less responsible for the outcome of his failed relationship with Martha, and ultimately his murder. Southern readers interpreted Nick's responsibility for what happened as nine points lower than non-Southern readers on a hundred-point scale. This may be because, for Southern readers, a key scene in *Jarrettsville* was Richard's public beating of Nick with a bullwhip. It is this violence at the hands of Richard that causes Nick to abandon Martha and leave Jarrettsville for Pennsylvania Amish country. In support of this characterization, for Southern readers, who hold Nick less responsible for leaving Martha and the town of Jarrettsville, the scene of Richard's beating of Nick rates twelve points higher on a hundred-point scale as a climactic scene of the novel than for non-Southern readers. For Southern readers this scene was as climactic as was Martha's murder of Nick for non-Southern readers. More generally, the more readers interpreted the beating of Nick at the hands of Richard as the climactic scene of the novel, the more they found Richard, racism, and the aftereffects of the Civil War as infusing what happened in the story; these readers were, in effect, honing in on the key scene—and structural factors that informed the scene—in Nixon's recrafting of *Martha's Version* into *Jarrettsville*.

Finding particular importance in Richard's beating of Nick, instead of placing primary blame on Nick for the dissolution of his relationship with Martha, Southern readers interpreted the aftereffects of the Civil War itself, a structural factor, as nine points higher on a hundred-point scale as a causal factor in the dissolution of their relationship than did non-Southern readers. The emphasis by Southern readers on the effects of the Civil War, and perhaps on Nick's beating as yet another aftereffect of the war, may be one reason why Southern readers also thought it less accurate to characterize *Jarrettsville* as a love story than did non-Southern readers by eight points. In these ways, while reading *Jarrettsville* Southern readers were in effect reading a slightly different novel than were non-Southern readers; their readings were more attuned to the violence and suffering in the text than to love and loss.

While readers diverged in their interpretations of *Jarrettsville* along several demographic lines, their interpretations also diverged based on their cultural tastes for different fiction genres. Broadly, readers tended to read *Jarrettsville* into the conventions of genres they preferred; they took what they were familiar with and read it into the novel, or alternately took the elements of the novel that fit their familiarities and preferences and accentuated them in their readings. By thirteen points on a hundred-point scale, fans of romance fiction thought it more accurate to characterize *Jarrettsville* as a romance novel than did non-fans of romance, and by eleven points they found it more accurate to generally characterize the book as a love story. Reading the novel toward one's prior preferences was also the case for readers of literary fiction, who by twenty points found it more accurate to characterize *Jarrettsville* as a work of literary fiction than did nonreaders of literary fiction. Fans of the horror genre, who as much or more than fans of any genre regularly encounter clear protagonists and antagonists and are unlikely to encounter female antagonists, read the largest divergence between Nick and Martha's culpability for the events in *Jarrettsville*, with Martha eleven points less responsible and Nick nine points more responsible for what happened, compared to the interpretations of non–horror fans.

Although fans of all genres found it most accurate to characterize *Jarrettsville* as a work of historical fiction, fans of historical fiction in particular read the story through the lens of history. Historical fiction fans, much like Civil War historical fiction author Nick Taylor who reviewed *Jarrettsville* in *The Rumpus*, interpreted the novel as more historically accurate by six points on a hundred-point scale than did others. Historical fiction fans also found the story to be more emotionally compelling, sadder, and more true to life than did others. *Jarrettsville* also made historical fiction fans think more about the nature of human relationships by seven points. Collectively these divergences suggest that fans of historical fiction, likely through their previous experiences with historical fiction, were more equipped or inclined to open themselves to a story and characters set in the post–Civil War period. They had, in effect, developed a skill for making emotional connections to historical stories.[18]

Overall, given a range of demographic characteristics and cultural tastes, readers diverged in both their evaluations and interpretations of *Jarrettsville* in significant ways. While most readers appeared to accept a baseline level of guidance from Nixon's intentions, they were not particularly constrained by them. Instead, personal factors related to readers such as their demographic backgrounds and previously derived cultural tastes were a salient lens through which they generated their evaluations and interpretations of *Jarrettsville*. Yet, implicitly suggested in this framework is that demographic or taste-based readings are the result of sociostructurally derived perspectives based on one's experiences in the world; to be older means to approach the world, or a new novel, differently from someone who is younger, just as to be a fan of historical fiction means to approach a new novel set in the past differently than others. If these evaluative and interpretive distinctions are truly experiential and not innate, they should be flexible, and we should be able to observe them unfold, retract, and expand in social processes. In other words, through interaction, readers, open to interpretation as they are, should be able to influence and affect each other's interpretations of texts.

MEANING IN INTERACTION

As most directly stated by Wendy Griswold, "Reading is social. It always has been."[19] While it is difficult, if not impossible, to pinpoint the precise factors across a reader's life that cause her to evaluate and interpret a novel as she does, some basic processes can be observed through readers in interaction. Book groups, in which people come together to discuss a book they have read, have a long history in the United States. Although Harvey Daniels dates the "literature circle" in the Americas back to the seventeenth century, it was not until the nineteenth century, and after the Civil War in particular, that the social phenomenon of book clubs emerged across the country. Since then, reading collectively has been further fostered by institutional developments such as the Book of the Month Club and Literary Guild in the first half of the twentieth century, and the Big Read and "One Book" programs in the twenty-first century.[20]

While most book groups are informal social gatherings, there is wide variation in how they are organized.[21] Most are made up of friends, acquaintances, or coworkers and take place within a private home; others are coordinated and hosted by libraries, bookstores, or community centers. Given their informal nature and reliance for membership on friendships, shared occupations, and neighborhoods, book groups are often demographically homogenous along lines of age, gender, income, race, and so on. It is also more likely than not that book group members enjoy the same "types" and genres of books as other members, lest they abandon the group or never be invited to join at all. Across book groups there are also finer-grained cultural distinctions around how the meeting will unfold and what "good" membership and participation consists of.

Some book groups double as dinner parties, with the food ordered in, cooked by the host, or organized as a potluck. Sometimes it is customary for the dishes served to relate somehow to the novel under discussion, a gustatory effort to really "get inside" the story.[22] At others, drinking alcohol is much more important than eating.[23] When selecting which books to read, some groups have formal nomination and voting procedures, whereas others rely on prepackaged or thematic lists (e.g., prize winners), and others still rely on a more haphazard and informal suggestion process from meeting to meeting. Discussion ground rules and informal codes of conduct also differ across groups. Some groups have a rotating "discussion leader" who does background research on the selected book for each meeting. Other groups begin each meeting with each member sharing first impressions before opening up the conversation. Other book groups have no overt ground rules for discussion and let it unfold organically. Book groups also differ in expectations for how much the book itself is actually discussed; is the text the focal point of the gathering or an excuse to get together?

While book groups differ, their conversations are always much deeper than simple back-and-forth evaluative statements. As Elizabeth Long explains the collaborative processes of meaning-making in book groups, "Conversations allow participants to clarify their own insights and opinions and also to integrate the various perspectives other readers bring to bear on the book. Through this integrative process, individuals—and sometimes the group as a whole—can reach new understandings, whether about life or about the text at hand. The discussion itself, then, can be a creative process, for it elicits a certain kind of value-oriented textual interpretation and encourages (through difference and disputation) a clearer articulation of partially formulated perceptions and implicit assumptions, whether about a specific book or about a personal experience."[24]

The collaborative and interactive process of meaning making within book groups can occur both for evaluations about the overall quality of a book and for its meaning along many different interpretive dimensions (e.g., how sympathetic various characters are, who is responsible for what). Within book groups, readers' evaluations of *Jarrettsville* were subjected to unfolding processes of interpersonal influence, and their evaluation of the book changed as they were influenced by the evaluations of other group members.[25] This is also true for a wide range of interpretive dimensions on which groups discussed *Jarrettsville*.

While all book group discussions included evaluative statements about the perceived overall quality of *Jarrettsville*, different book groups focused their talk on different elements of the novel. For groups in which a part of the story was not discussed, readers' interpretations of that part of the story were unchanged; readers were not influenced by each other's interpretations on things they did not talk about.[26] Yet, for groups that did discuss a particular interpretive dimension of the text, based on interpersonal influence through the contents of their discussion, readers (and their book groups) changed their interpretations of the novel as based on the contents of their discussions. For example, groups that spent focused time discussing topics related to how justified Nick was in leaving Jarrettsville after his beating at the hands of Richard could, and did, come to different conclusions, which resulted in a wide range of shifts in both positive and negative directions from where the groups had collectively started before their discussions (see Figure 9.3).

Consider from Figure 9.3 the largest group-level interpretive shifts in each direction. Through discussion, one group's collective interpretation of how justified Nick was in leaving Jarrettsville shifted *positively* by twenty-three points on a hundred-point scale. In contrast, for another group, through conversation their collective interpretation shifted *negatively* by twenty-nine points. The members of the group that shifted positively (i.e., in favor of Nick's justifiability) entered their meeting finding Nick slightly more justified in leaving Jarrettsville than readers overall. Within this group there were, however, a wide range of interpretations on Nick's justifiability; two members interpreted Nick's justifiability as a fifty on a hundred-point

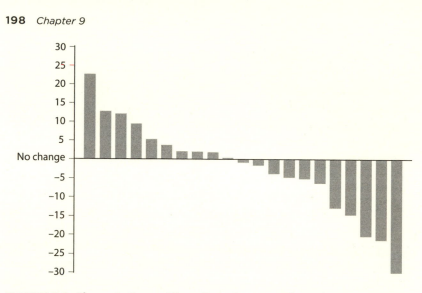

FIGURE 9.3. Change in Pre- and Post-discussion Means for Nick Being Justified in Leaving Jarrettsville, by Book Group.
Note: N = 21 Book Groups, 168 Readers. Book Groups (Along the X-axis) Sequenced in Order from Positive to Negative Change.

scale, two as a seventy, one as an eighty-five, and one as a ninety. The three members who considered Nick's actions the most justifiable were also the most influential in the discussion, according to the assessment of interpersonal influence among group members themselves. As their conversation unfolded, it did not take long for members to start discussing Nick's actions:

> Cheryl: I just don't understand why Nicholas did some of the things he did there, after, I don't know, I just wanted to smack him.

> Laura: And then moving out of his house instead of helping out, and going up the Pennsylvania line.

> Grace: Well that was after he was horse whipped and everything.

> Beth: Well, and I'm wondering how much of Nicholas's behavior was also explained by what happened to his father.

> Grace: Right.

> Mark: Right.

> Tammy: Well, that's true.

> Cheryl: And "turn the other cheek," that's how he had been raised.

Beth: Well it was clear that he and his family were not really safe.

Mark: Well they felt quite threatened, I mean, the ram was killed.

Grace: Right.

Beth: The ram was killed and his father was killed.

Mark: Well his father, yeah.

In this exchange, Cheryl first introduces Nick's behavior as unexplainable and frustrating, but at the suggestion of Grace and Beth, sympathetic context is offered to explain Nick's action. The group, including Cheryl who initially introduced the question, then follows Beth's lead and explores further background details to explain why Nick may have felt compelled to leave Jarrettsville. They conclude that rather than shirking responsibility, Nick left because his life was under genuine threat.

Later in the same discussion, the group returned to talk of Nick's pacifism. Members reminded one another that fighting back was not an option for Nick; one member pointed out that, barring his service in a Union militia, Nick had always retreated when faced with violence. The group also concluded that Nick left without a word to Martha because of his own humiliation at having been beaten, both physically and metaphorically, by her brother Richard. They decided that Nick's seemingly unreasonable behavior could be made sense of through culturally prescribed limitations around masculinity as they related to weakness and fear, especially given the time period. In contrast to Nick, Martha rebelled against the cultural limitations and gender norms of the time, the group concluded. As one group member summarized the main characters' relationship, "the question for Nick" was " 'we're going against the social norms but where does it go to? Where does it end up?' " They felt that Nick, perhaps rightly, saw that there could not be a peaceful resolution to their relationship given the circumstances of the place and time. As a result of this, they argued, Nick left to save both himself and Martha from future violence. What effect did this collaborative act of meaning making have on these readers' interpretations of the story? A group that entered the room collectively interpreting Nick's justification for leaving Jarrettsville as sixty-nine on a hundred-point scale left the room one hour later collectively interpreting it as ninety-two.

In contrast, a different group entered its conversation collectively thinking that Nick was slightly less justified in leaving Jarrettsville than did the average reader. But by the time they had concluded their conversation, their group mean for Nick's justification in leaving had dropped from forty-eight to eighteen on a hundred-point scale. What had happened? The interactive talk of Nick was introduced by one group member, Maria:

> Maria: If [Nick] could get his act together and leave the area . . . why didn't he tell [Martha] that Richard had assaulted him, and why not take her with him?
>
> Sarah: Right.
>
> Maria: It's just like, that's just stupid. It just made me mad. I was glad she shot him.
>
> *[group laughs]*
>
> Maria: He deserved it. I was like, well, she told you she was going to shoot you, and she wasn't joking, and she did. . . . Nick had all kinds of options for the things he could have done in that situation but he chose not to and he got shot.

Following Maria's opening salvo, the group delved deeper into Nick's failings of character, concluding, as one group member said, that he was "self-sabotaging." Another group member followed up by concluding that Nick's "excuses" for not staying in Jarrettsville "felt so transparent," and were just justifications "to walk away" from a relationship he did not want to be in anymore; walking away was, to her, simply "easier" than honoring his commitment to Martha. In this book group, unlike the first, Nick was not interpreted as a man trapped in a physically dangerous situation and in a time period characterized by rigid, oppressive gender roles. Instead, his flaws were his own. In the course of their conversation, the group came to interpret Nick's behavior as personal weakness; Nick had simply gotten "in over his head" with Martha and did the easier thing of walking away, rather than making it work.

Through their independent discussion of *Jarrettsville*, two groups that entered their respective meetings with a twenty-one point gap on Nick's actions ended their meetings with a seventy-four point gap on a hundred-point scale. Through conversation and interaction, what was once a small interpretative gap had grown. One group focused on what they believed to be very real dangers that threatened Nick in Jarrettsville; the other group came to understand those dangers as excuses for Nick's general weakness, self-sabotaging behavior, and moral flaws.

In this way, when making sense and meaning of *Jarrettsville* readers were no more confined by their demographic characteristics or tastes than they were by Nixon's intentions. Instead, readers entered their discussions with their own evaluations and interpretations; these were influenced by both general guideposts from Nixon and their own backgrounds and tastes. Once in discussion, however, readers were *also* open to different guideposts, suggestions, and collaborative sense making. What *Jarrettsville* was and what it meant to readers were conditioned not only on their individual characteristics, then, but also in interactive and collaborative processes of meaning making. This insight, rather than diminishing the effects of demographics and taste on the evaluation and interpretation of a new novel, represents a small step toward explaining how and from where interpretive differences among readers emerge.

WHY A MISANTHROPIC THUG MAY NOT BE ALL BAD

Richard Cairnes, Martha's brother, is in many ways *Jarrettsville*'s least sympathetic character. His father had died at the start of the war, preventing him from joining the Rebel forces so as not to lose the family farm, which caused him to settle for being a Southern militia member and co-conspirator with John Wilkes Booth in the assassination of Lincoln. In *Jarrettsville* other characters describe him as "yellow-bellied," a "hothead," and "arrogant." As the text alludes, Richard is but the most recent in a line of Cairnes family patriarchs who have raped and impregnated their current or former slaves. He also beats Sophie's brother, Tim, for having embarrassed him by leaving the farm due to Richard's sexual violence against his sister. When Nick gives Sophie and her family safe harbor on his land, Richard publicly accuses Nick of the rape, and evokes the Black Codes in post–Civil War Maryland to whip McComas for "defiling his property." He does not use the legally allowed horsewhip to do so, and instead uses a bullwhip to inflict more damage. McComas is left bloodied and near death.

For Nixon, Richard was never intended to be a character who evoked sympathy from her readers. Instead, she intended for Richard to be the closest character *Jarrettsville* had to an outright villain. She intended "sympathy" for him to be a five on a hundred-point scale, the lowest of all the characters. Yet she also did not intend him to be responsible for the ultimate outcome of the story; she intended Richard's responsibility to be twenty on the scale. For Nixon, it was the structural factors in Jarrettsville such as the lingering tensions of the Civil War (ninety) and the enduring presence of race and racism (one hundred) that were meant to be the ultimate drivers of the outcome of the novel. In addition to these structural factors, Nixon intended for equal blame to be placed on Nick and Martha in the dissolution of their relationship.

For readers, Richard was at once an unsympathetic character (seventeen), but was also much more responsible for the outcome of the story than Nixon had intended (sixty-six on the hundred-point scale). There were, however, differences among readers in their interpretations of Richard, and how he fit into the larger story of *Jarrettsville*. Southern readers in particular held Richard more responsible for the outcome of the story than did non-Southern readers, yet they were no more or less sympathetic to him as a character than were non-Southern readers. They instead saw the structural factors of racism and the war as infusing the outcome of the story more than did non-Southern readers. That Richard was more responsible for the outcome among Southern readers despite being no more or less sympathetic a character was, for them, a fact deeply intertwined in both the Civil War and the tragedy of the story.

Although Richard was discussed in all book groups, the discussion differed in Southern and Northern groups, as exemplified by a group of men in Massachusetts and a group of women in Nashville. For the men, Richard was less a character than a "caricature," as one group member put it. Richard was simply a misanthropic thug, as reviewers had characterized him, and thinly drawn at that; "just a Southern son-of-a-bitch," as a man in Massachusetts said. The same character was read and discussed by the women of Nashville quite differently.

While the women of Nashville started their discussion interpreting Richard as a no more or less sympathetic character than did other readers, through conversation their views shifted, and by the end of it there was a group-level shift of eight points on a hundred-point scale in favor of greater sympathy for Richard. This was the largest shift in favor of Richard for any group. Throughout the course of conversation among the women in Nashville, it became clear to them that neither *Jarrettsville* nor the character of Richard could be fully understood without having had firsthand experience with the masculinist code of Southern honor. Although the topic of "Southern honor" was first brought up in the group as they discussed Martha, they returned to it again in a later discussion of racism. It was during this discussion that a shift in feelings for Richard began to emerge, as the group concluded that Richard was, however appallingly, trapped in his time and place:

> Mary: It was really interesting to read inside the mind of Richard, who felt he owned [Sophie, Tim, and Creolia] and that he was helping them . . .

> Debra: It was so paternalistic, just completely paternalistic.

> Stacy: It's a disgrace.

Mary: . . . and they were his property.

Anna: But did you understand Southern honor better? I understood it. I mean, I didn't like it . . .

Mary: Yes, I did.

Judy: Yes.

Anna: . . . but I started to go "oh," I mean, it gave me a level of empathy which I never even wanted to consider, by reading the book.

Mary: Like feeling empathic with Richard?

Anna: Yeah.

Stacy: Yeah.

Debra: Oh. . . .

Stacy: Yeah, you know, coming from a deep South, rural family heritage from both sides, I mean, it's just, it's, it was a legacy from generation to generation.

Debra: But does it make you more empathic? Because I have come from that too and it makes me angry. It makes me very, very angry. It makes me disconnected from a character like Richard.

Stacy: Yeah, it does [make me feel empathetic]. I speak with my aunt about that to this day . . . [racism] was just something that had been passed down.

The Nashville book group's discussion of Southern honor, racism, and the lingering tensions of the Civil War—spurred by their analysis of the character of Richard—was the bluntest conversation about these politically charged topics across all groups. They were not, however, the only book group to engage them. But while other groups discussed if Richard was deserving of sympathy or not, among the Southern women of Nashville the question was instead if they could possibly *empathize* with Richard, a key distinction unique to them.

Across all groups, it was Southern groups who most often held the complex interpretation of both holding Richard responsible for the outcome of the story while also being sympathetic to him as a character. In fact, of the twenty-one book groups across the United States that participated in pre- and post-meeting surveys about their reading of *Jarrettsville*, there was one group that both before and after their meeting, more than any other group, thought that Richard was at the same time deserving of sympathy and responsible for what happened. This unique interpretation came from a book group in Harford County, Maryland, who hold their meetings at the local library branch in Jarrettsville.

In making this interpretation, the readers in Jarrettsville were more prone or equipped to think of Richard as a complex person: he was deserving of both sympathy for his difficult situation and scorn for how he reacted to it. They were in effect, as residents of Jarrettsville, both reading themselves onto Richard and reading Richard onto themselves. Yet they were far from the only readers to engage in this type of dialogical practice while discussing the story. Instead, across practically all groups the novel provided a low-stakes gateway through which readers could reflect and share stories with each other about their own experiences, regrets, and fears. Put another way, rather than just discussing the novel, readers also used *Jarrettsville* as a gateway through which they could further invest themselves and deepen the bonds of their reading communities: readers not only read their lives into the novel, but also read the novel into their lives.

READING NOVELS INTO LIFE

OR, HOW A STORY ABOUT THE PAST BECAME

A STORY ABOUT THE PRESENT

A WAR OF NORTH OR SOUTH

While discussing *Jarrettsville* over wine with her friends in Nashville, a woman remarked of residents of Jarrettsville, Maryland, "They're not Southern. I don't think that's the South." Another woman from the same group disagreed with this geographic interpretation, clarifying that for her "growing up in New Jersey [i.e., the North], you don't think about [slavery]," unlike "that part of the country." Over dinner with a group of men in San Francisco, a similar New Jersey exemption was proffered as evidence of *Jarrettsville*'s Southern setting. A man shared, "I grew up in Jersey City," about two hundred miles northeast of Jarrettsville, "so I didn't know about any of this."

In a book group in Santa Barbara, a woman who grew up in Washington, DC, about seventy miles south of Jarrettsville, shared how her family's belief that they were living in the North was probably not wholly accurate: "Washington, like Jarrettsville, we thought we were in the North, but I just told somebody recently I was a teenager before I knew that 'y'all' was two words. There was a very strong Southern bent. [But] then also, being Jewish, we never went into Virginia, because Virginia was farther south." A fuzziness on where Jarrettsville fell along a regional border was also evoked by a woman in Santa Cruz who had lived in Maryland. When describing the region to her mixed-gender book group, she called it an "anomalous place." Maryland, to her, is best typified as "being in the North but still really feeling like the South." She recalled that it had "towns with all-Black sections and white people living in these plantation houses, just like you were in Mississippi or something." To a different woman in San Francisco, being raised in Harford County, Maryland, meant growing up as much in the North as in the South. Raised on expansive property that adjoined the

Gunpowder River, she relayed how generations ago in the "in-between world" of Maryland, the "property owner both *had* slaves and *helped* slaves" escape to the North.

In Jarrettsville, this categorical battle over if the town was in the North or South was still being waged. On a temperate Monday afternoon in late October, a book group organized by the Jarrettsville branch of the Harford County Library sat down together to discuss *Jarrettsville*. The discussion leader casually opened the session by remarking, "I thought Southern sympathizers would be farther south" than Jarrettsville. To this statement a group member replied, "Maryland always had the 'are we the North or South?' connotation." The discussion leader, still unsure, offered, "You still see Confederate flags on porches in Cecil County [Maryland]," to which a Jarrettsville transplant from Connecticut said, "I still see them in Harford County!" Slightly perturbed by the direction of the conversation, a different woman inquired, slightly accusatively to the transplant, "Do you consider yourself a Southerner?" Quickly the transplant replied, "No. I grew up in Connecticut." The book group leader, a library employee who had grown up in Maryland, quickly realized the tension he had inadvertently introduced with his opening remark, and stumbled over his words as he backtracked: "See, I don't know where, I don't know where, I don't know for me if there's such a position." In response to the transplant saying she did not consider herself a Southerner, the questioner proclaimed, "Well, I do" and then as evidence offered that she had grown up in North Carolina. Another woman, who had been born and raised in Jarrettsville and was a bit annoyed that being from North Carolina was being treated as the northern-most mark of a true Southern identity, said, "I still consider *myself* Southern." With the room divided, the lifelong Jarrettsville resident doubled down on her position, citing that *Southern Living* magazine "declared Maryland a Southern state." To this, another group member objected, suggesting instead that "*Baltimore Magazine* dedicated a whole issue to asking if Maryland is a Northern or Southern state." Another woman, who identified as Northern, said "if you go south, we're definitely Northern," to which a woman who identified as Southern offered the rejoinder, "If you go north they think you have a Southern accent." The Northern-identifying woman conceded the point, concluding, "Oh, yes, they do." Offering support, the Connecticut transplant agreed, sharing, "I got accused of having a Southern accent after I'd been living here for five years." The Connecticut woman, who identified as Northern but with her comment was trying to find a common ground, failed to do so with at least one Southern-identifying woman in the room, who wrinkled her nose at the word choice of "accused."

READING NOVELS INTO LIFE

Readers both read their lives into novels, and read novels into their lives. To read one's life into a novel is to rely on one's background (such as demographics, experiences, and tastes) as the raw materials through which to make sense and meaning of the text. To know if *Jarrettsville* is about love or loss for a reader is also to ask if the reader is a romance fan or not, is Northern or Southern, and so on. To read a novel into one's life, however, is to instead treat the novel as the raw materials through which one turns over, reconsiders, or shares with others one's own experiences. Within this second framework, if the novel is about love or loss is all well and good, as the text is merely a gateway to *talk about* love or loss, to reconsider them, and to build new reflections and experiences in conversations. In this second framework even material culture such a novel, song, or television show can become a pathway to broader reconsideration, communication, collective understanding, and perhaps even action.

As Joshua Gamson has argued in defense of popular culture, the triviality for which it is sometimes impugned can instead be its strength. Due to the ephemerality and low stakes of popular culture, through it the discussion of difficult topics can be made permissible.[1] Because *Jarrettsville* is ultimately just a novel, and perhaps also because it provides the safety of "distance" by being set in the past, readers felt permission to treat it as the raw materials that could be read back into their own experiences in the present day. In this way, rather than novels just being good to read, they can also be "good to think with," and good to communicate with too.[2] Novels can be the building blocks through which readers form and deepen their communities.

In differentiating between novels as a thing to talk about and novels as vehicles through which to talk, some readers in book groups draw a distinction between "good books" and "good *book group* books." In this distinction, the former are worthy of praise for their quality (i.e., the time spent reading was time well spent), and the latter are praised for the quality of the discussion they elicit (i.e., the time spent discussing it was time well spent). A member of a neighborhood-based book group in Oakland described the difference: "Good books aren't always good book group books. Like we all thought *Let the Great World Spin* was a great book but didn't really have anything to say about it. . . . We just all really liked it but that was it." Just as a good book is not always great for discussion, a bad book can be great for discussion; to be one does not automatically mean to also be the other.

Underlying this classificatory system is a reader's differentiation between the evaluative dimensions of a book (i.e., is it good or bad?) and the interpretive dimensions of a book, and how useful they are for collaborative meaning making. The difference then, is that "good books" are exemplary pieces of culture, whereas "good book group books" are pieces of culture that are exemplary in opening up the opportunity to shift discussions from culture-as-object to culture-as-action. In this way, some books aren't "good" but provide "good" opportunities to hash out or reconsider ideas, values, and moral beliefs in conversation.

While some book groups found *Jarrettsville* to be neither a "good book" nor a "good book group book," for other groups *Jarrettsville* was good in both ways or not a great read but still a good book to make discussion with. In an example of *Jarrettsville* being good in both ways, in her opening remarks a woman in Southern California stated to her group, "I liked this book, it pushes your thinking." For a woman in Nashville, *Jarrettsville* was not a good book but was good for spurring conversation: "we haven't had that long of a discussion since [John Updike's] *Rabbit, Run*," she said approvingly. When *Jarrettsville* was a "good book group book," what began as a discussion of the novel regularly moved beyond the text; *Jarrettsville* was the initial raw materials through which readers shared stories with each other from their own lives. In these cases *Jarrettsville* often became a gateway through which to discuss two topics: inquisitive and oftentimes frank talk of personal romantic relationships, and distressing observations of, and encounters with, structural racism.

READING RELATIONSHIPS FROM *JARRETTSVILLE*

For an all-male book group in Northern California, *Jarrettsville* was overall not a good book, but led to potent discussion. Although talk of the novel was stilted, the discussion became livelier once one member shared the story of his own investigation of a murder in his family history. After passing around the nonfiction essay he had written about his family, the group mulled over the stakes involved in investigating one's past and fictionalizing a family story. Although a few of the men in the group lamented the time they spent reading *Jarrettsville*, in the course of discussion they found topics more interesting to them, and forged deeper connections to each other by learning more about the history of one of their members.

For a woman in a different book group in Northern California, reading *Jarrettsville* gave her an opportunity to connect with her school-aged son, who at the time was studying the Civil War. She liked both the novel and the relational opportunity reading it offered. Along a similar vein, a book group of women in Virginia transitioned from talking about Martha and

Nick's sexual relationship in *Jarrettsville* to constructing a piece of local "idioculture."[3] Together, they jokingly concluded that asking "where you're from" is actually coded language to ask where someone first had sex. The women spent the next ten minutes or so uproariously laughing as they shared with each other stories of where they were "from." In all of these cases, rather than being the topic of discussion, *Jarrettsville* was the conduit to deeper connections between people. These types of connections are not the stuff of "off-topic" discussion in book groups, but instead are often the mostly unspoken *point* of book group gatherings. As a different woman from Northern California described her book group, "We've been through weddings, and babies, and death. It's a support group too."

The lack of communication between Nick and Martha was a common theme of discussion both about and beyond *Jarrettsville*. For some readers, the lack of communication between the two main characters was just a plot device to propel the story, whereas for others it offered a chance to share and reexamine personal stories of when keeping secrets had devastating results. For a woman in a book group north of San Francisco, talk of Nick and Martha's lack of communication transitioned to consideration of her own difficulties with her mother, who "doesn't tell people when things upset her." In Virginia, what started as discussion of Martha and Nick's failure of communication led to talk of a secretive mother-in-law who hid from her family a child's adoption, and a different member's story about the discomfort of attending an uncle's wedding while having to keep the secret that he had been married before. Their stories were good reminders for the group as a whole that "friendships and relationships *end* because people won't talk," as one reader concluded.

Ruminations on communication and silence also emerged in talk from a group discussion of *Jarrettsville* by younger women in Berkeley. With Nick and Martha's relationship as a gateway, a woman who had recently broken up with her partner lamented the "wall of silence" that follows a breakup, and how she could not break through it: "I know where he is and I *can* go talk to him, but instead I spend all this money on therapy, and just, just talk about it with *myself*." Though fellow members of the book group laughed at her (intentionally humorous) lament, they shifted to serious and engaged discussion on the topic after she continued: "I don't know . . . rejection can just shut everything down when all of a sudden all communication just stopped. And people froze. In friendships, in anything, like, what happens when people just become paralyzed?"

While reflecting on the importance of communication in their lives, due to the central relationship between Martha and Nick in *Jarrettsville*, book groups also often used these experiences to reflect on gender norms. Following a discussion of Nick's actions in the story, a book group of men in the Northeast asked themselves, "if a woman is [sexually] aggressive does a man run," and if so, why? They worked together to understand if they, as middle-aged men, found a woman's aggression exciting or feared it was emasculating. They hypothesized that men might say they like equal and forward women but are really intimidated by them, or that they do like them but claim they don't, or maybe even really like to believe that they do even if they can't shake an underlying fear of emasculation. This group of men overall did not like *Jarrettsville*, but from it they collaborated in conversation to make sense of the intertwined topics of sexual desire, masculinity, and insecurity, all interspersed with the sharing of bawdy jokes and laughter along the way.

Talk of Nick's actions spurred a different book group, one composed of women, to consider if men could be trusted at all. For a group of younger women in Los Angeles the presence of fear in romantic relationships seemed like it related to one's own sense of self-worth. As one member concluded, "We've all been in relationships where, due to fear or a lack of feeling deserved, we pull back." Another member shared how after the dissolution of a relationship she, like Martha, behaved in ways that seemed foreign to her. "I went crazy after a breakup," she said, "I [was] a mad hatter." Offering support, her friend knowingly replied, "We've all been in that situation after a breakup." For the young women readers in Berkeley, their discussion of *Jarrettsville* turned into a discussion about the men they know. As one woman shared, "I am in this kind of relationship right now, a little bit, where I'm feeling really rejected, so it was super painful to be reading about this and it brought up so much fear for me." Another woman in the group, Jennifer, admitted that she did not make the connection between *Jarrettsville* and her own relationship until Amy, a friend and fellow book group member, made it for her:

> Jennifer: I didn't even attach the story [to my own life], so talk about powerful minds and detachment or denial. I did not even attach the story to my own relationship at all, until I talked to Amy, who was talking about men who are afraid to propose, and I was like, "What man was afraid to propose? I don't remember that from the story." I had no idea what she was talking about, and then I was like, "Oh, my partner of thirteen years who won't propose to me, oh, I hadn't thought of that." That was real, I hadn't thought of it. I did not connect Nick to James [my partner] at all . . .

Michelle: Oh, that's so rough.

Jennifer: . . . until I talked to Amy.

Nicole: Good job, Amy!

[group laughter, followed by a return to serious discussion]

Jennifer: . . . I thought a lot about the role of abuse or trauma in how, by Nick's example, he doesn't have a lot of tools to facilitate or process the whipping, or the war, whatever his trauma is . . .

Amy: Right.

Jennifer . . . and I can relate this to James without sharing too much, but I know how painful and hard it is for James to even cry, and how hard it is for some men to emote or move through things. For me that's a tool I use very regularly, crying, but that's a tool that men I know and love don't have.

As exemplified by Jennifer's story, rather than projecting her own life into *Jarrettsville*, a friend in the group had projected *Jarrettsville* onto her life. Though Jennifer hadn't made the connection, she did not oppose it, and in group discussion a retelling of the story drove her into a new, dialogical conversation with the text. She came to understand the actions of Nick through her own partner James, and came to understand James through her reflections on Nick. As such her disclosure to the group was not as much born out of her reading as it was born out of *talking about* reading. For readers across the country, no matter their evaluations of *Jarrettsville*, the book was used as an entry point to share and reflect on intimate relationships in unexpected, personal ways. Among group members, *Jarrettsville* also elicited talk about what it means to live in an unequal and racist society.

READING RACE FROM *JARRETTSVILLE*

It was nine fifteen in the evening at an apartment complex in Los Angeles when a group of younger white women discussing *Jarrettsville* heard someone yelling from the hallway: "Can you guys keep it down?!" The door to Rebecca's apartment had been slightly ajar, meaning that their conversation, filled with points of laughter, disagreement, cross-talk, and the sharing of personal stories could likely be heard out in the hallway. For the young women it was unclear if it was the noise of their conversation, the topic of their conversation, or both that had elicited the recrimination. They looked around to each other, dumbfounded about what had happened. "I've lived here for three years and I've never had anybody yell at me [for being too loud]," the host, Rebecca, said. "It's not like you're having a kegger," her friend replied. With mock sweetness and feigned indignation, her friend continued, role-playing her response to the woman in the hallway: "We're having a book club. You can tell your kids we're educating ourselves about racism!" The group laughed at the incongruity of the situation: they were being chided for speaking loudly while in the middle of a difficult discussion about American racism.

While readers shared stories with each other of their own romantic relationships through their collective reading of *Jarrettsville*, they also used the novel as a launching point to share their observations of and experiences with racism. Given the demographics of the book groups—their racial composition was almost entirely white—that the novel served as a gateway to sustained talk of racial inequality is perhaps even more intriguing than the talk of relationships.[4] With the historically accurate inclusion of slavery and racism in *Jarrettsville* as a form of low-stakes permission to discuss present-day racism, book group members shared painful and confusing stories with each other across three general themes: racism observed while growing up in one's hometown; racism observed in one's immediate family and experienced in others' reactions to young romantic love; and stories about racism's enduring violence, perpetuated among even the well-intentioned.

With *Jarrettsville* as an entry point, book group members shared childhood stories of racism. Southern readers talked of being in high school and rooting for teams called the "Rebels" while waving rebel flags, attending Dixie-themed proms and school events, and listening to "Dixie" at school assemblies and rallies. They shared these stories with a retrospective sense of shock about their seeming normalcy in childhood. One woman from Eastern Maryland shared a story with her book group of her first observation of racial hatred as a child: driving to the Maryland shore she saw "KKK" scrawled in large letters across a bus stop shelter immediately following the Cambridge Riot of 1963. A similar story was recounted by a teacher from Southern California whose family moved to a town in the Deep South when she was a child. Not knowing better, her mother was seen by the Black doctor in town instead of the white one, and had invited the nurse, also Black, who worked with the doctor to tea. "She was in deep trouble [with the other white women of the town for that]," the woman shared. "We didn't stay [in the town] that long." While sharing these types of stories, book group members did so from a place of shock about how overt the racism they had witnessed and been a part of had been, and how it had penetrated every facet of daily life. Another woman, after having moved to Louisiana, shared a story of unwittingly tripping over a racial fault line when offering beverages to potential new friends: "I can remember inviting some people from church to our house and saying 'does anyone want a Pepsi?' And they said, 'You can't drink Pepsi. That's what the Blacks drink.' And these were otherwise good-hearted people. We were told under no uncertain terms to avoid Pepsi. You drink Coke or 7-Up, and it's called 'pop.'"[5]

For the most part in these stories of encountering racism, readers cast themselves as passive observers who were silent witnesses to others' overt statements and acts. This was not always the case, however, as one woman in Nashville portrayed herself as a regretful perpetrator of racial insensitivity against a friend. Her story was spurred by the group's discussion of a scene in *Jarrettsville* in which Tim snaps at Martha for naïvely putting him, as a recently freed slave, in physical danger through a paternalistic effort to "help" him. The scene reminded her, she told the group, of an experience in high school when she was admonished by an African American friend for her own aloofness to racism and racial inequality: "I had a friend from high school, and we were talking about some racial issues that I was puzzled about. And she was like 'Mary! My great-grandmother was a slave! *Do you understand*?' And at that moment I was like 'holy shit,' you know, we're just a couple generations away, and I had read about slavery, but she was saying 'my relatives were slaves! Do you get it?' And somehow I hadn't gotten it until she said that to me."

While readers shared with each other stories of observing racism in schools and neighborhoods, they exchanged even richer stories about the racism displayed by trusted family members and community leaders. This was made particularly clear in instances of thwarted, or suspected, young romantic love across racial difference. A woman in Southern California shared a story of becoming friends in high school with her class president, who was Black, and being admonished for it by her father, who suspected they were romantically involved. He said to her, "You see him in the hallway and I want you to turn the other way."

In Virginia, a woman told the story of working at a tourist attraction with her brother who became friendly with an African American girl who also worked there. "My parents were teachers, you know, we were fairly educated for that area," the woman said before recalling coming home to her parents talking about their son's friendship. "It had come to their attention that my brother was paying a lot of attention to this girl," she shared. The next day her mother began asking her for information about what her brother was doing at work, "you know, do they go anywhere on their breaks?" Over time, the friendship between her brother and their coworker developed, and he wanted to pursue a romantic relationship. "He liked her, she played basketball like he did," the woman shared: "And I remember my mom, who is the most wonderful person, very open-minded, phenomenal, said to him, 'You cannot.' And I was like, 'What are you talking about? What do you mean he can't?' And she said 'No, he cannot do that. You know, your grandfather, your dad, it would be a mistake for him. He's got to live here and go to school here for two more years. We're not doing that. He can't do that. He can be her friend, but he can't date her.' And you know, it's just shocking to me."

Equally shocking to a young woman in Los Angeles (in the same book group that had been told to keep it down) was getting rebuked by her church pastor for questioning if interracial romantic relationships were unchristian: "There was a lot of interracial mixing in my school, and it was frowned upon, and I asked my pastor at the Baptist church. I said: 'Well, where in the Bible is it? If this is supposed to be wrong, I don't get it. If God doesn't care about this why is it wrong?' And he said, 'It's wrong because it creates a stumbling block in society.' And I'm like, I still don't get how that's wrong, I don't get it. But it was taboo, you did *not* go there, and it's really wild that those things still transcend time like that."

Updating to the present day, the woman then transitioned into a story about her Jewish boyfriend and their most recent visit to her family for Thanksgiving. "When we were leaving from Thanksgiving," she told her book group, "my dad gave him a bag of deer jerky in one hand and the New Testament in the other." Reminding her father with exasperation that her boyfriend was Jewish, he replied, "Yeah, but in case he wants to read about this, he was asking about it when we were [hiking] in the woods the other day." Her boyfriend, diffusing the situation at the doorway, in reference to the New Testament being offered, said to her with a wink, "Yeah, I'll take it. It's good for *Jeopardy.*" This story, like other group members' stories, started by recounting an example of observed racism from the speaker's childhood that was then translated into a more recent experience of racial or cultural intolerance. Just as *Jarrettsville* opened up pathways to conversations about personal experiences with racism, it also opened up pathways to broader conversations about the persistence of racism in American society, as a story about the past was transformed into stories about the present.

For the young women of Los Angeles, as their conversation about racism evolved out from the historical examples offered in *Jarrettsville*, they concluded that their own present-day friendships and romantic relationships were products of the intersection of race and class. "Now it's classism mixed with racism," one group member declared. "If someone's of a different race but they have money nobody will care," she said. A group of white women in a wealthy neighborhood in Oakland arrived at a similar conclusion when talking about the racial and economic contours of their own neighborhood. In confession to her book group, one woman recalled that upon moving to the Bay Area, she encountered African American neighbors "and truly thought 'gosh, they're just like I am.' I thought it was a racial thing [while growing up] but it was an economic thing." Similarly, to a group of elderly women at a Jewish community center in Southern California, *Jarrettsville*'s evocation of African American sharecropping in the post–Civil War South seemed to them comparable to the present-day treatment of Latino migrant workers in California's agricultural industry. "We don't cross paths, we don't see them," one woman suggested, to which her friend loudly disagreed, "We see them *every day*!"

A book group in Virginia also raised a comparison between historical racism and the present day. Their conversation, which built off of the racism described in *Jarrettsville*, turned toward recent history when a woman from Prince Edward County shared with her book group how in 1959, five years after *Brown v. Board of Education*, the county still refused to desegregate its public schools. Instead, they closed down the entire school system and rerouted public funds to nominally private, white-only segregation academies. It was not until 1964, when the Supreme Court outlawed the practice, that the public schools reopened. Recounting her own experiences of the public school system as a student in the 1980s, she shared, "There were three classes: a class of millionaires, the middle class, and a lower class that was all African American, which was basically the children of the parents who had been denied an education [in the early 1960s]." Since becoming an adult and staying in the area, she went on to say, "It has gotten increasingly better since the education is now there but there is still a major population that follows that same criteria." Building off the story, now several steps removed from the historical account of *Jarrettsville*, a fellow group member proclaimed, "And now they're doing the same thing to Hispanics." Everyone agreed, referring to the Virginia attorney general's memorandum and in-state practice at most public universities to entirely block admission to undocumented applicants.[6]

No matter which turns their respective conversations took, by starting from the raw material of *Jarrettsville*, readers shared stories of overt acts of racism they had witnessed in their own lives. Peppered with personal experiences of suspected or thwarted young interracial love, or reflections on the relationship between race and class, their conversations strayed in organic but important ways from the text. As each group's meeting flowed and evolved through its participants' contributions, what began as talk about one particular cultural object—a novel called *Jarrettsville*—became, through interaction, a different kind of talk entirely. In this way, readers read the novel into their own lives, although perhaps no reader found more connection between the text and her own life than did Sandy Sherman, herself a resident of Jarrettsville, Maryland.

READING JARRETTSVILLE FROM *JARRETTSVILLE*

Sandy Sherman first read *Jarrettsville* for her book group at the local Jarrettsville branch of the Harford County Library system; she is the Connecticut transplant who, despite her now Southern accent, did not consider herself a Southerner. As much as anyone, Sandy read *Jarrettsville* into her own life, as the novel, she said, "Brought things into focus for me." Reading *Jarrettsville*, "made it more real to me that all of these things are still alive and vital." For Sandy, *Jarrettsville* was good, if sometimes a bit painful, to think with, as for her reading the novel had dredged up twenty-one years of unpleasant memories and personal stories. Rather than just reading *Jarrettsville* from the standpoint of a longtime resident of Jarrettsville, from the novel *Jarrettsville* Sandy started to reread Jarrettsville the place, and its role in her life as her home. For this reason, reading the novel was "therapeutic" as it gave her the opportunity to compile the experiences she'd accumulated as a resident of Jarrettsville, and to give them real consideration.

Important to Sandy's experiences in both reading the book and living in Jarrettsville is that her marriage is an interracial one, as she is white and her husband is African American. Together, they first lived in Baltimore County, close to her in-laws, before moving to Jarrettsville to upgrade from an apartment to a house. In reference to their children, her husband described their move with a laugh, explaining, "Everyone *had* to have their own bedroom." As soon as they moved to Jarrettsville, Sandy started to experience "things that just make you scratch your head and wonder why." Right after they moved in, several neighbors on their block moved out. "Maybe just to go [to] Florida for the warm weather or something," she speculated, "I don't know." Then a different neighbor instructed his wife not to speak to Sandy's husband. "Now if [our neighbor's wife] speaks to me I'll reply, but I wouldn't initiate a conversation with her," Sandy's husband said.

Sandy doesn't know how many multigenerational African American families still reside in Jarrettsville; she's heard that in the late 1950s and early 1960s there were concerted efforts to push them out. One historical African American family in the area that she's friendly with had been willed the deed to the property they worked, along with their freedom, when their white owner died. The land and house had stayed in their family through the generations, despite repeated attempts by white land speculators to grab it from them, Sandy said. "I bet you keep that deed safe," Sandy remembered saying to the brother of the family member who held the deed at that time. "Both him and the deed are much safer just staying in the house," the brother replied with a grin.

Many of Sandy's stories that had resurfaced by reading *Jarrettsville* involved her children. When she first moved to Jarrettsville she told the principal at the elementary school that her two children were biracial, and asked how many nonwhite students attended the school. "There are two," the principal replied. "Two percent?" she asked incredulously, to which the principal said, "No, just two." In the early 1990s a white family whose daughter had befriended Sandy's eldest daughter had a BB shot through their front window. They told Sandy they wouldn't be reporting it to the sheriff's office. "They didn't want to stir the pot," she recalled, as "it had been a warning to them not to be friends with us."

Sandy also couldn't shake what happened when she went with her daughters and their Girl Scout troop to a nearby skating rink. "There were some high-school-aged boys who were behaving very rough around my girls," she remembered. The boys were "having these 'accidentally on purpose' accidents," Sandy said. When retelling the story, she buried any implication of racism within other possibilities before circling back around to her main suspicion that her daughters were being targeted for being African American: "It's nothing that you could put your finger on, you can't disprove that it wasn't an accident, it sure looked like an accident and you can't prove intent but why did it happen mostly around my girls, you have to ask yourself."

Sandy was straightforward about the hypothetical experiences that interracial families like hers might expect to face in Jarrettsville. The town is 96 percent white, and according to Sandy, "Nonwhites move out here but they don't stay long because they can't make friends." Instead, most of the newcomers to Jarrettsville, according to Sandy, are "white flight, quite frankly." The white flight had been, in essence, "a kind of a retreat from Baltimore, if you will," she said with a smile, evoking the Civil War setting of *Jarrettsville*. If, even unconsciously, someone is motivated to move "for racial separation," Sandy said, "maybe they seek out these areas where they can feel like they can live comfortably and maybe even gain some support for their views." She chuckled and recounted a story of seeing a young man at the Harford County Fair wearing a shirt that said, "If at first you don't secede, try, try again." And she remembered meeting another young man who had recently moved back to Jarrettsville. He said to her, " 'I'm coming back to defend the family property,' and I was like: 'From what?' It's just little exchanges that indicate to me the possibility of other motives." From reading *Jarrettsville*, and through Richard in particular, the mind-set had become clearer.

There are other examples of what Sandy called "the mentality" evident across Harford County, where Jarrettsville is located. At the post office in Bel Air an entire wall is covered with a mural of the Booth brothers. "And there he is on the post office wall, John Wilkes Booth, the famous actor," Sandy said with a wink. For shopping at Klein's, a Jewish-owned grocery store in the area, Sandy received withering looks from neighbors. "[The Kleins] have been here for several generations and they haven't proved themselves yet," she said, rolling her eyes. Most revealing to Sandy was the time that she mentioned a recent event of racial discrimination that her family had experienced to her dental hygienist, whom she described as "always really nice" and someone she's friendly with: "She was very honest with me, she said, 'Yeah, where I live, your family would definitely not be welcome.' Straight out, you know. She just said it, as a friend. Not to be mean, because it was true." This was an important interaction for Sandy, as it was for her a rare instance of frank talk about racism in the area with someone she didn't know well.

In her library-organized book group to discuss *Jarrettsville*, Sandy had opened up the doorway to discuss the current state of racism in the area when she stated she still saw Confederate flags in Harford County, but it was a doorway that others in the group didn't walk through. In the library-sponsored group the members were friendly, but for the most part were not friends independent of their membership. In that group, Sandy didn't share stories of her own experiences in Jarrettsville, nor did she share that she believed it was the particular racial configuration of her marriage that was most offensive to some: "I think out here [in Jarrettsville] an interracial couple moving in might even be more offensive than an African American couple, and particularly if that couple is an African American man and a white woman. . . . There's a long and not too flattering history of [white] men sleeping with African American women around here, like in [*Jarrettsville*], but the reverse, with a white woman married to a Black man, they think he's taken something." This was not a thought that had eluded her before, but from reading *Jarrettsville* and the scandalizing rumors of Tim potentially being responsible for Martha's pregnancy, it had been brought for her into clearer relief.

Yet for Sandy, *Jarrettsville* was not just good to think with, as she hoped it could be good to communicate with too. Her memories that had been exhumed through reading *Jarrettsville* were ones she had "never really talked with anyone here about much," as, she concluded, "I just don't know who to trust."[7] Yet she thought if others read the novel for them it too could be a gateway into these conversations and a way to open up into a discussion of what the town was like today. Sandy might be in the minority in her experiences, but she did not think she was alone.

It was from these thoughts that Sandy began to pass out copies of the novel to her friends, and formed her own ad hoc book group among them to discuss it. She also gave a copy to her swim instructor at the local community college, and circulated a book group sign-up sheet to draw recruits from the two or three swim classes held there every day, a way to use a shared interest in recreational swimming as a passageway to a shared reading of a work of fiction, and then maybe to a more free-ranging conversation about racism in present-day Jarrettsville. Even more than liking *Jarrettsville*, Sandy Sherman liked talking about it. When asked if she'd been organizing the ad hoc book groups so that she might have opportunities to engage with others in the types of stories she'd long held secret, Sandy replied with a warm and knowing smile: "There were indeed some selfish motives," she said.

All in all Sandy hadn't just read *Jarrettsville* into her life, she was also trying to use the novel as a way to *change* her life. Ultimately, Jarrettsville, Maryland, was where she lived, but she was hoping that through *Jarrettsville* she could change what the experience of living there had been like. She was in effect reading the town of Jarrettsville through the new eyes of a reader of *Jarrettsville*, and didn't always like what she saw. Reading it, she hoped, could be a pathway to action, and she could use the novel to speak with others about her experiences with relationships and racism in the town, and to hear about their experiences too. Maybe others could reread Jarrettsville if they just read *Jarrettsville*, she hoped.

HOW A STORY ABOUT THE PAST BECAME A STORY ABOUT THE PRESENT

Across over twenty book club discussions on *Jarrettsville*, readers compared plot points and events depicted in the novel to a wide range of current events and topics: post-Apartheid South Africa; the Israeli-Palestinian conflict; the October 6 national holiday in Egypt; and the passage of Proposition 8 in California. In discussions of whether or not Martha's murder of Nick could ever be understood as justified, readers discussed the murder of abortion providers and a recent news story about a teacher who had killed her husband. Discussions concerning a Union still divided after the Civil War evoked talk of current events such as modern secessionist movements in the United States, and a Ku Klux Klan rally held on the campus of Ole Miss after the chancellor removed "From Dixie with Love" from the marching band's repertoire. Across many book groups, some of which had read *Reading Lolita in Tehran* for prior meetings, the restrictive gender norms experienced by women in *Jarrettsville* were compared to theocratic law in some Middle Eastern countries. When a reader criticized Nick for retreating to the peaceful north of Amish country rather than staying to fight, her friend and fellow book group member said, "Oh, please. How is it any different than all of us wanting to move to Canada after Bush was reelected?" The thought of Nick and Richard becoming in-laws through Martha was compared to "the Bushes and the Obamas sitting down together for dinner every night," a comparison that fellow book group members approvingly agreed with. "This is about who we are as a nation," another reader said. "This is still going on."

For Cornelia Nixon, what had at first been a family story had become a novel, and it was a novel that she would end up literally taking back to Jarrettsville. As part of her book tour, Nixon was scheduled to spend a morning in Baltimore being interviewed by the local NPR affiliate, and then, that evening, to give a reading from *Jarrettsville* at the Jarrettsville branch of the Harford County Library. Nixon was more anxious than usual about the event. Would people from Jarrettsville come? If they did, how would she and her novel be received? Nixon was nervous for the same reasons she had waited so long to write *Jarrettsville*; through fiction she wanted to bring the historical story to life, not to offend.

For the crowd in Jarrettsville, Nixon had additional concerns. Members of the Archer family, for example, were characters in the novel, and it was likely that there would be Archers in the room at her book event. When writing Nick she hadn't considered what the McComas family might think of her portrayal of their murdered ancestor, and they very well could also be there. Martin Jarrett, whose family the town is named after, is also a character in *Jarrettsville*, and his portrait hung in the library in which Nixon was scheduled to read. *Jarrettsville* concludes with a jury of Southern sympathizers acquitting Martha of murder on the ad hoc grounds of "justifiable homicide," a true event that was as initially mind-boggling to Nixon as it was to many readers. But in the summers Nixon spent growing up on the family farm in Jarrettsville, she could remember coming across the types of people who may have taken a position like that, and they might be at her reading too. How would they react to Nixon's portrayal of events and her competing sympathies? More importantly, what would the residents of Jarrettsville today think about this controversial chapter in the town's history

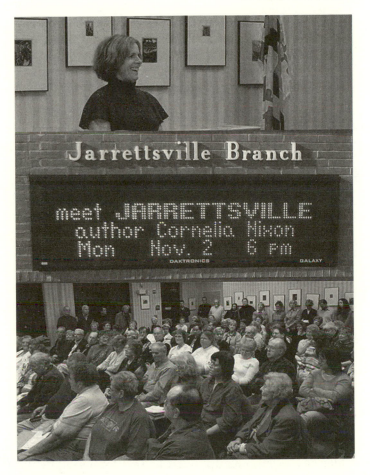

FIGURE 10.1: Nixon's Reading at the Jarrettsville Public Library.
Source: Upper and lower images with permission from *The Baltimore Sun*; middle image taken by the author.

released to the world in a published novel? "I think some people might not want that history dredged up," Sandy Sherman said while hypothesizing about the possible response to the novel in Jarrettsville.

Sandy Sherman was at the reading, as was the rest of the Jarrettsville Library book club. About a hundred people attended Nixon's reading, an impressive turnout for a town of about twenty-seven hundred. The assembled crowd was even too big to fit in the library's largest meeting room. After all the chairs were taken, it was standing room only against the back wall, and latecomers strained to see the proceedings from the hallway (see Figure 10.1). As for the reading itself, in Mississippi, the audience had cheered when Martin Jarrett referred to Nick McComas as a "Yankee bastard." In Jarrettsville, however, this same line, like the rest of Martin Jarrett's first-person narrative, was met with chuckles and laughter. The humor Nixon had tried to imbue in Jarrett's section, it seemed, was finally being appreciated and understood.

More memorable than the reading for Nixon was the Q&A and book signing. She would later remark how taxing the Q&A was due to the audience's prodigious historical knowledge of the place and time. Readers also shared their own stories with Nixon during the Q&A and book signing. "The longest line I've ever gotten," Nixon exclaimed. "And people wanted to talk too! God, they wanted to talk!" They recounted for her their own family histories, and their real-life ties to the novel's supporting characters. They wanted to talk about geography and street names, and how until the 1940s on opposite street corners sat redundant churches: one for Northerners and one for Southerners. A descendent of Nick's family also approached Nixon during the signing, and thanked her for having written the story. If there were people in Jarrettsville unhappy to have this chapter of the town's history dredged up, they did not seem to be at the library that night. Instead, from the conversations Nixon had with the audience, it seemed that excitement for her visit had been building for some time. A few people independently told Nixon that in the week prior they'd wandered through the graveyard back behind Bethel Church, in search of Martha and Nick's tombstones. "You won't believe what happened," one reader, who had visited the gravesites just earlier that day, said to Nixon. "I don't know who, but someone went out to Bethel Church and put flowers on Martha's grave." After looking at the grave and fresh-cut flowers for herself the following day, Nixon, filled with emotion, could only shake her head in wonder: "Can you believe it? Can you believe it? It's just the most amazing thing."

PART VI
CONNECTING THE CIRCUIT

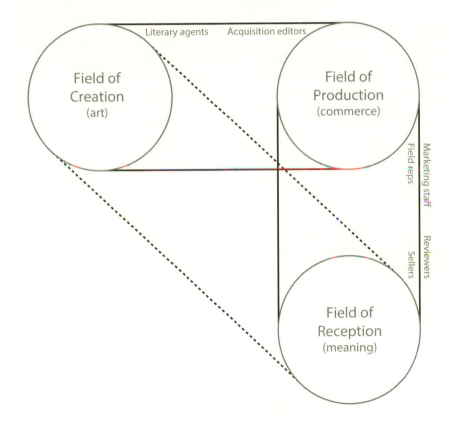

CONCLUSION

RECONNECTING CREATION,

PRODUCTION, AND RECEPTION

"A TYPICAL PUBLISHING STORY": WHAT THE
PEOPLE BEHIND *JARRETTSVILLE* LEARNED

Through her author tour and occasional fan mail Cornelia Nixon gained a window into the field of reception. Most pleasurable was how much Q&A time on her tour was taken up by historical questions from the audience. Before *Jarrettsville*, Nixon had never written a work of historical fiction. Given the substantial archival work the novel required, she relished the opportunity to answer readers' questions in detail. Much like winning the Shaara Prize for Civil War Fiction, these encounters were also, for Nixon, a salve against the critical review *Jarrettsville* had received in the *New York Times*. Despite the generally warm reception of *Jarrettsville*, Nixon did not think she'd ever write a work of historical fiction again. It was "just to tell that story," she imagined. After *Jarrettsville* she had been working on a new novel, *Beach Bunny*, about her time surfing as an undergraduate in Southern California. The Starbucks at Oxford and Center streets in Berkeley no longer felt like a good place to write, and she began writing at her desk at home. Over time *Beach Bunny* did not always feel like a good thing to write, and she began working on another novel too, which she referred to as her "divorce novel."

Nixon's progress was interrupted when her literary agent, Wendy Weil, passed away in 2012. Relying on the help of a name economy friend from the field of creation—Joyce Carol Oates—Nixon was matched with a new agent. For literary agents who straddle the fields of creation and production, a problem with Nixon's slower writing pace is that it is hard, if not almost impossible, for her to build momentum in her career. "He," Nixon said in reference to her new agent, "bemoans my utter lack of name recognition. He talks about having to 'reintroduce' me." After the mostly successful reintroduction of Nixon through *Jarrettsville*, it seemed that, should her new agent be able to secure a publishing contract for her, she would need to be introduced all over again.

For Nixon there was another aftereffect of *Jarrettsville*, which was more personal in nature. Her relationship with Jack Shoemaker at Counterpoint had first fractured over his decision to not release *Angels Go Naked* in paperback. At the time, sales of the hardback edition of *Angels* had not been strong enough to justify a paperback release, and Shoemaker knew how personally Nixon had taken it that the novel had never been given a second chance. His private hope had been that the sales of *Jarrettsville* would justify finally releasing *Angels* in paperback, and they had. Thirteen months after the release of *Jarrettsville*, *Angels* was back in print.

By 2016, Nixon and Shoemaker's relationship had no doubt been entirely repaired when he put in a bid for Counterpoint to publish her new novel, about divorce, titled *The Use of Fame*. For Nixon, fame *had* been useful. It was her brief flirtation with fame when Michiko Kakutani heaped praise on *Now You See It* that had partially carried her authorial career through *Jarrettsville*, and it was Oates's fame that led Nixon to her new agent, without which *The Use of Fame* would have likely never been published. Like everyone else involved with *Jarrettsville* it seemed, Nixon would also have stories to tell both before and after the novel.

Jarrettsville was, for Counterpoint CEO Charlie Winton, "A typical publishing story. It's sort of a great middle in publishing," Winton said, "where it's kind of like, 'okay, well, that was good, sort of.'" The "comp" title that Counterpoint and Publishers Group West had settled on for *Jarrettsville*, E. L. Doctorow's *The March*, had proven to be prophetic. That *Jarrettsville* had outsold its advance, but was not a hit like *The March*, meant the comp between them was actually good. *The March* had won the Pen/Faulkner Award, the National Book Critics Circle Award for fiction, and the Michael Shaara Award. *Jarrettsville*, by winning the Shaara Award but not the two larger awards, again proved the comp to be a good one. If *Jarrettsville* had actually performed to the level of *The March*, Counterpoint should have picked a more ambitious one, maybe even Winton's secretly hopeful comp *Cold Mountain*, which was a runaway best seller and won the National Book Award.

For Counterpoint, *Jarrettsville* had returned on investment—a success, given that around 85 percent of published books do not—but it had not been a hit. That is to say, the decision to publish *Jarrettsville* had not been a mistake, but it had not earned enough to cover many losses on what would be inevitable future mistakes. Despite not being a runaway success, however, *Jarrettsville* lived on. Books that are still selling are included toward the

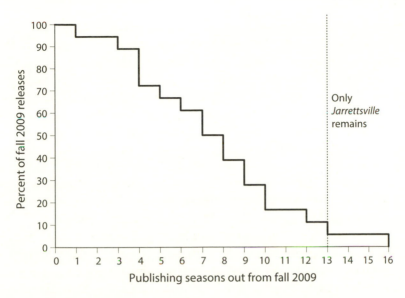

FIGURE 11.1: Survival Rate of Catalog Mentions for Fall 2009 Releases over the Next Five Years of Catalogs (2010–2014).

back in publishers' seasonal catalogs. Of the eighteen books Counterpoint released in fall 2009, *Jarrettsville* was the only one that appeared in each subsequent catalog over the next five years, and it was the last book remaining from the fall 2009 publishing season in Counterpoint's catalogs before finally dropping out (see Figure 11.1). By this measure *Jarrettsville* was not a typical publishing story, as it had lived an atypically long life.

As was the case for Nixon in writing *Jarrettsville*, for Counterpoint the experience of publishing the novel also caused small adjustments in their future actions. Winton regretted having entered into "co-op" with Borders, as the deal had, at the last moment, eaten into Counterpoint's reserve stock of the novel; it was reserve stock that would have been better served replenishing other outlets during the weeks leading up to Christmas instead of sitting unmoved in the Borders warehouses. "I don't know that we'll enter into co-op with the chains again," Winton would later say about the experience. He had been leery of co-ops with chains in the past, but the negative experience with *Jarrettsville* was, for him, a turning point.

For some of the readers of *Jarrettsville*, the book became an occasional reference point in their future reading and socializing. In discussing it readers made comparisons to a wide range of novels. To discuss *Jarrettsville* was also to discuss *Song Yet Sung* by James McBride, the Brian Copeland memoir *Not a Genuine Black Man*, *The Sound and the Fury*, *The Bridges of Madison*

County, Roots, Anna Karenina, Little Women, Cold Mountain, Reading Lolita in Tehran, and *The Help.* "Almost a hundred years separate them," a reader said of *Jarrettsville* and *The Help,* "which is just so sad." For one reader, Martha and Nick were just like "Edward and Bella" from the *Twilight* franchise, whereas for another they were like "Adam and Eve in the South." *Jarrettsville* was "not as good as *The Brief Wondrous Life of Oscar Wao*" but definitely "better than *American Pastoral*," said a woman who had read the novel by Philip Roth for her book group and clearly was not a fan. Among readers the most common comparison to *Jarrettsville* was *Gone with the Wind.* In a book group in Seattle, Martha was "a free spirit trapped by conventions," just like Scarlett O'Hara, whereas in Jarrettsville Martha was a "Scarlett O'Hara type," and in Nashville Martha was "about 30 percent Scarlett O'Hara."

More generally, a wide array of people across three fields had left their fingerprints on *Jarrettsville,* or had its fingerprints left on them. Some had lingered and some had moved on, though not entirely. By 2015 Nixon was divorced from Dean Young and was married to Hazard Adams, her former mentor, who in his own way had helped shape *Jarrettsville* by having long ago taught Nixon the Romantic poets who would sometimes inform her style. After working on *Jarrettsville,* Adam Krefman accepted an associate publisher position at McSweeney's, then returned home to Chicago, had two children, and transitioned over to marketing and sales for an online music magazine. *Jarrettsville* was the first book Krefman had shepherded through the field of production from start to finish, and it remained important to him. So did Jack Shoemaker, who had not only entrusted him with the sensitivity to be a good editor, but also modeled that sensitivity for him.

In 2013 Jack Shoemaker won the lifetime achievement award from PubWest, the widely recognized (within the field of production) trade organization for West Coast–based book publishers. He still works at Counterpoint. Charlie Winton stepped down as publisher in 2013 while still acquiring manuscripts and serving as CEO. In 2016 Counterpoint celebrated its twentieth anniversary as a for-profit publisher of "quality" literary fiction. In the pages of *Publishers Weekly* Winton surmised that Counterpoint may be the "only for-profit literary publisher west of the Hudson—and there aren't that many east of the Hudson." Counterpoint continued to maintain its balancing act: publishing books with commercial potential that could be promoted on the *Today* show, as well as books with long-term literary potential that could garner a *New York Times* review, or even better, both. "They believe in you artistically, even if you don't create a giant bottom line figure," a Counterpoint author said, while at the same time a Counterpoint staff member celebrated the press's "commercial" focus and discussed the possibility of growing through the acquisition of other publishing houses.[1]

In late August 2016, several days after Counterpoint put in an offer on Nixon's new novel, another major acquisition was brokered—their own. The upstart and independent Catapult Press acquired Counterpoint. In its one year of existence, Catapult, with offices in New York and Portland, Oregon, had made industry veteran Pat Strachan its editor in chief, and rounded out its editorial staff with established editors, as well as with well-reviewed authors who held industry experience. With the seed money for Catapult coming from CEO Elizabeth Koch—the publicly apolitical daughter of billionaire Charles Koch—the press seemed to be a twenty-first-century experiment in publishing: their books had already garnered major reviews and were distributed by Publishers Group West, but they were also focused on direct sales, had an online magazine for which writers were paid, and supplemented their authors' incomes by offering them opportunities to facilitate writing workshops.

Quite atypically in the industry, half of Catapult's editorial staff was also nonwhite. In the merger Shoemaker would stay on in his position at Counterpoint, while Winton stepped down as CEO and stayed on as an editor at large. Yuka Igarashi of Catapult (and former managing editor of Granta) would take over the editorial direction of Soft Skull while bringing the imprint back to New York. "Counterpoint is," said Catapult cofounder Andy Hunter in a statement, "one of the most important independent publishers in the United States, with an incredible list of literary fiction, incisive political nonfiction, and a countercultural ethos that makes it urgent and necessary.... Our goal is to support and continue the legacy Charlie Winton and his team have built, while innovating in our marketing and digital initiatives to make Counterpoint books an increasingly important part of our cultural conversation."[2] Catapult seemed to be saying all the right the things, but as with all experiments, what would end up happening remained to be seen.

* * *

As was the case in the introduction, the following sections are for sociologists and others interested in academic research on creation, production, and reception. If you do not feel inclined to these pursuits, Figure 11.2 is still worth considering, and there's a short and fun story waiting for you on pages 238–241. If you want some stories about how *this* book was born, they can be found in the methodological appendix.

LESSONS BEYOND *JARRETTSVILLE*: RECONNECTING CREATION, PRODUCTION, AND RECEPTION

In the early 1970s, while Cornelia Nixon was an undergraduate and living the life that she would reimagine in *Beach Bunny*, in sociology the study of material culture began to split. The move was necessitated by a need for more empirical precision, and a desire to scale down the study of cultural objects. Rather than treating media as a convenient window through which to investigate other interests (e.g., macro-level values systems, capitalist ideologies), culture scholars set out to study production and reception processes for what they were within the limited confines of concrete situations. Yet, nearly half a century later the old ghosts that had made the split of production from reception necessary no longer haunt sociologists. It is time to reconsider and knit back together the studies of creation, production, and reception. Somewhere in between overintegration and total estrangement lies three interdependent fields. In sociology the field concept is a powerful and increasingly prevalent one, but it is in need of further investigation and refinement.

RECONSIDERING ARRANGEMENTS WITHIN AND BETWEEN FIELDS

As this book shows, rather than occupying a single "literary field"—or even perfectly mirrored fields of production and consumption—authors, publishers, and readers are all for the most part operating in different fields.[3] It is through the insights of field theory that we know this to be true, as all of these fields have their own taken-for-granted realities, rules of the game, and fundamental laws that have been internalized by those within them. For a field to be a field, the players within it should also have a general sense of how it is structured and a sense of what other people are doing within it, and in the structural organization of their activities, they should be in competition with each other. None of this is true across these three fields, however.

While authors may compete with other authors for more literary acclaim or more readers, they don't struggle against readers for literary acclaim, nor do authors and readers engage in their authoring or reading in accordance with the same taken-for-granted realities. This is also true for a marketing director who can go about her work in the field of production knowing nothing about how authors position themselves against each other in the field of creation, or what's at stake for them in those internal field struggles. Similarly, an author can freely go about her work knowing nothing about the institutionalized norms, constraints, and conflicts faced by a marketing director in the field of production. To the extent she does know these things, she relies on secondary research or on repeating what she has heard from her agent or editor; when it comes to understanding the field of production, the words of her field-insider contacts become God.

To use an example from chapter 8, readers' expressions of status in the field of reception and authors' expressions of status in the field of creation are an entire field apart from a publisher's expression of her status when she criticizes another publisher for having too large of a booth at BookExpo America. Between players in the field of production, multiple meanings can be drawn out of a sarcastic four-word phrase, "well look at them." Yet for authors and readers to make sense of this meaning in context would take a preamble of background information, and the punch line, rather than being funny, may just make the speaker sound petty; to outsiders the offhand critiques of insiders about other insiders almost always sound trivial. Yet at the same time, as also discussed in chapter 8, for an author to break the code of *author omertà* would be seen by authors who follow the code as unfairly self-interested, whereas for a reader, were she to be aware of the code at all, its very existence seems unfairly self-interested, a field-level collusion of sorts. The practical existence of three interdependent fields also explains, as discussed in chapter 7, why having an author photo by Marion Ettlinger may serve as an objectified form of cultural capital for an author in the field of creation, while at the same time seeming like just another "crazy author" request in the field of production, and beyond perception in the field of reception.

Fields are often discussed as being "semiautonomous," although the study of them tends to emphasize the "autonomous" side of the phrase.[4] Yet due to the interdependency of these fields and their shared focus on novels, what happens in one field is far from entirely divorced from what happens in the next. Put differently, what "goes into" a novel in its creation and production is not entirely lost in its reception. As shown in chapter 9, readers are, at least in limited fashion, making meaning out of novels with the guiding hand of what authors have encoded into them. In being pitched in general interpretive directions by an author's intentions, readers are still free to make their own meanings—and more provocatively, as discussed in chapter 10, go a step further and read the novel into their lives—but at the same time they are not left entirely alone to make sense of things. What was unknowable when studying creation and reception independently from one another is now known at least in the case of *Jarrettsville*: readers who read the novel more in accordance with Nixon's intentions liked it more than readers who did not. By following the life cycle of *Jarrettsville* across the length of this book, it becomes impossible to avoid that when novels travel across fields they bring with them the work that has gone into them.

Field theory in sociology, particularly through the work of Bourdieu on cultural fields, focuses on the "poles" of fields (i.e., the outer reaches of the field at each side of it) at the expense of the majority of activity, which occurs in between.[5] However, as highlighted in chapter 6, at least in the field of production, art and commerce exist in a continuum, and in many cases their relationship is complementary rather than antagonistic. This tweak on Bourdieusian field theory may reflect a difference in focus, as while in Bourdieu's literary field there are no shortages of people and objects, his account tends not to focus on organizations.[6] In the field of production it is at the organizational level that the mutual dependency of "artistic" works and "commercial" works is most clear. Publishers, at the very least dating back to the "golden age" of literary publishing in the mid-twentieth century, have sought a balance of "big-bet" commercial books that provide quick and large shocks of revenue (or quick and large losses of revenue) and "small-bet" literary books from which revenue is hoped to be consistent over the long run so as to keep the publisher afloat when "big-bet" books do not pay off. While the relationship between commercial and literary books can be fraught with tension and acrimony when the dual imperatives fall out of balance, it can also, most of the time, be mutually dependent and harmonious. As corroborated across several other recent studies of the relationship between art and commerce in culture-producing organizations, tensions can occur, but to treat this occurrence as the typical state of affairs is a misunderstanding of how many culture-producing organizations operate in day-to-day practice.[7]

With field theory's emphasis on structural relations, the approach is also often treated as antithetical to network or symbolic interactionist approaches.[8] Yet as this book shows, even within fields the importance of substantive interactions in collaborative decision and meaning making cannot be discounted. Such is the case for readers in book groups in chapter 9, who walk into their meetings having made meanings that are at least partially informed by their structural positions, but then through interpersonal discussion leave their meetings with sometimes very divergent interpretations from the ones with which they entered.

More generally, within each field, the making and remaking of novels are deeply social and interactive processes. At first, be it with an author, acquisition editor, or reader, an individual mostly does the sense- and meaning-making work on a novel. Her position as embedded within a field informs how she goes about this work, but once the first pass is done, other field participants are brought in for refinement and collaborative creative exchange.

Authors receive feedback and suggestions from others in the field of creation, just as a copy editor, cover designer, and various marketing reps come
on board in the field of production once an editor has finished her work.
Readers often interact with other readers about the novels they're reading or
have read, collaboratively influencing and refining the meanings they make
of novels. In this way, we can think of the social lives of novels as shaped like
a series of hourglasses: from broad influences, a person distills down into
her work on an object, and then through direct interpersonal exchange the
horizons of that object are broadened again.

The importance of substantive interactions in each field is necessitated
by the inescapable uncertainties of writing, publishing, and reading novels;
uncertainty is mitigated through bringing reinforcements (and hopefully,
collaborative new ideas) into the processes. Bringing in others for feedback
and suggestions—a new title for *Jarrettsville* in chapter 2; changes based on
editors' rejection letters in chapter 5; the selection of comp titles in chapter 7; changing one's opinions on the justifiability of a character's actions
through conversation as discussed in chapter 10—is a regular strategy to
manage inherently uncertain processes. Social feedback is also used to win-
now through an oversupply of things, be it for an author choosing from too
many possible narrative directions in which to go, an agent or editor choosing from too many available books upon which to work, a bookstore buyer
or reviewer choosing from too many books to promote, or a reader choosing from too many books to read. As a result, in all three fields uncertainty
and oversupply create the conditions under which social and relational exchange become paramount.

Real networks of relational exchange are also the conduits through which
novels are transported from one field into the next; these relationships work
to knit together the relationships *between* fields.[9] The structural positions of
people in these exchanges matter when, for example, determining whether
an agent is legitimate or illegitimate (as discussed in chapter 4) or what type
of press Counterpoint is (as discussed in chapter 6). But there is a duality
between the structural positions of people and the substantive relationships between them, as novels cannot pass from one field into the next if
not through the "pipes" or "circuits" that span them.[10] Were we to reduce
acquisition editors to their structural positions, the finely curated list of editors Weil had sent *Martha's Version* to in chapter 5 would not have been so
unpredictably idiosyncratic in their evaluations of what was right and wrong
with the manuscript.

More generally, a good example of how both structural similarity and interpersonal relations are important in transitioning novels across fields can be
found in the relationships between agents and editors. As an example of the

former, as discussed in chapter 4, the extended profiles on new editors in the AAR's newsletter exist as dispositional dating profiles for agents. Yet, at the same time, due to their interdependence and the multiplex way in which over time agents and editors can grow closer with each other, both *what* to work on and *how* to work on it can become increasingly symbiotic. The same is true in the next field transition for the relationships between field reps and bookstore buyers; trust and shared sensibilities developed through repeated exchange make their jobs easier, and make talking about novels together both easier and more emotionally rewarding. As discussed in chapters 5 and 7, both within and between fields, for novels to travel requires *emotional contagion* to be fomented through direct interpersonal interactions. As shown in the case of *Jarrettsville*, the fomentation of emotional contagion happens between people, not through positional osmosis.

In further evidence of the necessity of substantive interaction to transport novels from here to there, part of their transportation requires translating their meaning from what made sense where they were, to what makes sense where they need to go. This too is done through real conversations between people. In transitioning a novel across fields, a literary agent (with one foot in the field of creation) and an editor (with one foot in the field of production) meet somewhere in between, and together develop a blended language that allows for the importation of a novel across fields. It is not a literary agent's job to know only what an author thinks her book is, or why authors in other positions in the field of creation might herald it or disparage it, although she probably has a sense for these things. Instead, she has to be able to translate these things with an editor into stories about the book that those firmly in the field of production are equipped to care about and understand.

By way of example of how the talk of novels changes based on their locations, of the stories about Nixon's creative process as told in chapter 2, Wendy Weil (her agent) knew some of them, Adam Krefman (her editor) knew very few of them, and beyond *Jarrettsville* being based on a true family story, Abbye Simkowitz (Counterpoint's publicity director) knew or cared about none of them at all. In the four-step path between Nixon and Simkowitz, almost all the interesting things about *Jarrettsville* had changed. Likewise, for Simkowitz and the review outlets she was pitching, the "important" stories about *Jarrettsville* would again have to change (e.g., "don't talk about the plot too much"). Through Simkowitz's pitch, review outlets took all the information about how Counterpoint thought about the book (who liked it and why; where it fit on their list; Nixon's previous record of reviews) and again translated it into meanings that would matter in the field of reception: What is the book "about"? Where does it fit with other books in the field? Is it successful in its aims? Is it worth reading? Simkowitz's pitch—just as is the

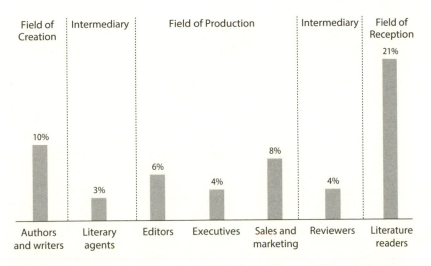

FIGURE 11.2: Percentage African American/Black and Latino/Hispanic by Position and Field.
Source: Authors and writers from 2015 Bureau of Labor Statistics. Literary agents from original data. Literature readers from NEA 2009 "Reading on the Rise." All other data from the 2015 Diversity Baseline Survey.

case for a screenwriter's pitch to a network or studio or a journalist's pitch to her newsroom—was ultimately about translating the values of an object so that it could transition across fields. Yet pitchers, as the metaphor goes, also require catchers, and it is through cooperative and repetitive interactions that pitchers and catchers adjust to each other in learning how to best work together.

It is also through network relations (both within and across fields) that cultural reproduction may occur, as personal connections and shared sensibilities, interests, and tastes become paramount in generating enthusiasm for novels. The twinning of identity and personal experience with enthusiasm and work specialization can have very real consequences for which novels are transported across and through fields, and which novels are not. Such is the case for the lack of racial and ethnic diversity across fields as discussed most directly in chapters 3 through 5. Perhaps most troubling is that across the tripartite field structure, the lowest rates of racial and ethnic diversity are found among those in boundary-spanning roles across fields; the conduits through which novels are passed—or not—from one field to the next (see Figure 11.2).

Of the three fields it is also the field of production, situated in between the fields of creation and reception, that is most racially homogenous. As stated in chapter 4, it is quite possible that there would be more Black and

Latino authors if there were more Black and Latino agents (who are more willing to represent "ethnic" or "multicultural" fiction than are white agents) and editors who might take an interest in their work: "We don't need more Latina authors. We need more Latina acquisition editors," former Simon & Schuster editor Marcela Landres has said.[11] A similar predicament occurs in the next field transition to readers, who may be better directed to books they would enjoy (the premise on which the field transition is based) with more sales and marketing staff (or reviewers) who had a better grasp on at least some of their preferences and tastes. In an interdependent system, a problem in input can also affect outputs. As it currently stands in the United States, for about every hundred thousand white readers of literature there is a white literary agent, whereas there is one Black or Latino literary agent for about every one million Black or Latino readers of literature. As these fields are interdependent and novels are built to travel, a lack of diversity at the center can impact not only which works from the field of creation gain access, but also the activities of authors themselves, as discussed of the authors Damon and Maxine in chapter 5.

FORCES OF CHANGE ACROSS THREE INTERDEPENDENT FIELDS

Fields are oriented toward reproduction, which does a lot to limit endogenous change.[12] More generally, popular theories of production and reception are more equipped to deal with endogenous change than is field theory.[13] By way of example, as discussed in chapter 3, the rise of literary agents is a story of changes in the market and organizational form (a "production of culture" story) much more than it is the story of capital accumulation or positional strivings (a field story). In turn, the rise of short stories in the field of creation is a story most easily explained through indirect governmental intervention, changing field-level organization, and changing career structures with the rise of MFA programs. Yet endogenous changes in fields can also be described through stories that are friendlier to field theory, as long as one is willing to accept that people sometimes don't know what to do, and sometimes try to experiment to figure it out.[14] In these instances, endogenous change can occur due to the unavoidability of experimentation when dealing with novels that are by definition all at least a little bit unique, which can lead to change through imitation (or shifting conventions) as a regular tool to mitigate against uncertainty.

Consider, for instance, the case described in chapter 7 in which Counterpoint and PGW had to decide if it was "acceptable" to release *Jarrettsville* with a blurb on the front cover (and as a paperback original) with the work still garnering reviews and being understood as literature within the field of production. While *Jarrettsville* could certainly be typified and "comped" to other novels, as a new novel it was also by definition at least marginally unique, making small experimentations unavoidable (e.g., popular fiction can have blurbs on the front cover and literary fiction can maybe have blurbs on the front cover, but what about *Jarrettsville*?). Yet, at the same time, the question of experimentation was also imitative: the question was if it was wise to imitate publishers of literary fiction who had put blurbs on their front covers, or if the press should align with the publishers who were not doing so. Counterpoint's decision was also, in its own small way, something other publishers may react to; to put a blurb or not on the front cover was to cast one's vote on the trend, as to do so could cause the trend to further cascade. Were we to ask if Counterpoint deciding to put a blurb on the front cover of *Jarrettsville* was a cause or effect of the increasing usage of the practice in the field of production, this story would present an endogeneity "problem." If, however, our question is about how endogenous change within the field of production may occur, rather than presenting an endogeneity "problem" the story provides a solution.

More typically in field theory the evolution of fields is explained through exogenous forces of change; conditions outside the field ripple through it, be it rising education levels or the entrance of new cohorts of upstarts challenging the established.[15] Good examples of exogenous change as related to novels are the effect of change in US copyright law on US fiction in the nineteenth century, and the effect of oil prices on Nigerian novel production in the 1980s.[16] When considering creation, production, and reception as proximate and interdependent fields, however, even smaller, meso-level shifts—rather than international markets forces, national governmental policy, generational change, or rising education levels lifting all boats—in one field can be an exogenous force of change for companion fields. By way of example, as discussed in chapter 2, the field of production found itself positioned between a field of creation from which fiction authors were increasingly producing short stories in MFA programs, and a field of reception for which there was not a robust demand for volumes of short stories. As a result, a small change in the field of production was needed to bring what was happening in companion fields back into balance: thus, the "novel in stories" device became ascendant. This is a case of a large change in the field of creation—the rise of the MFA program and the latent effects it had on which forms of fiction were being produced—leading to a small and proximate change in the field of production so as to maintain good relations with both authors and readers.

Another example of a small exogenous force causing change across fields is the adoption of eBook technology, and what in chapter 8 is referred to as the rise of the *uninvested inclusivity* publishing model used by outlets such as Amazon. This technological change in the field of production rippled through the field of creation, altering some authors' income streams, as discussed in chapter 3. While in field theory exogenous forces are usually big forces that result in big changes, by scaling down to interdependent fields of creation, production, and reception—and by studying them simultaneously—we can also make sense of much more modest exogenous forces that lead to more modest changes; we can make sense of smaller shifts and adjustments in addition to larger ruptures.

A second, and more common, force of small exogenous change across these fields is success. Change frequently occurs in reaction to success achieved in the field of reception, but also in response to perceptions of success in the fields of creation and production. To illustrate this point, consider the following field-traversing story: the path from Anne Rice's 1976 *Interview with the Vampire* to E. L. James's 2011 *Fifty Shades of Grey*.

FROM *INTERVIEW WITH THE VAMPIRE* TO *FIFTY SHADES OF GREY*

In the late 1960s, while a PhD student in English at Berkeley, Anne Rice decided she'd rather be a writer than study literature. She wrote a short story about a vampire, which she then revised into a novel after switching paths and enrolling as an MFA student in creative writing at San Francisco State University. It was not until several years later, however, that Rice met a literary agent at a writers conference who, after many rejections, shepherded her vampire story into the field of production, selling it to Knopf for a then-high advance of $12,000. The book was met with mixed reviews and overall middling sales, and Rice spent the next decade or so publishing two works of historical fiction under her own name, and five works of erotica under two different pen names. While this could have been the end of *Interview with the Vampire*, instead, in the mid-eighties Rice returned to the novel, turning it into a series, *The Vampire Chronicles*, which was a runaway success.

Several years later, at the turn of the 1990s, back in the field of production the publisher HarperCollins had noticed the success of Rice's vampire books in the field of reception and turned to Alloy Entertainment, a book packager, to find an author to translate Rice's vampires into the young adult genre. In the field of production Alloy Entertainment sketched out the basic contours of the idea and then turned to the field of creation to find an author to enact their vision. The author they found was L. J. Smith, and the books she produced were titled *The Vampire Diaries*. Smith had planned on writing a trilogy, but due to demand in the field of reception, the first series became a quartet of novels instead.

Even if one is unfamiliar with *The Vampire Diaries* books, the basic contours of the plot may be familiar. Although Stephenie Meyer claims that the plot of her *Twilight* series of young adult books came to her in a dream and that she was inspired by a range of literary classics, since the series' release in the mid-2000s passionate fans of *The Vampire Diaries* in the field of reception have objected to what they see as Meyer's clear influence for *Twilight*. Both series feature a small-town setting in which a teenage girl finds herself in a love triangle with two exceptionally old mythical creatures, which are both masquerading as humans in her high school. The one she will end up with is complicated and brooding, and as they fall in love she wants him to drink her blood so they can live together as immortals, but he resists. In *The Vampire Diaries* the girl's name is Elena, and the mythical creatures are brothers, both vampires, named Stefan and Damon. In the *Twilight* series the girl's name is Bella, and the mythical creatures are Edward, a vampire, and Jacob, a werewolf.

Although *Vampire Diaries* book fans in the field of reception accuse Meyer of not crediting the inspiration for her work, fans of the *Twilight Series* reverse the accusation in reference to *The Vampire Diaries* television series, which was brought to air in 2009. Sometimes this reverse-inspiration claim by *Twilight* fans is because they are unaware that *The Vampire Diaries* show is based on a book series that predates Meyer's first *Twilight* novel by fourteen years. Other times it is because they rightly recognize that the packaging of *The Vampire Diaries* into a television show in the field of production in 2009 came on the heels of *Twilight*'s massive success in the field of reception as both a book and a film series. With regard to the second accusation, *The Vampire Diaries* was reborn as a television series because of *Twilight*'s multiformat success, and the co-creators of the *Diaries* television series, Julie Plec and Kevin Williamson, were open about similarities between the two properties when developing the show. The "why here, why now?" question about the *Vampire Diaries* television show can be answered in a single word: *Twilight*.

In addition to *Twilight* playing a role in porting *The Vampire Diaries* to television, it also, back in the field of creation, begot what would eventually become the *Fifty Shades of Grey* book series. In this success-induced field transition E. L. James, after having read the *Twilight* trilogy in five days, wrote a work of *Twilight* fan fiction titled *Master of the Universe* under the pen name "Snowdragon Icequeen." After uploading it to FanFiction.net, the work became a runaway success by that community's standards, garnering around forty thousand reviews. After *Master of the Universe* was removed from the site, James took it and "filed off its serial numbers," a term common in the fan fiction community to describe the process through which fan fiction is transitioned away from its source material (in this case, *Twilight*) so that the work can be saleable without violating copyright claims (e.g., creating analogous character names, settings, and so on). Renaming *Master* as *Fifty Shades of Grey* and rewriting about 10 percent of the text, James partnered with the Australian virtual publishing company The Writers' Coffee Shop to release *Fifty Shades* as a series of eBooks. This release sold around a quarter million copies and made it onto the *New York Times*' eBook fiction best-seller list, at which point the rights were purchased for a sum in the seven figures by the editor Anne Messitte at Vintage (a division of Random House and paperback imprint of Knopf), for whom *Fifty Shades* went on to sell over a hundred million copies.

In a final turn, from *Fifty Shades of Grey*'s success in the field of reception we circle back to the fields of creation in which writers then created their own *Fifty Shades* fan fiction out of what had originally been James's *Twilight* fan fiction.[17] At the same time, in the field of production in reaction to the success of *Fifty Shades*, publishers began looking back into their catalogues for works of erotica they could rerelease to capitalize on what they hoped would become a trend of mass consumption for that genre. For the publisher Penguin, from their back catalogue they rereleased a box set of three erotica novels titled the *Sleeping Beauty Trilogy*, which had been written by A. N. Roquelaure over thirty years prior. Back then, Roquelaure had written the *Sleeping Beauty* novels in between writing another series of novels, which she had originally crafted as a short story about vampires while enrolled as a PhD student in English. When writing erotica, Roquelaure was the pen name used by Anne Rice, the author of *Interview with the Vampire* (see Figure 11.3).[18]

As was the case with the example of the "novel in stories" device, this example of a multistep process of cross-field reactivity is decidedly not a story of massive changes or ruptures within any field as the result of exogenous pressure. Instead, it's a subtler story based on activities and adjustments caused by small and nearby forces rather than large and distant ones.

Also suggested in this story is that field players are reactive, and more or less capable of acting strategically, as did Rice when she pivoted to write erotica after *Interview* was first poorly received, Alloy Entertainment when they repackaged *Interview* for the young adult genre, Smith when she turned her trilogy into a tetralogy, Meyer when she declined to cite influence from *Diaries*, James when she "filed off the serial numbers" for *Fifty*

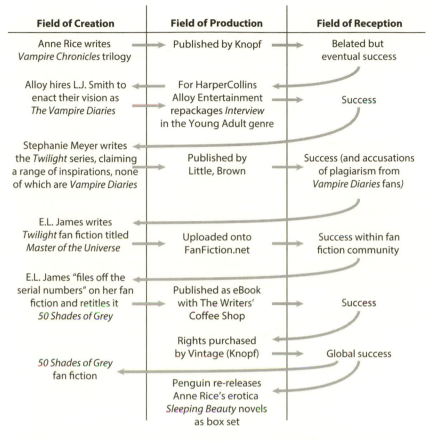

Field of Creation	Field of Production	Field of Reception
Anne Rice writes *Vampire Chronicles* trilogy	Published by Knopf	Belated but eventual success
Alloy hires L.J. Smith to enact their vision as *The Vampire Diaries*	For HarperCollins Alloy Entertainment repackages *Interview* in the Young Adult genre	Success
Stephanie Meyer writes the *Twilight* series, claiming a range of inspirations, none of which are *Vampire Diaries*	Published by Little, Brown	Success (and accusations of plagiarism from *Vampire Diaries* fans)
E.L. James writes *Twilight* fan fiction titled *Master of the Universe*	Uploaded onto FanFiction.net	Success within fan fiction community
E.L. James "files off the serial numbers" on her fan fiction and retitles it *50 Shades of Grey*	Published as eBook with The Writers' Coffee Shop	Success
50 Shades of Grey fan fiction	Rights purchased by Vintage (Knopf)	Global success
	Penguin re-releases Anne Rice's erotica *Sleeping Beauty* novels as box set	

FIGURE 11.3: From *Interview with the Vampire* to *Fifty Shades of Grey*.

Shades, and Penguin when they rereleased Rice's erotica novels. It is, in fact, through big and small strategic actions across many iterative changes that we can trace a path from Rice's sexless vampires to James's work of BDSM erotica. If it were not for these strategic actions and interdependent cross-field reactivity, this would have either been a story of thirty-five years stuck in a recursive sexless vampire loop, or there would not have been a path to follow at all. Through the structure of three interdependent fields we can document both reproduction and change within fields, and across fields.

ARE BOOKS SPECIAL?

Books have historically been treated as special objects: as vehicles to pass down accumulated knowledge, as parables for living, as status symbols, as tokens of affection, and as matters of community. The quasi-sacred status of books seems to exist beyond their actual contents. To engage in the public destruction of even the most disreputable of books (such as *Mein Kampf* or *The Turner Diaries*) would for many still create discomfort. The specialness of books also exists beyond any abstract specialness afforded to the written word. To keep all of the newspapers or magazines one has ever read might be considered hoarding, yet to unceremoniously throw out one's books would also introduce suspicion.

Starting in the 1920s, home furnishing catalogs centered their representation of ideal, middle-class lifestyles on the prominent display of books.[19] The "buy independent" social movements of the 1980s and 1990s found their most persuasive frame through the image of the independent bookstore. As independent hardware stores, electronics stores, and grocers have become increasingly replaced by national and international chains, it is through independent bookstores that these movements continue to find their clearest articulation of the vitality of local community.

In a further testament to the power of the book, unlike the proprietors of independent outlets for other types of retail goods, the independent bookstore has made a substantial and measurable comeback. While the fields of recorded music and news journalism have been entirely upended by digital transitions, digital transitions in book publishing have been far more gradual, and in 2015 their growth has at least temporarily leveled off at around 25 to 30 percent of the book market. Even if this is only a temporary slowdown, unlike in news journalism and recorded music, the doomsday predictions for book publishing have not yet come to pass. Publishers still regularly discuss digital transitions more as potentially profitable opportunities than as disastrous challenges. One of the advantages of the digital transition for publishers is it allows them to imagine a world in which they're not regularly destroying books; about 25 to 30 percent of all books produced go unsold and are first dramatically discounted (sometimes sold at 10 cents per pound) before the rest are remaindered. It's a fact of the field of production that's not often discussed in the fields of creation or consumption, and due to the special status of books, readers may even prefer that the treatment of books as "garbage" scheduled for destruction is kept hidden behind the curtain of another field.[20] Yet while books are afforded a special status, this does not necessarily mean that the nuts and bolts of their creation, production, and reception are also special. Put another way, across other cultural arenas, is the tripartite structure of interdependent fields that exists for fiction generalizable, or is it unique?

When comparing the creation, production, and reception of novels to other cultural arenas (e.g., music, film, art, stand-up comedy, advertising, and so on) the tripartite field structure is more readily apparent for books, as field locations also tend to geographically map onto the real world.[21] Unlike "creatives" in advertising firms or chefs in restaurants, authors do not write novels in offices at publishing houses. As a result, from the perspective of a publisher a novelist is writing "out there somewhere" in both a field and a physical geographic sense; the same is not true for advertising creatives or chefs, nor is it true for architects, actors, or studio musicians. Similarly, unlike for authors, who give readings but do not make their livings through performance, audiences are not "far away" for stage actors, musicians, chefs, and stand-up comedians; they may be interacting in a different field but nonetheless regularly see consumers face-to-face. Unlike many of these other cultural fields, the creation, production, and reception of literature also have people in salaried positions who are formally employed in transitioning cultural objects across them, as is the case with the relationship between agents and editors, and field reps and bookstore buyers. For television and film, agents handle contractual obligations, while the artist herself frames the artistic project—within production imperatives—in pitch meetings with the "suits." In this way, for books in particular, both the boundaries of these fields and the "who is doing what where" may be atypically clear. This is not meant to suggest that a tripartite field structure applies only to books, but rather that the generalizability of the structure across cultural arenas is an open empirical question.

To answer that question, it is prudent to return to the rise of the production of culture perspective starting in the early 1970s. One of the major goals of the approach was to study a wide range of industries, rather than to assume a uniform black box of ideologically driven cultural production. The goal to "scale up" from particular industries to general rules of cultural production has in the intervening years borne fruit. From this collaborative effort we now know of the irreducible nature of uncertainty in cultural production, and the reliance on genres and the classification of objects for sense making and to organize activity. We know that interpersonal connections and internships are the primary access points into these industries, and that "talent" and "ability" are treated as inborn and ineffable qualities. As the "scaling up" from industry-specific cases to generalizable rules worked for the study of production, perhaps it too can work for the study of the relationship between creation, production, and reception. Just as there is no shortage of boundary-traversing relationships hiding under the covers of books, there is likely no shortage of them hiding under the covers of fields.

METHODOLOGICAL APPENDIX

FROM THERE TO HERE

The genesis of this project was a conversation with Simonetta Falasca-Zamponi. I had recently completed an MA thesis on the mid-nineties transition in daytime television from "trash talk" (e.g., *The Jerry Springer Show*) to "syndi-court" (e.g., *Judge Judy*) programming. It was a content analysis that I had tried and failed to dress up as a study of production or reception. My motive in that work was as much personal as intellectual; I wanted Josh Gamson, for whom I had worked as a research assistant and whose work I still admire, to read it and think I was smart. While speaking with Falasca-Zamponi about my next project, she asked a sensible question: do you want to do a study of production or reception? Quite naïvely, and still unaware of the implications of my response, I blithely said "both." Generous as she is, and probably imputing more intentionality in my response than I possessed at that time, Falasca-Zamponi encouraged me.

For a variety of reasons, both personal and strategic, I decided to study a novel. Powell's (1985) *Getting into Print* was an early, and still important, inspiration for me in the study of production, as were Long's (2003) *Book Clubs* and Radway's (1984) *Reading the Romance* for reception. There was, however, one project that did both: Griswold's (2000) pathbreaking study of the Nigerian "fiction complex." Although I wanted to follow the life cycle of a single book rather than a nation's literature, *Bearing Witness* was evidence that what I wanted to do could be done.

Figuring I should start at the "beginning," I paired up with an author of mystery novels, who generously kept a diary of his creative process as he began drafting a new manuscript. From this first experience I realized I had two problems: (1) the creative process can be long and messy, and (2) it's much easier to find authors who will let you study them than it is to find publishers who will do the same. What I thought was my start turned out to be a false one, but it brought me to the conclusion that my point of entry had to be a publisher. I figured that once I found a publisher amenable to my nosiness, I could get paired up with an author whose manuscript they had accepted for publication. For this reason, the data I collected on Cornelia Nixon, inclusive of her creative processes in writing *Jarrettsville* and her network of authors and friends in the field of creation, were retrospective.

With generosity I could not expect or deserve, Nixon opened her life to me, and over time, in addition to our regular interviews, she introduced me to others involved in her authoring process. She also provided me with multiple drafts of her novel and boxes of the archival material she used to write *Jarrettsville*. She had, thankfully, written copious memos to herself on these documents, through which, in addition to our interviews, I could examine her research and authorial process. She spent a marathon session going over these drafts and archival materials with me, comparing them side by side. Wendy Weil also gave to me all of the rejection letters for *Martha's Version* as analyzed in chapter 5, another important archival data source. I raise the issue of retrospective data collection here because if there is a bias to retrospective accounts, it's that they can end up reconstructing messy processes and chance occurrences into narratives that seem purposeful, planned, and linear. As seen in chapter 2, however, the account of *Jarrettsville*'s creation describes a process that was far from planned or linear; when cross-checked against personal and archival records, retrospective accounts can still offer insights into the "messiness" of creativity in real life.

But I'm getting ahead of myself. To find an author, I had to first find a publisher, and Counterpoint Press wasn't the first publisher I found. Not knowing much, I contacted a friend from middle school who worked as an assistant to a literary agent. I interviewed her, and then interviewed friends of hers who also worked in publishing. Three steps removed from my initial contact, I was put in touch with an editor who then put me in touch with his publisher, who agreed to let me study his independent publishing house. The house specialized in literary fiction and had several hits to its name. I moved to the city where the publishing house was located about a week before my study of the press was to begin. That Friday, I emailed the publisher to say hello and reiterate how grateful I was to be starting my fieldwork. The publisher emailed back to say that just the week before he had been forced to downsize his entire staff and put all operations on hold. Literally and metaphorically dressed up with no place to go, I did not know what to do.

Because I had no publishing house to study, I had lots of free time. I decided that if I couldn't study a publisher, I might as well start interviewing editors and fiction authors. Editors were people whose roles in the chain of production, as described by Powell's *Getting into Print* and Coser, Kadushin, and Powell's (1982) *Books*, fascinated me. I found authors and editors through referrals from those I'd already interviewed, and also through reading *Publishers Weekly*. In particular, I wrote down the names of editors who appeared in its pages, and began contacting them. I also went to a neighborhood bookstore and wrote down the names of the editors of recent fiction releases (which can be found in the acknowledgments pages) and, when I could find their contact information, cold-contacted them for interviews as well. During this time my goal was still to find a publisher. With a passing knowledge of social psychology, I alternated between "foot in the door" and "door in the face" techniques: asking some editors if I could study them and their publishing house and, when they declined, asking instead for a sixty-minute interview, and vice versa.[1]

At the time I felt quite clever for using this strategy, but it didn't work. Yet fortunately the experience of interviewing editors made me realize that for my eventual case study I needed to interview people who were unaffiliated with the novel that would be at its center (e.g., other authors, agents, editors, etc.) at every step in the chain, lest I not be able to differentiate between the particular and generalizable. Similarly, if during my hypothetical case study I came up against an unforthcoming publicity director, without interviewing other publicity directors, I wouldn't be able to say anything about publicity directors at all.

This was an important realization that greatly shaped both the structure and contents of this book, but I still did not have a publisher to study, and most editors I contacted, as one would expect, did not write me back or return my calls. Stuck, and now a little bit more desperate, I again turned to a friend, this time one who occasionally babysat the children of two exceptionally well-known authors. I gave my project proposal to him, and he gave it to them, asking if they could think of anyone to put me in touch with. Shortly thereafter they had their assistants email me with a list of editors to contact, clarifying that I had their permission to include their names as the reference. All of the editors I contacted from that list wrote me back by the end of the day, and from those emails, two publishers agreed to let me study them. It was from this experience that the power of name-economy authors as discussed in chapter 3 first emerged.

Both presses were independent and on the West Coast, causing me to be concerned that a study of them would not be representative of the field of production in the United States, for which the epicenter is Manhattan. Fortunately I had already interviewed editors at imprints in New York, meaning this was not a question that would have to be left unanswered. As a result, I was able to answer some of the specifics of that question in Childress (2015), and some more generalities of it in chapter 6 of this book. Having already experienced one independent press go out of business, and knowing how quickly staff can turn over in book publishing, I opted to concurrently study *both* agreeable presses at the same time. Each set me up with an author they had accepted for publication, and for a while I studied both authors and presses simultaneously, until it became clear that the author of the book I was studying that was not *Jarrettsville* was moving at a much slower pace; the book was ultimately released two years after *Jarrettsville*.

At Counterpoint, Charlie Winton, Jack Shoemaker, Adam Krefman, and the rest of the staff were incredibly generous. Winton agreed to let me intern and to sit in on editorial and noneditorial meetings. Over six months at Counterpoint, I formally interned on the editorial side for three days a week for about sixteen weeks (the production of their fall season), while dropping in with semiregularity for a while after that. While interning at Counterpoint, Winton, Shoemaker, Krefman, and others began to share with me sundry internal office memos, their email exchanges related to *Jarrettsville*, and so on. They did this knowing that I was happy to share with them what I wrote in advance of publication but that my reports and impressions were ultimately my own.

Regarding names and pseudonyms, before starting my fieldwork on *Jarrettsville* I discussed with those directly involved the impossibilities of preserving true anonymity. *Jarrettsville*'s author, editor, publisher, and so on would be in the public record, and in order to offer genuine anonymity to those people I'd have had to write a whole book about *Jarrettsville* while keeping the book itself unidentifiable. As a result, in this work, real names are used when discussing individuals as they directly interact with *Jarrettsville* in the fields of creation and production, and in all other cases pseudonyms or all-purpose identifiers ("an editor" or "an agent") are used. In my experiences, literary authors and those in book publishing by default assume a journalistic standard in which their names are attached to their quotes. Yet although the pro forma anonymization of quotes in sociology is an important subject of debate, in my experience, even for my generally well-off, non-vulnerable population of interlocutors who were sharing with me everyday stories of work life, offering to withhold specifying details resulted in participants telling me things they may otherwise not have said.

Those who could conceivably be identified, by name or by description, were also given the opportunity to read this book in advance of its publication in order to offer factual corrections and share any possible concerns.

Sharing a draft of my work with my respondents prior to publication allowed for the correction of several small factual errors in my account, which otherwise would still be present here. As speech that sounds normal in conversation can sometimes seem clunky on paper, by request, in quoting I have also sometimes lightly cleaned up my interlocutors' grammar or phrasing, but nothing more. Identifying terminology is also sometimes inconsistent (e.g., "African American" or "Black") based on respondents' preferences. My interlocutors were also given the opportunity to self-select their own pseudonyms, although for the most part they seemed to find this offer uninteresting or burdensome.

Several respondents also, provided with a pen and blank sheet of paper, "mapped out" for me their place in the field in which they participated, as well as their broader understanding of its relations. Their maps were incredibly helpful for me to make sense of the worlds they inhabit. Noteworthy also is that, without prompting, those who completed these "idio-maps" for me also tended to draw out their worlds both spatially (as one would see in a multiple correspondence analysis) and with connective lines (like edges on a networks diagram). From this I began to learn that my respondents thought of their own social worlds as existing in an overlapping Bourdieusian-style and networks-style space. This was, in part, the inspiration for the discussion on this point in chapter 11. I do not reproduce their idio-maps in this book, as to do so would just be to present a series of lines and boxes with all identifiers blacked out. Instead, I treated these idio-maps as supplementary to the interviews rather than their own formally collected and analyzed body of data.

It took a while to "get in" at Counterpoint. In the first month or so, people spoke carefully in my presence, sometimes glancing over to me before choosing their words. During this stage, I tried to keep my jottings to a minimum when in public and would write my field notes during lunch and after work. During the next stage, my presence and motives for being at Counterpoint became the subject of friendly office banter. One day in the office someone burped loudly and yelled across the room to me, "is *that* going in your book?" At the time I just laughed and surreptitiously jotted down that the joke had been made, but now it has.

In a second instance at around the same time someone at Counterpoint agreed to audio record an important meeting for me, as I could not be there. Before the meeting she announced that the proceedings were being recorded, but Winton arrived late and consequently had not heard this. As a sensitive business matter unrelated to this study began to be discussed, the person recording for me interjected to let Winton know that, if he cared, he was being recorded. "Oh, what? Why?" Winton asked. Upon hearing the explanation, Winton (it seemed) picked up the recorder, put it to his lips, and theatrically said "Clayton, you're a dog!" before continuing on with the sensitive line of discussion. In this instance, my "presence" was both a joke and generally accepted (i.e., neither Winton nor the colleague stopped the audio recording, or the discussion). At the same time, this example reveals how during this phase of study the boundaries of what I should be privy to at Counterpoint were still a bit amorphous. During this second phase, when people had become more comfortable with my presence and observations, I started asking them out to lunch for interviews. My reasoning was that they might then be a bit more comfortable and forthcoming in answering my questions about broader issues and the minutiae of what I was observing in my research, which proved true.

It was not until my last couple months at Counterpoint that I truly felt I was "in." The signal to me was that people started telling me things that, as a researcher, they should not have if they didn't trust me to protect their confidentiality, or to be able to parse between on- and off-the-record observations. At the same time that people increasingly said off-the-record things to me, they had also stopped verbally clarifying that what they were saying was so.² During this phase of observations people also started to forget how little I knew, treating me as an insider who was (or should be) familiar with jargon I was not. When an editor-friend was under the gun, I mentioned that I was just puttering between tasks and available to help out. "Great!" she said, handing me the page proofs for a novel. "Could you give this a quick check for orphans and widows?" As I tried to process her request, she started laughing about my confusion, explaining that orphans and widows are typesetting terms, and I was not supposed to hurriedly scan the manuscript for orphaned or widowed characters. "That's right," she said with a friendly smile, as if to say "I forgot that you are not one of us."

Although this was a momentary lapse and I do not believe that anyone ever truly forgot that I wasn't really a "member of the team," by the time I traveled with the staff to BookExpo America I was at least member-adjacent (e.g., it was rightly assumed that I would be helping with carrying and unpacking boxes of books, setting up the booth, etc.). Concurrently, I was also attending author readings and sundry publishing events, both to get a better sense for the field and to approach more unaffiliated people for off-hour interviews. During this stage, with less time on my hands due to increased inclusion at my field site, my jottings were increasingly taken on scraps of paper or in emails to myself, and on most days I'd have to wake up early and complete my field notes in the morning.

Beyond interviews and fieldwork, other data sources have helped fill gaps in the data collection. This includes secondary sources, industry trade publications, other data sets I constructed, overlapping roles (e.g., an author interviewed due to her status as an author with whom I also spoke about her work as a reviewer), and exchange partners (e.g., what, in a discussion of agents, editors have to say about agents). A good example of this is the discussion of the inner workings of the *Times'* book review process as discussed in chapter 8. Without access to the behind-the-scenes operation, I instead relied on secondary sources of the *Times'* staff publicly discussing their process, and explanations from publicity directors about how they have pitched outlets like the *Times*. It is a similar case with the database of literary agents and their demographics as discussed in chapter 4; nothing like that existed, and while writing the manuscript I took a detour into new data collection because I figured it very well should. In that instance, to be fair, part of the motivation was also to have something to say about literary agents that had not already been said by John B. Thompson in his exquisite chapter on them in *Merchants of Culture*.

In total 202 readers of *Jarrettsville* filled out surveys about their reading experiences. I constructed the survey questions with input from both Nixon and Krefman. Nixon filled out the survey with regard to her intentions rather than interpretations. As a PhD in English, she understood quite intimately what I was up to. Krefman filled out the survey with regard to his interpretations. There's no way to establish the population that read *Jarrettsville*, so the survey respondents are neither a "representative sample" of *Jarrettsville* readers nor even entirely a "sample" of that population, as the majority of them were recruited into reading the book (i.e., to consider them a "sample" of the population that read *Jarrettsville* would be tautological). About thirty of the survey respondents were found on Goodreads.com. They had reviewed *Jarrettsville*, and I contacted them through the Goodreads interface asking if they'd be willing to fill out a survey in exchange for a $5 gift card to Amazon or Powell's. All other survey respondents were members of book groups.

Groups were recruited in three ways: (1) through two-step friend and familial networks, (2) through a snowball sample from early participating book groups, and (3) from interview respondents (e.g., bookstore buyers and employees) who contacted me to tell me that a local book group was going to read *Jarrettsville* and might be amenable to being studied. A lone exception is a group of friends from graduate school who self-organized to read and discuss *Jarrettsville*, for which I am grateful. The full survey protocol is discussed in more detail in Childress and Friedkin (2012). For

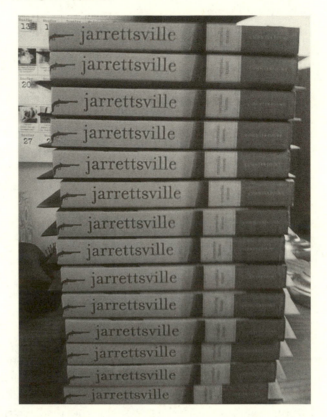

FIGURE 12.1: A Stack of *Jarrettsville* Copies Stuffed with Surveys before Drop-Off.

the reception component of this research, I chose to study book groups both because of my enjoyment of Long's (2003) book, and because while designing the study I was taking Noah Friedkin's social networks graduate course. Book groups, I figured, could work as a naturally occurring setting in which to apply Friedkin's research on interpersonal influence. I provided book group members with copies of *Jarrettsville*, lest they incur financial cost to participate, and perhaps be stuck having purchased a book they did not even like (see Figure 12.1).

Under instruction to not speak with each other about *Jarrettsville* before their group discussions, book group readers filled out a survey about *Jarrettsville*, in addition to a general interpersonal influence survey about their group, adapted from Friedkin's surveys. The data reported through the bulk of chapter 9 are from these pre-discussion surveys. I attended and recorded all book group discussions of *Jarrettsville*, save for two. In those cases, I mailed a box of books, instructions, and a recorder. Immediately following their discussions group members filled out the same survey about *Jarretts-ville* that they had completed prior to the meeting. In addition, they filled out a second influence survey about that particular meeting. The only hic-cup was that some group members balked at completing the first (general) interpersonal influence survey. A few of these respondents shared more spe-cifically that they did not finish that survey because it did not make sense to them; influence in their meetings, they thought, is unstable and is instead dependent on a range of factors: who knows what about the book (i.e., has visited the locale of the story); who recommended it to the group or picked it; who is the group leader for the discussion (in groups that have rotating discussion leaders); or who has an established taste or distaste for the type of novel being read (i.e., if a member complains every time the group reads a potboiler, her opinions might be discounted for potboilers, but be very influential when not reading potboilers).

After group members completed their post-meeting surveys, but before the close of the meeting, as a form of reciprocity (in addition to supplying the books for reading) I would answer any questions they wanted to ask about the creation and production of *Jarrettsville*. While doing so I passed around documents such as the alternative covers for *Jarrettsville* reproduced in chapter 7, and the early visual inspirations for Martha from chapter 2. As might be expected, interesting comparison points or "takes" on *Jarrettsville* often emerged during these post-meeting debriefings, although I did not treat anything said during these debriefs as data, and they were effectively thrown out. Also important is that only in limited cases did I make a point to confirm the veracity of the stories book group members told about their personal lives as they related to relationships and racism, as discussed in chapter 10. In quoting these stories I treat them as cultural data; for the purposes of this research, they are relevant as stories that people shared with each other about their lives.

Last, it should be noted that save for the pre- and post-discussion sur-veys, the bulk of this research draws from inductive design. I thought I was studying production and reception until I began to speak with authors, and realized that they are generally unaware—and sometimes quite gratefully unaware—of the ins and outs of how book publishing works, often even after having published many novels. By asking them about their creative processes, who they talk to about their work, who they share it with, and so on, it became quickly apparent to me that the field of creation is a field unto itself; though authors and editors interact with each other, for the most part they are living in different worlds. Along similar lines, early in my research I had a jarring realization that the fields of creation and reception do not quite align as much as I had assumed. During an interview, an author whose work I very much enjoy gave me a withering look upon hearing which other authors' works I enjoy. What I, as a regular fiction reader two decades or so in the making, thought of as a coherency in my tastes violated something in how he grouped novelists, or saw himself as differing from the other novelists I had named. From reading his novels I thought I had spent time in his world, but that wasn't quite right, and it was probably mostly only his novels that we shared in common.[3] With regard to these types of inductive observations, part of tracking a novel through its creation, production, and reception, I learned, is giving up one's preconceptions and being willing to follow the story wherever it goes.

ACKNOWLEDGMENTS

My uncle Johnny owns an art gallery, and as a child he told me that outsiders to the field are interested in paintings. They, he said with a wink, know so little they have nothing to look at but the art. Experts, he contrasted, want to know about the agents, gallerists, and collectors; those are the people that they're fans of. Having studied book publishing and now also having written my own book, I say with all sincerity that I am a fan of Meagan Levinson, and you should be too. Eric Schwartz, who signed this book before moving on to be Editorial Director at Columbia, also could not be more wonderful. From the perspective of an author, most of the time an editor is a publisher and a publisher is an editor, but that's not always the case. Joseph Dahm, Heather Jones, Meghan Kanabay, Dimitri Karetnikov, Samantha Nader, Amanda Weiss, and Jenny Wolkowicki prove the point, and the attention and care they gave this project cannot be discounted.

There is no conceivable scenario in which this book would exist without Bill Hoynes, who, when I was a directionless twenty-one-year-old, sat me down and told me that if I wanted to I could be a professional sociologist. I had never let myself imagine such a thing. Leonard Nevarez and Josh Gamson sent me to Santa Barbara, where Simonetta Falasca-Zamponi, Noah Friedkin, and John Mohr showed me how. Noah sat knee to knee with me and taught me how to actually write an article. John gave me the confidence and freedom to fail, and never lost his own in me when I did. I went to Paul DiMaggio for a year of finishing school, and what a year it was. In a moment of imposter syndrome that is common to many academics, I had the first panic attack of my life the first time I walked onto the Princeton campus to meet Paul for lunch. He was too kind, and too generous, to let me get away with that crippling fear for long. Anything that I have or will do right in my career was first observed as the "natural" thing to do by one or all of these people.

As Cornelia Nixon told me one day at the Starbucks at the corner of Oxford and Center streets in Berkeley, California, an acknowledgments page must always be inadequate. If you take anything away from this book it is that in the creation, production, and reception of a book there are enough uncredited people to fill another book. In addition to those named above, the following list is limited to those who were kind enough to read and comment on sections of this book, and sometimes the whole book: Shyon Baumann, Jenny Carlson, Hae Yeon Choo, Angèle Christin, Paul DiMaggio, Alison Gerber, Wendy Griswold, Paul Hirsch, Vanina Leschziner, Kathy Liddle, Omar Lizardo, Neda Maghbouleh, Ashley Mears, Dan Menchik, John Mohr, Ann Mullen, Jean-François Nault, Matt Norton, Simone Polillo, Craig Rawlings, Dan Silver, Adam Slez, and Alison Teal. To this too-short list of people without whom this book could not be possible, also included are those who opened their lives, homes, emails, notes, and journals to me, not least of whom was Cornelia Nixon, who shared them all. This is a work of social science, and data are reported as they occurred, yet to the people who gifted me their thoughts and time, on an interpersonal level I do not feign objectivity.

This book also would not have been possible without the people who provided the material and emotional support that allowed for it to take shape. I was able to study Counterpoint and crisscross the country going to book groups because of UCSB's Graduate Research Mentorship Program, and when that money was spent, the University of California Humanities Research Institute kicked in for yet another trip. Klaus Nathaus (then at Bielefeld) and Brian Moeran (then at Copenhagen Business School) allowed for me to have the space and time to figure things out, probably before I even felt deserving of that space and time. Through the Center for the Study of Social Organization at Princeton University I had the time to take what I had figured out and then figure it out again in the structure of a book. To actually write this book took the space and time afforded me by the University of Toronto, and the intellectual and emotional support afforded me by my colleagues. It was not part of Patricia Landolt's job as chair to listen to me kvetch about how awful writing a book is, nor was this anyone else's job. Yet my colleagues at the University of Toronto allowed me to bogart conversations with the minutiae of my unhappiness. It's the same case for friends, both academic and nonacademic. Now on the other side, I owe a lot of people a lot of listening.

Since my daughter Neelu started talking she has heard way too many times that "Daddy has to work." Too many times the sentence was clipped short, and it should have been "Daddy has to work, even though Daddy does not want to work, because Daddy wants to be spending time with you." Neda and I have been together for a decade now, and I still haven't come across a single thing I'd rather do without her. She's the only other person who has read every word of this damn thing multiple times.

If you found this book to be lacking I accept all blame. For any successes in this book, you now have a list of their rightful mothers and fathers. One time over beers after politely listening to me try and fail to explain what my work was about, Neda's friend Ethan said, "Oh, so you study an author's acknowledgments page?" That's quite right. Thanks to him too.

NOTES

CHAPTER 1: INTRODUCTION

1. In the (widely diffused) Indian parable from which the elephant metaphor here is derived, the describers of different elephant parts are blind, or are feeling different parts of the elephant while in the dark. I include this footnote to convey that to study cultural production (for instance) is unequivocally to not be "blind" or "in the dark." Instead, to focus on cultural production in the life cycle of cultural objects is to specialize, and specialization is *incredibly* useful. Yet it is also useful to step back and look at how different areas of specialization do and do not relate to each other.
2. See Kroeber 1919.
3. Although credited to Taylor, the first time this theory appears in print is in Nystrom 1928.
4. On "nothing-but" formulations of the relationship between culture and economy, see Zelizer 2010.
5. See, for instance, Rosenberg and White 1957; "The Triumph of Mass Idols" in Lowenthal 1983; Parsons and White 1960; Lomax 1968.
6. As Peterson (1979) writes, "When American sociologists did look at expressive symbols, it was not because these were presumed to be important but because they made possible an ingenious research strategy. Whether functionalists or Marxists, these researchers posited that culture mirrors society, or some aspect thereof, and so examined [popular culture] . . . in order better to understand the less visible aspects of social relations" (138).
7. See Peterson and Anand 2004: 312.
8. This point was most clearly articulated in Corse 1995; Griswold 1981; Peterson 1990.

9. For early harbingers, see White and White 1965; Hirsch 1972; Stinchcombe 1959; and Lowenthal 1961. For many good cases on the point, see Becker 1982; Bielby and Bielby 1994; Bourdieu 1984; 1993; 1996; Denisoff and Levine 1971; Gamson 1998b; Gitlin 1983; Godart and Mears 2009; Grindstaff 2002; Hall 1980; Hirsch 1972; Griswold 1987b; Jhally and Lewis 1992; Johnston and Baumann 2009; Leschziner 2015; Liebes and Katz 1990; Mears 2011; Negus 2013; Powell 1985; Radway 1984; Rossman 2012; Shively 1992; Thompson 2010.

10. As is always the case with figures, Figure 1.1 one could be further complicated at the expense of readability. By way of example, consumer culture theory approaches fall somewhere in between the "reception" and "consumption" quadrants; work on categories would be out toward the "context" side of the x-axis and above or below it depending on the study; work on artistic careers would be closer to the "production" side of the y-axis, somewhere in the top left quadrant. If you'd like to use this figure to make sense of the structure of this book, I'm going to try to force you to use Figure 1.2 instead, but you can do so as follows: going clockwise, the first (top left) quadrant is mostly covered in chapters 2–4; the next (top right) quadrant is chapters 5–8; the third (bottom right) quadrant shows up in chapter 8 but is most squarely in chapter 9; the last (bottom left) quadrant starts toward the bottom of chapter 9 but is most squarely in chapter 10.

11. As famously written by William Goldman and referenced in Caves 2000, "nobody knows anything" when it comes to knowing if a movie will return on investment or not. Similarly for television, despite efforts to convince advertisers to the contrary, "all hits are flukes" (Bielby and Bielby 1994).

12. "Circumstances," in this sense, being a more casual way to say "inputs" or "facets," such as is this case for the "six facet" model that forms the basic architecture of the production of culture approach (see Peterson and Anand 2004 for review; see also Peterson 1976; Coser 1978; Crane 1992 for earlier formulations of the approach).

13. See Peterson 1994: 184. Peterson here seems to be using "sociology" as a synonym for "empiricism." On the empirical study of culture and meaning in sociology, see Mohr 1994; 1998; Mohr and Duquenne 1997.

14. See Griswold 1987b: 4.

15. For more consumption-oriented work that investigates social boundaries through cultural tastes, see Bryson 1996; Goldberg 2011; Mark 2003; Peterson and Kern 1996; Lamont 1992; Lizardo and Skiles 2016. Here too the question is "what do people do with culture" rather than "what does culture do with people," although for that perspective see Mark 1998, in addition to the references in note 16.

16. On the counterpoint, see Griswold 1993; Lizardo 2006; Long 2004; McDonnell 2010; Rubio and Silva 2013; Schudson 1989; Vaisey and Lizardo 2010.

17. See DiMaggio 1987: 442.

18. As Griswold (1993) suggested, "Connections should be made between the institutional and the reader-response mode of analysis" (464). For the quote in the sentence, see Peterson (2000: 230).

19. See Warde 2015: 129. Of note, there is a similar predicament in media studies, as Rodney Benson (1999) explains: "Media researchers tend to study either the 'objective' processes that generate media messages [i.e., production] or the 'subjective' processes of audience interpretation, but not both" (484).

20. See Griswold 1993: 465. This is not meant to suggest a lack of work on artistic careers and trajectories (e.g., Anheier, Gerhards, and Romo 1995; Craig and Dubois 2010; de Nooy 2002; Ekelund and Börjesson 2002; Giuffre 1999). Rather, the point is simply to suggest that the creative *processes* of authors and other creators have gone comparatively understudied, although see Leschziner 2015 for a notable exception.

21. On the call more generally to move "upstream" see Becker, Faulkner, and Kirshenblatt-Gimblett 2006; on the specific phrasing of "mental and material workshop," see Menger 2006: 62. See also Menger 2014.

22. The exception to this statement is the work on photography by Bourdieu, Boltanski, Castel, Chamboredon, and Schnapper, which on its cover is attributed to Bourdieu (see Bourdieu and Whiteside 1996), and is sometimes listed as "Bourdieu and associates." On the statement, however, see Bourdieu 1984; 1993; 1996. See also Du Gay et al. 1997, which appears only in endnotes not because it is unimportant, but because by modern sociological standards it does not empirically make it all the way to reception, although it certainly does in theory (in both senses). See also Van Rees and Dorleijn 2001.

23. See Griswold 1986; 2000. See also Griswold 1987b; 2004 for more on the "framework" or "accounting device" being used.

24. See Martin (2003) on the history and trajectory of field theory. The three main branches in sociology are Bourdieusian (1993; 1996), the neo-institutional account of DiMaggio and Powell (1983; 1991), and Fligstein and McAdam's strategic action fields (2012). The work of Pierre Bourdieu, as an early importer of field theory to sociology, has most influenced the others. DiMaggio and Powell (1991) see a "natural affinity" between their field theory and Bourdieu's, whereas Fligstein and McAdam cite Bourdieu as a direct influence (38). Although the metaphors are different and in name it is not an offshoot of field theory, Abbott's (2005) "linked ecologies" approach belongs here too. Albeit some meaningful differences, building off from Liu and Emirbayer's (2016: 66) excellent examples, Bourdieu's "positions" are Abbott's "ligations," and in processes Bourdieu's "homologies" are DiMaggio and Powell's "isomorphism" and Abbott's "hinges" or "avatars" (if about people it would be "homologous," "isomorphic," and "alliance").

25. In four steps (and true of all three of the main variants of field theory in sociology): the fields are (1) semiautonomous, meso-level social orders, in which (2) actors have a shared orientation to the field but heterogeneous

self or normative interests within it, which (3) are dependent on their location in field, causing (4) variation in conscious or unconscious efforts to achieve status through the procurement of structural, physical, financial, or symbolic resources. The language here has been slightly tweaked from Childress 2015. The turn of phrase "meso-level social order" is from Fligstein and McAdam's (2012) definition.

26. For relationships between fields, see Benson 1999; Fligstein and McAdam 2012. Also see Eyal (2013), who notes that Bourdieu's field theory is "quite rigorous in applying [a] relational approach" within fields, but "between *fields themselves* . . . it is as if the relational approach stopped short" (158). On that point, for Bourdieu sometimes creation, production, and reception seem to all be occurring in the same field (e.g., Bourdieu 1993: 49), whereas at other times there is a "field of production" and "field of consumption." In these latter cases, due to the rigid homologies in his theory that cause the fields to be mirror images of each other, the conceptualization errs on the side of an overly integrated system that Griswold warns about. Such is the case when the "social characteristics of the audience [are] . . . *perfectly congruent* [with the] characteristics of the authors . . . the works, and the theatrical businesses themselves" (Bourdieu 1993: 84), or when due to their homologous positions writers and publishers are characterized as a "*double personage*" (Bourdieu 1996: 216).

27. See Leschziner and Green (2013).

28. This is not to suggest that there are not "routines" or routine action in fields. Instead, this book recalibrates the balance away from an overemphasis on just routines and routine action, as wonderfully spelled out in Leschziner and Green (2013).

29. Namely, these are social network analysis and symbolic interactionism. For examples, see Becker and Pessin 2006; Bottero and Crossley 2011.

30. One way to know these are different fields is that they have different *nomos*, or fundamental laws, which all fields have (Bourdieu 1997). Further evidence for these being different fields is that the "rules of the game" vary across them (Bourdieu and Wacquant 1992: 232). Likewise, to be in a field is to "have a sense of what others are doing" in the field (Fligstein and McAdam 2012: 4), which, save for those who shepherd books across fields, is most typically *not* the case across the fields of creation, production, and reception.

31. These are the fundamental laws discussed in note 30.

32. Getting "inside" is in reference to Gitlin's (1983) study of *Hill Street Blues*, titled *Inside Prime Time*.

33. "To watch a book be born" is an allusion to Keith Gessen's detailed reportage on the creation and production of Chad Harbach's *The Art of Fielding*, first published in *Vanity Fair* under the title "The Book on Publishing," and then released in expanded version as a Kindle Single under the title *How a Book Is Born* (see Gessen 2011).

34. "From start to finish" here, as well as throughout, is a turn of phrase in reference to Becker, Faulkner, and Kirshenblatt-Gimblett's (2006) *Art from Start to Finish*.

CHAPTER 2: THE STRUCTURE OF CREATIVITY

1. Draugsvold 2000: 86.
2. See Adler and Adler 2003.
3. As Heinich (1997) writes of "writing what you know" being viewed as a mark of artistic authenticity, for artists there is a homologous "personalization of the object . . . [and] symmetrical objectification of the artist as a person" (115). See also Bourdieu (1993) on Flaubert: "the work of formalization [through writing] gave the writer the opportunity to work on himself and thereby allowed him to objectify not only the positions in the field and their occupants he opposed, but also, through the space that included him, his own position" (207).
4. In sociology, this is mostly thanks to Howard Becker. See Becker 1974; 1982.
5. See Baker and Faulkner (1991) on the upsides of these role specializations. See Baumann (2007b) on the rise of the director as the authorial voice of a film. Interestingly, for television, as directors are swapped in and out across episodes, the director is more like "support personnel" in Becker's formulation, and it is the showrunner who is treated as the authorial voice. On the rise of the showrunner, see the very good insider accounts in Martin (2013) or the discussions of Lorne Michaels in Shales and Miller (2008). Interestingly, for television, it is also sometimes the network executive who is treated as the "visionary" of the endeavor, as is the case in Salkin (2013) for the Food Network and Klickstein (2013) for Nickelodeon.
6. See Faulkner and Becker 2009; de Laat 2015.
7. On the "writer who writes alone" formulation, see Brodkey 1987: 55–59.
8. This characterization fuses what Anheier and Gerhards (1991) refer to as the two component elements that make up the myth of authors: the writer as *homo singularis* and the writer as *prophet and genius* (813–814).
9. Hargadon and Bechky 2006: 484.
10. See Gross 2009: xv.
11. Kurtzberg and Amabile 2001: 285.
12. See Farrell 2003.
13. Rather than positioning themselves and others in the field of creation depending on "failure" or "success" in these companion fields, in the field of creation novelists position themselves and others along different matrices: the "deservedness" of success, or the "art"-based metric of positioning, rather than one based on financial or popular success. This harkens back to Stebbins's (1968) work on group formation in jazz communities, in which musicians sort and group with each other on the basis of perceived artistic

ability rather than economic returns or viability. Although treated by Stebbins as a "special theory" of jazz, it is also true of novelists in the field of creation, and may more broadly be true across different fields of creation in the arts.

14. As the novelist Brad Leithauser has written, "you know you're *really* fond of somebody when his or her books make you almost as nervous as your own" (see Leithauser 2013).

15. See Childress and Gerber 2015.

16. See Harbach 2014.

17. The rise of creative writing programs, as discussed in chapter 3, may have done more than anything to increase the social capital and enlarge the social circles of novelists in the past forty years. See Kingston and Cole 1986; Frenette and Tepper 2016. See also Anheier, Gerhards, and Romo 1995 on the social networks and resultant "social topography" of writers.

18. This is what Harrison and Rouse (2014) describe as "elastic coordination" in their study of the creative processes of modern dancers.

CHAPTER 3: AUTHORIAL CAREERS

1. See Trollope 1883: 245.

2. See Zelizer 2010 for the multiplex, relational nature of everyday economic transactions, and the variable meanings drawn out of them. See also Wherry 2014 on the role of meanings in particular.

3. See Bourdieu 1993: 40. Rather than just being about money, this interest in disinterestedness can cover a wide swath of cultural terrain, and even fandom itself (see Friedman 2014).

4. See Lee 1961.

5. See Bauer 2015.

6. As documented by Tuchman and Fortin (1984), with the realization that money could be made through writing novels in the mid-eighteenth century, men began to write more novels, and over time "edged women out" of the English literary tradition.

7. See Gessen 2014: 314.

8. The NEA reports median incomes for "writers and authors" inclusive of advertising writers, authors, biographers, copywriters, crossword-puzzle creators, film writers, magazine writers, novelists, playwrights, sports writers, and lyricists. Of writers by this definition, 84 percent hold a bachelor's degree or higher, and the median income is $42,074. There is not, unfortunately, good data that disaggregates beyond these very different writerly occupations.

9. See Kingston and Cole (1986) for the most complete, albeit now out of date, social scientific work on writers' income. On the point of definition, Bourdieu (1993) argues that "every literary field is the site of struggle over the definition of the writer," and that "every survey aimed at establishing the hierarchy of writers predetermines the hierarchy by determining the popula-

tion deemed worthy of helping to establish it." Given this predicament, "the *boundary* of the field is a stake of struggles, and the social scientist's task is not to draw a dividing-line between agents involved in it, by imposing so-called operational definitions" (42). One way around Bourdieu's concern may be the usage of respondent-driven sampling (Heckathorn 2002). See Heckathorn and Jeffri (2001) for jazz musicians across four cities; see Jeffri, Heckathorn, and Spiller (2011) for visual artists in New York City. See Salganik and Heckathorn (2004) more generally, although see Salganik (2006) and Goel and Salganik (2010) for questions and limitations of the method. Griswold (2000) defines being a Nigerian novelist as being Nigerian and having published a novel, finding the existence of several hundred Nigerian novelists across several decades. This is both an appropriate and a pragmatic definition for her case and research question.

10. See Gerber 2017. As suggested throughout this chapter, the latter, more holistic view, unlike the "object-centered" view, allows us to explain how the vast majority of novelists can actually *afford* to be novelists.
11. See Thompson 2010.
12. See Caves 2000; Merton 1968; Rosen 1981.
13. See Moeran 2003. See also Rawlings 2001.
14. On about one-third of revenue, see Purdum 2015; on sixteen members of the team, see Swanson 2016.
15. See Mahler 2010.
16. See Alter 2016. For the romance novels in the series, rather than listing an author, the novellas will rely on a "James Patterson Presents" imprimatur.
17. In order, see Kellner 2002; Maslin 2004; Mozes 2010.
18. See Colacello 1990: 208.
19. See Kellner 2002.
20. See McDowell 1984.
21. See Siddique 2013. While for name-economy authors it can be wonderful to publish without hype or expectation, this does, of course, assume that their work would be published without hype or expectation, as Lessing's experiment showed. Such was also the case in 1975 when as an experiment a writer resubmitted Jerzy Kosinski's National Book Award–winning short story collection *Steps* to fourteen publishers and thirteen literary agents under the penname Erik Demos. All the agents and publishers, including *Steps'* original publisher Random House, rejected the manuscript.
22. See Bosman 2012.
23. See Shank 2012.
24. See Trachtenberg 2010.
25. See Caves 2000 on the "nobody knows anything" principle. See also Salganik, Dodds, and Watts 2006; Salganik and Watts 2008 for an exceedingly clever experimental design showing why this is the case.
26. See Oshinsky 2007.

27. See Leong 2010.
28. See chapter 6 for a more extended discussion of this system.
29. See Stolls 2008: 5–6.
30. See Semonche 2007: 83.
31. In a 2010 interview, Charles Plymell makes reference to Allen Ginsberg's "VW [bus that the] Guggenheim bought him" (see Blaine 2010).
32. See McGurl (2009: 24). On reasons for student attendance in MFA programs, despite financial costs, see Childress and Gerber 2015. On self-reported skills obtained, satisfaction, and job outcomes for MFA holders (which are certainly not as dour as is sometimes assumed), see Frenette and Tepper 2016.
33. Under the NEA's definition of writers, 57 percent are women, compared to 46 percent for all artists. Even compared to all artists, writers under the NEA's definition are disproportionately white, with only 13 percent being nonwhite, as compared to 20 percent of all artists and 32 percent of the total labor force (see NEA 2011: 8–11).
34. See Harbach 2014: 12.
35. Although the term "self-publishing" is used throughout this section, see chapter 8 on the distinction between *invested exclusivity* and *uninvested inclusivity* publishing models, the latter of which so-called "self-publishing" falls under. The term "self-publishing" makes sense insofar as we are discussing who is taking on the financial risks, but generally it is more clear to avoid referring to a particular publishing model using a phrase that suggests its nonexistence.
36. See Cornford and Lewis 2012.
37. See Dale 2016.
38. See Weinberg 2014.
39. See Puzo 1972: 34.
40. See Puzo 1972: 33.
41. In 2015 dollars, by Puzo's estimate, after receiving his advance for *The Godfather*, over a couple decades or so he had earned about $75,000 from book writing and had about $130,000 in debts.
42. See Puzo 1972: 41.
43. This and subsequent amounts in this paragraph are in 2015 dollars.

CHAPTER 4: LITERARY AGENTS AND DOUBLE DUTIES

1. See Kakutani 1991.
2. While Reynold's agency is generally believed to be the first in the United States, literary agents in the United Kingdom likely predated it. In November 1893, the same year that Reynold's founded his agency, in the *Athenaeum*, the English publisher William Heinemann dismissed literary agents as "parasites" in a tongue-in-cheek explanation of how to grow one's business as a literary agent. Thompson (2010) hypothesizes that Heinemann's disdain

was likely being directed at A. P. Watt, widely believed to be the first literary agent.

3. See Zelizer 2010; for editors in particular in this formulation, see Galassi 1980.
4. See de Bellaigue 2008.
5. See Thompson 2010: 58–99.
6. See Arnold 1999.
7. See Coser, Kadushin, and Powell 1982.
8. Notable exceptions to this general rule about size are William Morris and ICM Partners, which both have literary divisions, but are top global agencies for talent across many creative industries.
9. In this way, the consolidation of literary agents into agencies is somewhat like a more formalized version of competitive poker players who buy stakes in each other's winnings.
10. See Reynolds 1966: 113.
11. Rather than being particular to the transition between these two particular fields, in creative industries in which generally unregulated intermediaries negotiate the passageways between "talent" and "producers," scammers are a problem (see Mears 2011). The existence of scammers in these roles is evidence of "talent" and "producers" occupying different fields, as it is the "talent's" unawareness of the rules of the game in the field of production on which scammers thrive. In this way "scammer" is a predictable structural position resulting from cross-field arrangements.
12. The Science Fiction & Fantasy Writers of America offers the most comprehensive list of predatory practices on its "Writer Beware" blog and website, which can be accessed at http://www.sfwa.org/other-resources/for-authors/writer-beware/.
13. The "about two-thirds" figure (65.3 percent) is derived from a database of literary agents in the United States constructed by the author. Job history was obtained from public data available on LinkedIn.com, in which 56 percent of all agents in the database had reported prior work experiences.
14. The AAR was formed in 1991 through the merger of the Society of Authors' Representatives (founded in 1928) and the Independent Literary Agents Association (founded in 1977).
15. The AAR Canon of Ethics can be found at http://aaronline.org/canon.
16. See Bourne 2012.
17. See Bourne 2012.
18. Do new generations of literary fiction writers disproportionately come from MFA programs in creative writing because these people have self-selected into them, or because the people in them are simply more "searchable" given the strategies that literary agents employ to find young authors? There are no reliable data on this question, but it's likely a bit of both.
19. On the underemphasized role of emotional connection to cultural objects, see Benzecry 2011.

20. See Ferrari-Adler 2009.
21. See Rivera 2012. See also Lamont, Beljean, and Clair 2014.
22. In the language of networks, this would be the case of status homophily (e.g., race and gender) being either confused or correctly identified as a stand-in for values homophily.
23. See Lee 2013.
24. Aragi is legally classified as white in the United States, although due to her Lebanese background is more generally treated as nonwhite (see Maghbouleh 2017).
25. An intense informal pressure to network is common across media industries (see Hesmondhalgh and Baker 2010), and it is possible that the "three martinis" were used to make the obligation of networking more pleasurable. Through this lens the expense account of the publishing industry as an incentive to network is the inverse of the on-site free meals, dry cleaning, and so on of the tech industry: one with perks that incentivize interaction *between* organizations without proprietary concerns, and the other with perks that incentivize interactions *within* organizations with proprietary concerns.
26. The email reports agency-to-publisher sales on a five-point monetary scale along with names of the selling agent, purchasing editor, and author and the genre designation of the book along with a brief description of it.
27. On the relational work accomplished in trade association journals and magazines more broadly, see Spillman 2012.

CHAPTER 5: DECISION MAKING, TASTE, AND FINANCIAL COMMITMENT TO CULTURE

1. See Zelizer 2010: 153.
2. See Gologorsky 2000.
3. See Aronson 1993: 13.
4. See Hirsch 1972.
5. See Aronson 1993: 15.
6. See Hardwick 2000.
7. See Donald 2002: 376–377.
8. See Aronson 1993: 11.
9. See Aronson 1993: 16.
10. This is for two reasons. First, in exposure to new or unknown objects (and particularly those like books that take a long time commitment to familiarize oneself with and evaluate) categorical comparison is a useful shorthand to signal what things are. Second, there is an oversupply problem in these field transitions: most written books won't be published, just as most published books won't be widely read. For this reason categorical comparison winnows the oversupply down to categories of books that would be considered in the first place.

11. Although not on books, on the basic point, see Zuckerman 1999.
12. In contrast to Baker and Faulkner's (1991) findings regarding role separation in Hollywood, in this example overlapping artistic and commercial roles (i.e., "double duties") are mitigated as both concerns are handled by dyadic pairs on opposite sides of the table, rather than both being held by a single individual.
13. See Sale 1993: 269.
14. This sentence is Paul DiMaggio's phrasing, which was used to summarize the point in response to an earlier draft. Credit for clarity and brevity goes to him.
15. These causes include: (1) the reliance on preexisting social networks to hire new entrants in the field, (2) the reliance on a protégé/mentorship model, which can reproduce existing demographic patterns, (3) low or nonexistent starting salaries, which restrict barriers to entry, (4) what one respondent referred to as a "passable production" of nonwhite authors, which insulates the industry from criticism, (5) unclear skills demands and no formal credentialing process, which can cause other implicit biases to slip into evaluations of "potential."
16. According to the 2014 *Publishers Weekly* Salary Survey, three-quarters of editors at publishing houses agree with the statement "the publishing industry suffers from a lack of racial diversity," with only 5 percent in disagreement.
17. See Wade 1993: 74.
18. See Powell 1985.
19. See Donadio 2006.
20. See Schuster 1993: 23.
21. Save for publishing name-economy authors, publishers' usage of numerical data for forecasting purposes is best described by the Carnegie School approach to organizational behavior: editors have choices about which books to publish, and then look for ways to validate their feelings by drumming up problems or solutions using numbers (see Cohen, March, and Olsen 1972).
22. The use of storytelling in this quote serves as a good empirical example of Beckert's (2013) discussion of "fictional expectations" and how they can be used to motivate action (in this case, deciding to publish a book).
23. On predicting "hits" being a signal of poor judgment, see Denrell and Fang 2010.
24. In this way lists of comparable titles in book publishing are quite different from a real estate agent's construction of "comparable" properties (also referred to as "comps") when estimating the value of a property. For a real estate agent the goal is numerical accuracy, whereas for an editor or publisher the goal is to tell a numerical story about sales, regardless of if they will be ultimately achieved or not.
25. See Walker 1993: 264.
26. See Hochschild 1983; for broader review, see Steinberg and Figart 1999.

27. See Jackall 1988.
28. For a more relational approach (such as suggested here) to emotions in economic exchange and organizational settings, see Bandelj (2009) and Rivera (2015). See also Collins (2004), whose perspective particularly informs the latter, which is probably the closest corollary example to the explanation offered in this section. That said, emotions as a form of capital, as discussed in Reay (2000), are more about having the emotional reserves to deal with trying situations than is implied in the usage of the term here. In this case, rather than moderating one's emotions being a tool to deal with difficult situations, the idea here is that emotions are a useful tool to *generate* preferred situations. To be clear, the goal is not to introduce a "new" form of Bourdieusian capital (which is particularly the case for one that has already been introduced), but rather to suggest that editors' usage of enthusiasm fits within a broader Bourdieusian framework of capital exchange. Also worth saying is that despite the general truth of this, editors (and agents, for that matter) perform emotional labor too. Most frequently this is with authors and is about managing their expectations and demands once their books have traveled into a field they don't understand.
29. See Curran 2011: 177.
30. See DiMaggio 1977 on the "pure brokerage" style of administration under which editors operate in trade publishing.
31. "Writing quality" can be considered as a distinct subset of evaluative statements that may or may not build up into more global evaluations of "literary quality." For instance, for an editor a novel can be beautifully written but still more "plot-based" than "character-based," thus having a high quality of writing but still lacking literary quality. This is also the case for "capturing the time period" versus broader characterizations of how the work fits into the "historical fiction genre," in which a work can fail as historical fiction because the author too obsessively captures the time period at the expense of the story, or because the author fails to capture the time period enough to tell a credible story. Alternately, a work can also be evaluated as a piece of historical fiction *independent* of historical accuracy (e.g., saturation of the historical fiction market, the editor does not have a taste for historical fiction, the story is not captivating enough to sustain a work of historical fiction, etc.).

CHAPTER 6: INDUSTRY STRUCTURE AND THE POSITION AND DISPOSITION OF PUBLISHERS

1. For a theoretical overview of research on categories in organizational sociology, see Negro, Koçak, and Hsu 2010. On genre classifications, see also DiMaggio 1987; Lena 2012.
2. See Parker 2002. More generally on the history of Farrar, Straus and Giroux, see Kachka 2013.

3. See Parker 2002.
4. See Woll 2002. See also Thompson (2010: 221–222) on the retail revolution and declining significance of the backlist. While Thompson notes that Amazon may have changed the match of this back a bit, the pendulum may be swinging even further back to the backlist with the growth of the eBook market, as keeping a book "in print" no longer requires the capital expenditure it used to.
5. See Thompson 2010.
6. On this point in the Hollywood film industry, see Rossman and Schilke 2014. See also Elberse 2013: 42. While Elberse is looking at a single season of Grand Central's publishing list in which none of the would-be hits dramatically flopped, the imprint is taking a diversified strategy, and hoping that over time some of their low-cost books will generate slow and steady sales over the long term (or even better, one might become a surprise hit with a return on investment that cannot be matched even by would-be hits that do hit).
7. See Donadio 2006.
8. Bourdieu differentiates between these types of books as "the bestsellers with no tomorrow" versus the "classics" that live on through educational adoption. The difference here is that between these books, Bourdieu writes, "the opposition is total," whereas these types of books are dependent on each other not only for definition by negation, but also for a publisher's survival (see Bourdieu 1996: 147).
9. See DiMaggio and Powell 1983; White 1992.
10. A book "too good not to publish" is not only a mark of quality of the book under question, but also a status claim. It is to say "I, as someone who cares and feels deeply about books, am the sort to publish the unpublishable out of adoration and love."
11. Rather than coming from my fieldwork, this anecdote was shared with me by Paul DiMaggio, who also noted that in the 1976 Mel Brooks film *Silent Movie*, Gulf and Western was satirized as Engulf and Devour for their takeover of Paramount Pictures.
12. To be fair Bourdieu (1980: 262) acknowledges the existence of blended publishing strategies, but seems to treat the general rules as exceptional cases (e.g., it is " 'great' publishers which combine economic prudence . . . with intellectual daring," and Lindon is an exceptional case for publishing books he likes while staying in business). This may be due to fundamental differences between the French and US literary fields, or may be due to Bourdieu reconciling what he knows about publishers with his broader theory of how cultural fields are structured (i.e., as long as the cases remain exceptional, a balancing of artistic passion and financial prudence at the organization level does not impinge on a polarized conception of fields).
13. See Thompson 2010.
14. See Greco 2005.

15. The two waves of conglomeration in book publishing are most adroitly sum-marized and discussed in Thompson 2010. Although this is also a topic of dis-cussion in my own data collection, in this section I lean heavily on Thompson's exquisite account. See also Thornton 2004 for the case of higher education publishing.

16. On "open systems," see Lopes 1992, which Thompson 2010 refers to as a "federal" model in reference to book publishing. See also Dowd 2004 on the same point.

17. See Peterson and Berger 1975, for which Lopes 1992 and Dowd 2004 are rejoinders.

18. For this type of resource partitioning (a subset class of niche differentiation) in other cultural markets, see Carroll and Swaminathan 2000 (on beer) and Boone, Van Witteloostuijn, and Carroll 2002 (on newspapers).

19. For Bourdieu, as part of their *habitus*, people have dispositions both to some objects over others and to some actions over others in particular situations. Book publishers (or publishing imprints), it is argued here, also have dispo-sitions that outlast the individuals who enact them. Schocken Books, for in-stance, has and will continue to publish books on Jewish-themed topics re-gardless of who is actually making the publishing decisions. Most typically editors and publishers seek to "match" the disposition of the press with the disposition of the editor so that one need not take primacy over the other. As those matches aren't always perfect, sometimes the tactic is to find some-one with the know-how or reputation to work on books that fit the publish-er's disposition, while also giving the editor leeway to pursue a tract that interests her, provided that it doesn't invalidate what the publisher is already doing (e.g., for sociology, Princeton University Press is known for doing books that crosscut culture, economy, and organization, and depending on the editor, the press might also build a focus on ethnography, gender, social movements, and so on). On the idea that publishers in the field are arrayed in relational space, see Bourdieu 2008.

CHAPTER 7: STORYTELLING AND MYTHMAKING

1. These emails have been reproduced with permission from both parties.

2. Despite usage of the word, "lead" title does not always mean only a single title. More often an imprint or publisher might have a lead fiction and a lead nonfiction title, or several, in which case a book would be described as "one of our lead titles."

3. See Hirsch 1972.

4. See Dyckhoff 2001.

5. See Siegel 2004. The second half of Siegel's sentence is more biting, and is "regardless of whether anyone besides your mother and your cat knows who you are." It is relegated to a note here because while it's an accurate bit of

sarcasm for the fields of production and reception, in the field of creation, which is the field to which the Ettlinger signal is being sent, it is a useful piece of symbolic capital through which to signal who you are or where in the field you are aspiring to, particularly to those who do not already know.

6. This might be seen as somewhat reckless or dangerous behavior by a young and new editor like Krefman, but it was motivated by the same thing that made him *good at his job*: he was advocating for his book and his vision for it. More generally, as discussed later in this chapter, part of what was happening in this instance was that as a young editor Krefman was struggling with the increasing interest in *Jarrettsville* within Counterpoint, and his resultant loss of control over the project. At McSweeney's, where he attained his entrance into book publishing through an internship, the system was atypical in that the editor maintained full control and final say over decisions at every step of the publishing process. To first publish in "POB" was very much a McSweeney's thing to do, just as to first publish in PBO was quickly becoming a Counterpoint thing to do. As discussed in chapter 5, Krefman's dispositional sensibility about books in this case didn't match his position at Counterpoint (and concomitantly Counterpoint's dispositional sensibility as a press), and he ultimately did what many editors do in these types of situations: when later a position opened at McSweeney's, he took it and left Counterpoint.

7. In media industries this is known as "windowing." See also Franssen and Velthuis (2016) on hardcover pricing.

8. Although in his publishing tastes Shoemaker had a strong preference for the artistic (and sometimes esoteric), he also had a strong populist streak, and more generally believed that once books of artistic merit were published, it only made sense to package them in ways that might appeal to readers.

9. The outlier to the upper left of the graph in Figure 7.3, which received a lot of discussion time despite low projected initial sell-in, also made sense: it was a novel for which the movie rights had been optioned and that already had major stars attached but was not yet in production. As such, it was a more long-term bet, and worth a comparatively lot of talk, even if the sell-in would be coming much later, after the film was hopefully released.

CHAPTER 8: RETAILERS AND REVIEWERS

1. If there had been regular readers allowed at the event, "let the locusts descend" could have had an unflattering edge to it, but as only insiders were present and the statement was made by an insider, it was a "we are locusts" joke rather than a "they are locusts" joke.

2. On field-configuring events in cultural arenas, see Anand and Jones 2008; Moeran and Pedersen 2011.

3. See also Franssen and Kuipers (2013) for how publishers' catalogs are used in selecting titles for international rights.

4. Secondary texts are those *about* texts (or "primary" texts). Think of a book review, a jacket synopsis, a reader report, or an agent's summary in submission; these are all writings *about* the thing rather than the thing itself. Secondary texts rise to prominence in field transitions, and tend to recede from prominence once texts are safely embedded within fields. See Fiske 1987.

5. See Clines 2016.

6. On resource space and specialization, see Carroll and Swaminathan 2000.

7. Part of the logic here is a financial one: if a publisher can ride the wave and keep the book in stock, there is a high return on investment for surprise hits, as the associated costs of advances, publicity, and marketing are low. If the advance and promotional costs are high, rather than holding out hope for a surprise hit, there can be nervousness that the book "better be" a hit.

8. Unlike major publishers, which are all located in New York, "focal" independent bookstores are spread out across the country because readers are also diffuse. As the theory goes, if Prairie Lights gets behind a book, other independent presses in the Midwest will be reactive to Prairie Light's position, just as other independent bookstores in the mid-Atlantic may be reactive to Politics and Prose's position. That Prairie Lights is a block away from the University of Iowa, home to the country's most prestigious MFA program in creative writing, also helps.

9. Being evoked here is Rossman (2014) on gift exchange in obfuscatory relational work. As the chapter progress, the reader might also note that the gift exchange between independent bookstores and publishers becomes something more akin to payola with chain stores, which evolves into something closer to blackmail with Amazon. In Rossman (2012) the processual nature of these relationships (between radio stations and record labels) is cyclical over time and describes the industry as a whole, whereas here, at least to date, the relationships differ based on type of trading partner and over time have been more stable. More generally, legality and government intervention drive Rossman's cycles, whereas in this case there's sometimes a more straightforward transactional story about who has the coordinated power in the exchange to demand what.

10. Although she has nowhere near the buying power of Hensley, Pennie Clark Ianniciello, the book buyer for Costco, plays a similar role. Clark Ianniciello, like Hensley for Barnes & Noble, makes the books at Costco stand out from those at other "big box" retailers, as while Costco is reactive to consumer demand (i.e., only filling its shelves with hits), because of Clark Ianniciello, Costco sometimes *creates* hits: "She has an uncanny knack for leading customers to buy books, for molding their taste," then director of distributor sales for HarperCollins, Jeff Rogart, once commented (Batchelor 2008: 167).

11. See Miller 2009.

12. See Brown and Wiley 2011.

13. Due to the fights between publishers and department stores in the first half of the twentieth century, "agency pricing" is legal, although in the early 2010s Apple and the "big five" publishers were found by the Department of Justice to be guilty of price fixing, as the publishers had coordinated (through Apple) in their adoption of an agency pricing model.

14. In generating revenue out of authors' pockets for assorted services in an *uninvested inclusivity* model, Amazon is like "vanity presses" of days past, but unlike the old vanity press model (and what makes Amazon more than just a vanity press) is that Amazon can actually offer distribution, so there's the, albeit small, chance of real success for authors who do not already have followings. As is always the case in these types of scenarios, however, the same few occasional success stories are routinely trotted out in a way that tries to evade (but at the same time undergirds) the exceptionality of these cases. One imagines that if the modal self-published author through Amazon was having success, Amazon would release these numbers, which the company has not. As a result it is unknown if the modal self-published author on Amazon is making gains or taking losses through payment for services, although both scenarios are feasible (see chapter 3).

15. See Stone 2013: 242.

16. See Ghose, Smith, and Telang 2006.

17. See Lumenello 2007: 4.

18. See Sullivan 2015.

19. On work in this tradition, see Ahlkvist and Faulkner 2002; Rossman 2012; Shrum 1991.

20. As Bourdieu writes, "Every critic declares not only his judgement of the work, but also his claim to the right to talk about it and judge it" (Bourdieu 1993: 36). For work in this tradition, see also Baumann 2007b; Janssen 1997; Van Rees 1987; Verboord 2010.

21. See Janssen 1998.

22. See Hardwick 1959: 138.

23. See Lumenello 2007: 4.

24. *Omertà* is a masculinist Southern Italian code of honor, most frequently associated with the Sicilian Mafia. The code consists of three parts: (1) not interfering with others' actions, (2) not reporting on others' malfeasance to authorities, and (3) maintaining silence about others' doings, and particularly wrongdoings.

25. In particular, see the closing two paragraphs of Foreman 2012.

26. See Rich 2009.

27. Consider, for instance, the evaluative and condemnatory first two words of the anonymous *Kirkus* review for David Egger's debut book, *A Heartbreaking Work of Staggering Genius*, which simply stated, "It isn't." This is in direct contrast to the non-anonymized rules of engagement in the field of creation,

which Adelle Waldman (2003) describes as "find something positive to say, and proceed gently from there."

28. See Goodheart 2009.

29. Also a factor was that Borders was on the downswing. The company declared bankruptcy in the United Kingdom and started closing UK stores just a month after *Jarrettsville*'s release, and then declared bankruptcy in the United States about fifteen months later. Although often attributed to Amazon, Borders' inability to outlast Barnes & Noble was fourfold: (1) in the early days its edge was its back-end distribution system, which over time became a hindrance due to a lack of updating (i.e., a first mover problem in the space), (2) Borders had competed with Barnes by having stores with even larger footprints, making them particularly susceptible to damage in the 2008 economic downturn, (3) the company made a series of bad bets, dedicating much of its stores' floor space to CD sales as that market declined and then to DVD sales as that market declined, and (4) rather than deducing the growing importance of controlling online bookselling, Borders contracted that wing of its operations out to Amazon.

30. These figures are for 2009–2010, as reported by BookScan, which captures an estimated 85 percent of all US book sales. In rank order, sales per one million residents by region using 2010 census data are 33.1 for the South Atlantic, 22.3 Mountain, 17.9 Northeast, 12.8 Pacific, 8.3 Middle Atlantic, 7.8 West North Central, 6.8 East North Central, and 3.7 South Central.

CHAPTER 9: READING LIFE INTO NOVELS

1. See Goolrick 2009.

2. See Anonymous 2009a.

3. See Anonymous 2009b.

4. See Taylor 2009.

5. See Goodheart 2009.

6. Although this is a point that has been empirically proven many times over, for a few classics in the genre, see Bryson 1996; Griswold 1987a; Liebes and Katz 1990; Shively 1992.

7. Textual constraints, through the framework of author's intentions, were expressly dismissed in the poststructuralist literary tradition (see Barthes 1974; Fish 1980; Foucault 2002). Did sociologists believe this? Either way, scholars of reception and consumption have been focused on questions that have not necessitated an answer: How do consumers use cultural objects to make boundaries or signal statuses, and how do the structural positions of readers affect the ways they read and the meanings they draw out of cultural objects?

8. See Griswold 1993, emphasis added.

9. See Escarpit 1971: 83.

10. See Manguel 2014.
11. See Butler 2011.
12. Results differ from those of Childress and Friedkin (2012) due to (1) additional survey responses outside of the framework of that article (i.e., readers not in book groups, etc.), and (2) an incorporation of more survey dimensions as they relate to the broader discussions in this chapter versus the narrower discussion of that work. See the methodological appendix and Childress and Friedkin (2012) for more detail on survey design and differences between these works.
13. For all correlations relayed throughout this chapter, $p < .05$.
14. See Griswold and Wright (2004).
15. These eleven genres were action, fantasy, historical, horror, literary, mystery, popular, romance, sci-fi, thriller, and young adult.
16. On the reading class, see Griswold 2008.
17. Genre is based on the standardized summated divergence from Nixon's intentions across the four genre designations for *Jarrettsville* surveyed (coef. = -6.23, $SE = 1.51$, $p < .001$). Interpretation is based on the standardized summated divergence from Nixon's intentions across all interpretive variables surveyed net of genre designations (coef. = -8.35, $SE = 1.48$, $p < .001$). The negative coefficients signal an inverse relationship between diverging from Nixon's intentions and liking *Jarrettsville*.
18. See Zerubavel 2009 on lenses.
19. See Griswold 2008: 161.
20. See Daniels 2002. On book groups in the United States, see Long 2003, and on those in the United Kingdom, see Hartley 2001. On the Book of the Month Club, see Radway 1997. On One Book programs, see Griswold and Wohl 2015.
21. Readers used the terms "book group" and "book club" interchangeably. Throughout this section the word "group" is used to describe the small and informal to quasi-formal gatherings under discussion.
22. For two book groups in California, Southern-style food was purposefully cooked and shared in accordance with reading *Jarrettsville*. A book group of men in Massachusetts discussed *Jarrettsville* while drinking beer and eating pizza; a group of men in San Francisco discussed the novel while eating a home-cooked meal provided by the host and his partner around a formally set dining room table; others just had light snacks, and others still had only wine. For book groups meeting at a local bookstore, a coffee shop, a religious community center, and a library, food and drink were not constitutive parts of the gatherings. More generally, among the twenty-one book groups that participated in the study, groups that met during the day included light snacks at most and groups that met during the night included light snacks at least.
23. The convivially raucous and tipsy character of some book groups was best expressed by a group member who, deep into a loud and consistently

overlapping conversation about *Jarrettsville*, shouted out, "Everyone shut up because I need to say something, and I'm drunk, and this is important." Her group mates laughed and granted her the stage.

24. See Long 2003: 187.
25. See Childress and Friedkin 2012.
26. This would also be the result of a book group in which the given interpretive dimension was discussed but none of the discussants were influenced by each other.

CHAPTER 10: READING NOVELS INTO LIFE

1. See Gamson 1998a.
2. Being "good to read" versus "good to think with" is evoking Lévi-Strauss's (1963) discussion of totems, and animals being not just "good to eat" but also "good to think with" (89). In turn, "good to communicate with" is an evocation of Douglas (1972).
3. Fine (1979) defines idioculture as "a system of knowledge, beliefs, behaviors, and customs shared by members of an interacting group to which members can refer and employ as the basis of further interaction" (734).
4. As found by Bonilla-Silva (2006), middle- and upper-class white Americans—such as those who made up the book groups who read *Jarrettsville*—can become atypically inarticulate when discussing topics of race and racism. Such was overwhelmingly not the case for the *Jarrettsville* book groups. Had they been purposefully convened to talk about race and racism, perhaps they would have been less articulate and shared less. But, often in the privacy of their own homes, they had gathered to talk about a novel, which served as the gateway to frank, coherent, and oftentimes revealing discussions.
5. On the racialized distinction between Coke and Pepsi in the first half of the twentieth century, see Capparell 2007.
6. See López and López 2009: 68.
7. Sandy Sherman is a pseudonym. The real Sandy Sherman read this section prior to publication and gave approval for its inclusion.

CHAPTER 11: CONCLUSION

1. See Gross 2015.
2. See Milliot 2016.
3. "Perfectly mirrored fields" is in reference to Bourdieu's "homology" between the fields of production and consumption, as he views the homology between writers, publishers, and readers as being "perfectly congruent" (Bourdieu 1980: 269). The congruency is so perfect for him that writers and their publishers are a "double personage," or structurally what amounts to the same person in two different places and bodies at once (Bourdieu 1996:

216). For rhetorical effect Bourdieu calls this a "coincidence so miraculous" (Bourdieu 1996: 162), and even argues that every work of art that does not find its corresponding "natural place" in the field of production is "doomed to failure" in the field of consumption (1996: 165). This is Bourdieu, theorizing without data, at his most mechanistic. Despite the theorizing, back out in the world the randomness of success for cultural objects as they transition into new fields—all operating according to their own arrangements and principles (see Salganik, Dodds, and Watts 2006 for the case of reception)—is too high to take these types of statements seriously. As all producers know, you can do everything right and still be doomed to failure, just as those who may seem structurally doomed to failure (i.e., a "nobody" publisher publishing something it has no experience with and little expectations for) can and often do have surprise hits. See also failures that at a later date become successes, such as *Lord of the Flies*, as discussed in chapter 3, or *Moby-Dick* (see Barker-Nunn and Fine 1998). More generally, the issue here is that if production and consumption perfectly mirror each other, this impinges on most everything else that would make studying either of them interesting.

4. See Benson 1999 for an exception. For Bourdieu, fields are nested in other fields, which are sometimes overlapped by the "field of power." Like Eyal (2013), I do not find this formulation convincing. The idea of a field is itself a bit of an abstraction. Unlike, say, the gastronomic field or the literary field, the field of power is an abstraction built on top of an abstraction. Power, according to the argument here, is a *dynamic* that operates internally *within* fields (i.e., they have power over us), or operates relationally *across* fields (i.e., what's happening over in that field is going to necessitate changes to what we're doing in this field, and we'd be wise to make them), rather than actually being a field itself.

5. See Bourdieu 1993; 1996. Part of this may be due to the metaphor of "poles" in field theory dovetailing with the "forces" present in a magnetic "field." As Martin (2003: 29) notes, sometimes Bourdieu treats his fields as magnetic fields, and at other times he criticizes others for thinking of fields as magnetic fields. No bother, though. Bourdieu, in a blessing and a curse, is too influential to escape critique over his metaphors, be they about magnets or about economics.

6. On this point, see Martin 2003; Swartz 1997. See also Emirbayer and Johnson 2008. See Bourdieu 2008 for an instance in which the focus is expressly on organizations.

7. See Christin 2014; Mears 2011.

8. As Bourdieu and Wacquant (1992) write, "to think in terms of field demands a conversion of the whole ordinary vision of the social world which fastens only on visible things," and "the structure of a field . . . is different from the . . . networks through which it manifests itself" (96, 113–114). Elsewhere

Bourdieu writes that "the truth of the interaction is not to be found in the interaction itself" (Bourdieu 2005: 148). At other times Bourdieu softens this statement by writing that "the truth of the interaction never lies *entirely* in the interaction," although at the same time in this instance, he argues that dedicating interest to the interaction itself is to fall prey to the "occasionalist illusion" (Bourdieu 1990: 291, emphasis added). On the incorporation of networks into a Bourdieusian field approach, see Anheier, Gerhards, and Romo 1995; Bottero and Crossley 2011; de Nooy 2003; Mohr 2013.

9. This is part of what Fligstein and McAdam (2012) refer to as a transition away from a "fieldcentric" approach to one that also considers fields themselves as operating in relational systems (57). See also Eyal (2013) on this point.

10. On the pipe metaphor, see Podolny 2001. On the circuit metaphor, see Zelizer 2010.

11. For the quote, see Lista 2013. On the point, the ACS occupational definition of "authors and writers" as used in Figure 11.2 is based upon the following prompt: "Current or most recent job activity: Describe clearly this person's *chief job activity* or business last week. If this person had more than one job, describe the one at which this person *worked the most hours*" (emphases added). The implication is that those who cannot find work as writers and authors as their primary job activity are not recorded as writers or authors (i.e., aspirants who cannot get published, regardless of the reason, are left out of the recorded data).

12. See Bourdieu 1985: 736. Endogenous change is possible as capitals can ostensibly be leveraged in the hostile takeover of better positions (i.e., strivings) and ultimately into controlling definitions, although the field is organized to prevent these internal ruptures. Very loosely applied, the accumulation of capitals serves the same purpose as "social skill" in Fligstein and McAdam's field theory (2012), although they also rely on social movements theory to explain endogenous change within fields. See also Baumann (2007a) on the application of social movements theory to artistic legitimation. See also DiMaggio and Powell (1983) in which the change is reproduction. More generally see Childress (2015) on these three strains of field theory.

13. The "six facet" model of the production of culture perspective is, in essence, a framework for understanding cultural change. On the reception side, as texts are multivocal and meanings are socially constructed, that interpretation and evaluation would be unstable over time is not a difficult proposition to agree with (i.e., a lack of longitudinal studies of meaning should not be confused with theoretical difficulty in explaining how change occurs).

14. See Leschziner and Green (2013) for the quite elegant and incredibly useful insight into how this perspective can be woven into field theory without violating its other assumptions.

15. See Bourdieu 1996: 150–161 (Figure 6 in particular). On education Bourdieu writes, "Among these changes, the most determining is no doubt the growth . . . of the educated population (at all levels of the school system) that underlies two parallel processes: the rise in the number of producers who can live by their pen . . . and the expansion of the market of potential readers" (Bourdieu 1996: 127).
16. See Griswold 1981; 2000: 36–38.
17. See Italie 2012.
18. Of note, while Rice wrote *Interview* as an MFA student at San Francisco State after leaving a PhD program in English at Berkeley, one of her fellow students in that program in 1972, Cornelia Nixon, took the reverse path by starting in the SF State MFA program in creative writing before going across the Bay to the PhD program in English at Berkeley.
19. See Striphas 2009.
20. The word "garbage" comes from Mike Ward, president of discounter Thrift Books, when explaining the business he's in: "We are taking garbage [and] running it through a very sophisticated salvage process in our warehouses, to create or find or discover products people want, and then we sell them at a very, very cheap price" (Nosowitz 2015).
21. On fields being located in physical space, see Childress 2015; Leschziner 2015; Martin, Slez, and Borkenhagen 2016; Sallaz 2012.

METHODOLOGICAL APPENDIX

1. For a more detailed description of interviews with these editors, which were semistructured, see Childress (2012).
2. There are no cases in which these distinctions posed a problem for this study. Off-topic banter included such things as the use of sarcasm for sport, general office gossip, gossip about the reputations of different authors or people in publishing, and so on.
3. In listening to interviews between stand-up comics on podcasts or while watching authors interview other authors, make note of how the interviewer-insiders avoid the (taken to be) "boring" and "hack" questions that readers and nonpractitioner interviewers always ask, and reflexively apologize or acknowledge when a question is of a type that would come from a field outsider rather than insider.

REFERENCES

Abbott, A. (2005). Linked ecologies: States and universities as environments for professions. *Sociological Theory*, 23(3): 245–274.

Adler, P. A., and Adler, P. (2003). The reluctant respondent. In J. Holstein and J. Gubrium (Eds.), *Inside interviewing: New lenses, new concerns*. Sage: 153–173.

Ahlkvist, J. A., and Faulkner, R. (2002). "Will this record work for us?" Managing music formats in commercial radio. *Qualitative Sociology*, 25(2): 189–215.

Alter, A. (2016). James Patterson has a big plan for small books. *New York Times*, March 21.

Anand, N., and Jones, B. C. (2008). Tournament rituals, category dynamics, and field configuration: The case of the Booker Prize. *Journal of Management Studies*, 45(6): 1036–1060.

Anheier, H. K., and Gerhards, J. (1991). Literary myths and social structure. *Social Forces*, 69(3): 811–830.

Anheier, H. K., Gerhards, J., and Romo, F. P. (1995). Forms of capital and social structure in cultural fields: Examining Bourdieu's social topography. *American Journal of Sociology*, 100(4): 859–903.

Anonymous. (2009a). Fiction book review: Jarrettsville by Cornelia Nixon. *Publishers Weekly*, August 10.

———. (2009b). Jarrettsville. *Kirkus Reviews*, August 15. https://www.kirkus reviews.com/book-reviews/cornelia-nixon/jarrettsville/.

Arnold, M. (1999). Why editors become agents. *New York Times*, November 10.

Aronson, M. (1993). The evolution of the American editor. In E. Gross (Ed.), *Editors on editing: What writers need to know about what editors do*. Grove Press: 10–21.

Baker, W. E., and Faulkner, R. R. (1991). Role as resource in the Hollywood film industry. *American Journal of Sociology*, 97(2): 279–309.

Bandelj, N. (2009). Emotions in economic action and interaction. *Theory and Society*, 38(4): 347–366.

Barker-Nunn, J., and Fine, G. A. (1998). The vortex of creation: Literary politics and the demise of Herman Melville's reputation. *Poetics*, 26(2): 81–98.

Barthes, R. (1974). *S/Z*. Hill & Wang.

Batchelor, B. (2008). *American pop: Popular culture decade by decade*. ABC-CLIO.

Bauer, A. (2015). "Sponsored" by my husband: Why it's a problem that writers never talk about where their money comes from. *Salon*, January 25. http://www.salon.com/2015/01/25/sponsored_by_my_husband_why_its_a_problem_that_writers_never_talk_about_where_their_money_comes_from/.

Baumann, S. (2007a). A general theory of artistic legitimation: How art worlds are like social movements. *Poetics*, 35(1): 47–65.

———. (2007b). *Hollywood highbrow: From entertainment to art*. Princeton University Press.

Becker, H. S. (1974). Art as collective action. *American Sociological Review*, 39(6): 767–776.

———. (1982). *Art worlds*. University of California Press.

Becker, H. S., Faulkner, R. R., and Kirshenblatt-Gimblett, B. (Eds.). (2006). *Art from start to finish: Jazz, painting, writing, and other improvisations*. University of Chicago Press.

Becker, H. S., and Pessin, A. (2006). A dialogue on the ideas of "World" and "Field." *Sociological Forum*, 21(2): 275–286.

Beckert, J. (2013). Imagined futures: Fictional expectations in the economy. *Theory and Society*, 42(3): 219–240.

Benson, R. (1999). Field theory in comparative context: A new paradigm for media studies. *Theory and Society*, 28(3): 463–498.

Benzecry, C. E. (2011). *The opera fanatic: Ethnography of an obsession*. University of Chicago Press.

Bielby, W. T., and Bielby, D. D. (1994). "All hits are flukes": Institutionalized decision making and the rhetoric of network prime-time program development. *American Journal of Sociology*, 99: 1287–1313.

Blaine, D. (2010). Interview with Charles Plymell. *Carbon-Based Lifeform Blues*, January 13. http://blues.gr/profiles/blogs/an-interview-with-charles-plymell-early-beat-generation-poet-1.

Bonilla-Silva, E. (2006). *Racism without racists: Color-blind racism and the persistence of racial inequality in the United States*. Rowman & Littlefield.

Boone, C., Van Witteloostuijn, A., and Carroll, G. R. (2002). Resource distributions and market partitioning: Dutch daily newspapers, 1968 to 1994. *American Sociological Review*, 67: 408–431.

Bosman, J. (2012). Book is judged by the name of its cover. *New York Times*, February 22.

Bottero, W., and Crossley, N. (2011). Worlds, fields and networks: Becker, Bourdieu and the structures of social relations. *Cultural Sociology*, 5(1): 99–119.

Bourdieu, P. (1980). The production of belief: Contribution to an economy of symbolic goods. *Media, Culture, and Society*, 2(3): 261–293.

———. (1984). *Distinction: A social critique of the judgment of taste.* Harvard University Press.

———. (1985). The social space and the genesis of the groups. *Theory and Society,* 14(6): 723–744.

———. (1990). *The logic of practice.* Stanford University Press.

———. (1993). *The field of cultural production: Essays on art and literature.* Columbia University Press.

———. (1996). *The rules of art: Genesis and structure of the literary field.* Stanford University Press.

———. (1997). *Pascalian Meditations.* Stanford University Press.

———. (2005). *The Social Structures of the Economy.* Polity Press.

———. (2008). A conservative revolution in publishing. *Translation Studies,* 1(2): 123–153.

Bourdieu, P., and Wacquant, L. J. (1992). *An invitation to reflexive sociology.* University of Chicago Press.

Bourdieu, P., and Whiteside, S. (1996). *Photography: A middle-brow art.* Stanford University Press.

Bourne, M. (2012). A right fit: Navigating the world of literary agents. *The Millions,* August 15. http://www.themillions.com/2012/08/a-right-fit-navigating-the -world-of-literary-agents.html.

Brodkey, L. (1987). *Academic writing as social practice.* Temple University Press.

Brown, E. F., and Wiley, J., Jr. (2011). *Margaret Mitchell's* Gone With the Wind: *A bestseller's odyssey from Atlanta to Hollywood.* Taylor Trade Publications.

Bryson, B. (1996). "Anything but heavy metal": Symbolic exclusion and musical dislikes. *American Sociological Review,* 61(5): 884–899.

Butler, S. F. (2011). Document: The symbolism survey. *Paris Review,* December 5.

Capparell, S. (2007). *The real Pepsi challenge: The inspirational story of breaking the color barrier in American business.* Simon & Schuster.

Carroll, G. R., and Swaminathan, A. (2000). Why the microbrewery movement? Organizational dynamics of resource partitioning in the US brewing industry. *American Journal of Sociology,* 106(3): 715–762.

Caves, R. E. (2000). *Creative industries: Contracts between art and commerce.* Harvard University Press.

Childress, C. C. (2012). Decision-making, market logic and the rating mindset: Negotiating BookScan in the field of US trade publishing. *European Journal of Cultural Studies,* 15(5): 604–620.

———. (2015). Regionalism and the publishing class: Conflicted isomorphism and negotiated identity in a nested field of American publishing. *Cultural Sociology,* 9(3): 364–381.

Childress, C. C., and Friedkin, N. E. (2012). Cultural reception and production: The social construction of meaning in book clubs. *American Sociological Review,* 77(1): 45–68.

Childress, C. C., and Gerber, A. (2015). The MFA in creative writing: The uses of a "useless" credential. *Professions and Professionalism*, 5(2): 1–16.

Christin, A. (2014). Clicks or Pulitzers? Web journalists and their work in the United States and France. Dissertation, Princeton University.

Clines, F. X. (2016). Indie bookstores are back, with a passion. *New York Times*, February 12.

Cohen, M. D., March, J. G., and Olsen, J. P. (1972). A garbage can model of organizational choice. *Administrative Science Quarterly*, 17: 1–25.

Colacello, B. (1990). *Holy terror: Andy Warhol close up*. HarperCollins.

Collins, R. (2004). *Interaction ritual chains*. Princeton University Press.

Cornford, D., and Lewis, S. (2012). *Not a gold rush*. Taleist.

Corse, S. M. (1995). Nations and novels: Cultural politics and literary use. *Social Forces*, 73(4): 1279–1308.

Coser, L. A. (Ed.). (1978). The production of culture. *Social Research*, 48(2).

Coser, L. A., Kadushin, C., and Powell, W. W. (1982). *Books: The culture & commerce of publishing*. Basic Books.

Craig, A., and Dubois, S. (2010). Between art and money: The social space of public readings in contemporary poetry economies and careers. *Poetics*, 38(5): 441–460.

Crane, D. (1992). *The production of culture*. Sage.

Curran, J. (2011). *Media and democracy*. Routledge.

Dale, B. (2016). Hugh Howey has no patience for book lovers who don't read books. *New York Observer*, March 30.

Daniels, H. (2002). *Literature circles: Voice and choice in book clubs and reading groups*. Stenhouse.

de Bellaigue, E. (2008). "Trust me. I'm an agent": The ever-changing balance between author, agent, and publisher. *LOGOS: Journal of the World Book Community*, 19(3): 109–119.

de Laat, K. (2015). "Write a word, get a third": Managing conflict and rewards in professional songwriting teams. *Work and Occupations*, 42(2): 225–256.

Denisoff, R. S., and Levine, M. H. (1971). The popular protest song: The case of "Eve of Destruction." *Public Opinion Quarterly*, 35(1): 117–122.

de Nooy, W. (2002). The dynamics of artistic prestige. *Poetics*, 30(3): 147–167.

———. (2003). Fields and networks: Correspondence analysis and social network analysis in the framework of field theory. *Poetics*, 31(5): 305–327.

Denrell, J., and Fang, C. (2010). Predicting the next big thing: Success as a signal of poor judgment. *Management Science*, 56(10): 1653–1667.

DiMaggio, P. (1977). Market structure, the creative process, and popular culture: Toward an organizational reinterpretation of mass-culture theory. *Journal of Popular Culture*, 11(2): 436–452.

———. (1987). Classification in art. *American Sociological Review*, 52(4): 440–455.

DiMaggio, P., and Powell, W. W. (1983). The iron cage revisited: Collective rationality and institutional isomorphism in organizational fields. *American Sociological Review*, 48(2): 147–160.

———. (1991). Introduction. In W. W. Powell and P. J. DiMaggio (Eds.), *The new institutionalism in organizational analysis*. University of Chicago Press: 1–38.

Donadio, R. (2006). Promotional intelligence. *New York Times*, May 20.

Donald, D. H. (2002). *Look homeward: A life of Thomas Wolfe*. Harvard University Press.

Douglas, M. (1972). Deciphering a meal. *Daedalus*, 101(1): 61–81.

Dowd, T. J. (2004). Concentration and diversity revisited: Production logics and the US mainstream recording market, 1940–1990. *Social Forces*, 82(4): 1411–1455.

Draugsvold, O. G. (Ed.). (2000). *Nobel writers on writing*. McFarland.

Du Gay, P., Hall, S., Janes, L., Madsen, A. K., Mackay, H., and Negus, K. (1997). *Doing cultural studies: The story of the Sony Walkman*. Sage.

Dyckhoff, T. (2001). They've got it covered. *Guardian*, September 15.

Ekelund, B. G., and Börjesson, M. (2002). The shape of the literary career: An analysis of publishing trajectories. *Poetics*, 30(5): 341–364.

Elberse, A. (2013). *Blockbusters: Hit-making, risk-taking, and the big business of entertainment*. Macmillan.

Emirbayer, M., and Johnson, V. (2008). Bourdieu and organizational analysis. *Theory and Society*, 37(1): 1–44.

Escarpit, R. (1971). *Sociology of literature*. Vol. 4. Routledge.

Eyal, G. (2013). Spaces between fields. In P. Gorski (Ed.), *Bourdieu and historical analysis*. Duke University Press: 158–182.

Farrell, M. P. (2003). *Collaborative circles: Friendship dynamics and creative work*. University of Chicago Press.

Faulkner, R. R., and Becker, H. S. (2009). *"Do you know . . . ?" The jazz repertoire in action*. University of Chicago Press.

Ferrari-Adler, J. (2009). Agents & editors: A Q&A with four young literary agents. *Poets & Writers*, January/February.

Fine, G. A. (1979). Small groups and culture creation: The idioculture of Little League baseball teams. *American Sociological Review*, 44(5): 733–745.

Fish, S. E. (1980). *Is there a text in this class? The authority of interpretive communities*. Harvard University Press.

Fiske, J. (1987). *Television culture*. London: Routledge.

Fligstein, N., and McAdam, D. (2012). *A theory of fields*. Oxford University Press.

Foreman, A. (2012). New faces of evil: "Casual Vacancy," by J. K. Rowling. *New York Times*, October 26.

Foucault, M. (2002). What is an author? In D. Finkelstein and A. McCleery (Eds.), *The book history reader*. Psychology Press: 225–230.

Franssen, T., and Kuipers, G. (2013). Coping with uncertainty, abundance and strife: Decision-making processes of Dutch acquisition editors in the global market for translations. *Poetics*, 41(1): 48–74.

Franssen, T., and Velthuis, O. (2016). Making materiality matter: A sociological analysis of prices on the Dutch fiction book market, 1980–2009. *Socio-Economic Review*, 14: 363–381.

Frenette, A., and Tepper, S. J. (2016). What difference does it make? Assessing the effects of arts-based training on career pathways. In R. Comunian and A. Gilmore (Eds.), *Higher education and the creative economy: Beyond the campus.* Routledge: 83–101.

Friedman, S. (2014). *Comedy and distinction: The cultural currency of a "good" sense of humour.* Routledge.

Galassi, J. (1980). The double agent: The role of the literary editor in the commercial publishing house. In B. Henderson (Ed.), *The art of literary publishing: Editors on their craft.* Pushcart Press: 78–87.

Gamson, J. (1998a). The depths of shallow culture. *Newsletter of the Sociology of Culture Section of the American Sociological Association,* 12(3): 1–6.

———. (1998b). *Freaks talk back: Tabloid talk shows and sexual nonconformity.* University of Chicago Press.

Gerber, A. (2017). *The work of art.* Stanford University Press.

Gessen, K. (2011). *How a book is born: The making of the art of fielding.* Vanity Fair.

———. (2014). Money. In *Happiness: Ten Years of n+1.* Faber & Faber: 307–335.

Ghose, A., Smith, M. D., and Telang, R. (2006). Internet exchanges for used books: An empirical analysis of product cannibalization and welfare impact. *Information Systems Research,* 17(1): 3–19.

Gitlin, T. (1983). *Inside prime time.* Pantheon.

Giuffre, K. (1999). Sandpiles of opportunity: Success in the art world. *Social Forces,* 77(3): 815–832.

Godart, F. C., and Mears, A. (2009). How do cultural producers make creative decisions? Lessons from the catwalk. *Social Forces,* 88(2): 671–692.

Goel, S., and Salganik, M. J. (2010). Assessing respondent-driven sampling. *Proceedings of the National Academy of Sciences,* 107(15): 6743–6747.

Goldberg, A. (2011). Mapping shared understandings using relational class analysis: The case of the cultural omnivore reexamined. *American Journal of Sociology,* 116(5): 1397–1436.

Gologorsky, B. (2000). The odd couple. *New York Times,* April 16.

Goodheart, A. (2009). The war at home. *New York Times,* October 22.

Goolrick, R. (2009). An unsettled town in an unsettled time. *Washington Post,* October 24.

Greco, A. N. (2005). *The book publishing industry.* Lawrence Erlbaum.

Grindstaff, L. (2002). *The money shot: Trash, class, and the making of TV talk shows.* University of Chicago Press.

Griswold, W. (1981). American character and the American novel: An expansion of reflection theory in the sociology of literature. *American Journal of Sociology,* 86: 740–765.

———. (1986). *Renaissance revivals: City comedy and revenge tragedy in the London theatre.* University of Chicago Press.

————. (1987a). The fabrication of meaning: Literary interpretation in the United States, Great Britain, and the West Indies. *American Journal of Sociology*, 92(5): 1077–1117.

————. (1987b). A methodological framework for the sociology of culture. *Sociological Methodology*, 17(1): 1–35.

————. (1993). Recent moves in the sociology of literature. *Annual Review of Sociology*, 19: 455–467.

————. (2000). *Bearing witness: Readers, writers, and the novel in Nigeria*. Princeton University Press.

————. (2004). *Cultures and societies in a changing world*. Sage.

————. (2008). *Regionalism and the reading class*. University of Chicago Press.

Griswold, W., and Wohl, H. (2015). Evangelists of culture: One Book programs and the agents who define literature, shape tastes, and reproduce regionalism. *Poetics*, 50: 96–109.

Griswold, W., and Wright, N. (2004). Cowbirds, locals, and the dynamic endurance of regionalism. *American Journal of Sociology*, 109(6): 1411–1451.

Gross, A. (2015). Counterpoint Press marks 20 years. *Publishers Weekly*, November 6.

Gross, N. (2009). *Richard Rorty: The making of an American philosopher*. University of Chicago Press.

Hall, S. (1980): Encoding/decoding. In Centre for Contemporary Cultural Studies (Ed.), *Culture, media, language: Working papers in cultural studies, 1972–79*. Hutchinson: 128–138.

Harbach, C. (Ed.). (2014). *MFA vs NYC: The two cultures of American fiction*. Macmillan.

Hardwick, E. (1959). The decline of book reviewing. *Harper's*, 138–143.

————. (2000). The torrents of Wolfe. *New York Review of Books*, November 16.

Hargadon, A. B., and Bechky, B. A. (2006). When collections of creatives become creative collectives: A field study of problem solving at work. *Organization Science*, 17(4): 484–500.

Harrison, S. H., and Rouse, E. D. (2014). Let's dance! Elastic coordination in creative group work: A qualitative study of modern dancers. *Academy of Management Journal*, 57(5): 1256–1283.

Hartley, J. (2001). *Reading groups*. Oxford University Press.

Heckathorn, D. D. (2002). Respondent-driven sampling II: Deriving valid population estimates from chain-referral samples of hidden populations. *Social Problems*, 49(1): 11–34.

Heckathorn, D. D., and Jeffri, J. (2001). Finding the beat: Using respondent-driven sampling to study jazz musicians. *Poetics*, 28(4): 307–329.

Heinich, N. (1997). *The glory of Van Gogh: An anthropology of admiration*. Princeton University Press.

Hesmondhalgh, D., and Baker, S. (2010). "A very complicated version of free-dom": Conditions and experiences of creative labour in three cultural indus-tries. *Poetics*, 38(1): 4–20.

Hirsch, P. M. (1972). Processing fads and fashions: An organization-set analysis of cultural industry systems. *American Journal of Sociology*, 77(4): 639–659.

Hochschild, A. R. (1983). *The managed heart: Commercialization of human feeling*. University of California Press.

Italie, L. (2012). "Fifty Shades" books now have fan fiction of their own. *Today*, May 24.

Jackall, R. (1988). Moral mazes: The world of corporate managers. *International Journal of Politics, Culture, and Society*, 1(4): 598–614.

Janssen, S. (1997). Reviewing as social practice: Institutional constraints on critics' attention for contemporary fiction. *Poetics*, 24(5): 275–297.

———. (1998). Side-roads to success: The effect of sideline activities on the status of writers. *Poetics*, 25(5): 265–280.

Jeffri, J., Heckathorn, D. D., and Spiller, M. W. (2011). Painting your life: A study of aging visual artists in New York City. *Poetics*, 39(1): 19–43.

Jhally, S., and Lewis, J. (1992). *Enlightened racism: The Cosby Show, audiences and the myth of the American dream*. Westview Press.

Johnston, J., and Baumann, S. (2009). *Foodies: Democracy and distinction in the gourmet foodscape*. Routledge.

Kachka, B. (2013). *Hothouse: The art of survival and the survival of art at America's most celebrated publishing house, Farrar, Straus, and Giroux*. Simon & Schuster.

Kakutani, M. (1991). Books of the *Times*: Portrait of a family from shifting points of view. *New York Times*, March 28.

Kellner, T. (2002). Stranger than fiction. *Forbes*, October 28.

Kingston, P. W., and Cole, J. (1986). *The wages of writing: Per word, per piece, or perhaps*. Columbia University Press.

Klickstein, M. (2013). *Slimed: An oral history of Nickelodeon's golden age*. Plume.

Kroeber, A. L. (1919). On the principle of order in civilization as exemplified by changes of fashion. *American Anthropologist*, 21(3): 235–263.

Kurtzberg, T. R., and Amabile, T. M. (2001). From Guilford to creative synergy: Opening the black box of team-level creativity. *Creativity Research Journal*, 13(3–4): 285–294.

Lamont, M. (1992). *Cultivating differences: Symbolic boundaries and the making of inequality*. University of Chicago Press.

Lamont, M., Beljean, S., and Clair, M. (2014). What is missing? Cultural processes and causal pathways to inequality. *Socio-Economic Review*, 12(3): 573–608.

Lee, H. (1961). Christmas to me. *McCall's*, December.

Lee, J. (2013). Literary culture clash. *Guernica*, July 1. https://www.guernicamag .com/literary-culture-clash/.

Leithauser, B. (2013). Reading your friends' novels. *New Yorker*, January 7.

Lena, J. C. (2012). *Banding together: How communities create genres in popular music*. Princeton University Press.

Leong, M. (2010). The $4,000 tip jar: David Sedaris on a life spent on tour. *National Post*, December 7.

Leschziner, V. (2015). *At the chef's table: Culinary creativity in elite restaurants*. Stanford University Press.

Leschziner, V., and Green, A. I. (2013). Thinking about food and sex: Deliberate cognition in the routine practices of a field. *Sociological Theory*, 31(2): 116–144.

Lévi-Strauss, C. (1963). *Totemism*. No. 157. Beacon.

Liebes, T., and Katz, E. (1990). *The export of meaning: Cross-cultural readings of Dallas*. Oxford University Press.

Lista, L. (2013). Video: Latina book editor shares insights on how to get published in today's book industry. *Latina Lista*, September 24. http://latinalista.com /culture-2/books/tuesday-video-marcela-landres-why-we-need-more-latino -acquisition-editors.

Liu, S., and Emirbayer, M. (2016). Field and ecology. *Sociological Theory*, 34(1): 62–79.

Lizardo, O. (2006). How cultural tastes shape personal networks. *American Sociological Review*, 71(5): 778–807.

Lizardo, O., and Skiles, S. (2016). Cultural objects as prisms: perceived audience composition of musical genres as a resource for symbolic exclusion. *Socius: Sociological Research for a Dynamic World*, 2: 2378023116641695.

Lomax, A. (1968). *Folk song style and culture*. Vol. 88. Transaction.

Long, E. (2003). *Book clubs: Women and the uses of reading in everyday life*. University of Chicago Press.

———. (2004). Literature as a spur to collective action: The diverse perspectives of nineteenth-and twentieth-century reading groups. *Poetics Today*, 25(2): 335–359.

Lopes, P. D. (1992). Innovation and diversity in the popular music industry, 1969 to 1990. *American Sociological Review*, 57(1): 56–71.

López, M. P., and López, G. R. (2009). *Persistent inequality: Contemporary realities in the education of undocumented Latina/o students*. Routledge.

Low, J. T. (2016). Where is the diversity in publishing? The 2015 Diversity Baseline Survey results. *Lee & Low Books Blog*, January 26. http://blog.leeandlow .com/2016/01/26/where-is-the-diversity-in-publishing-the-2015-diversity -baseline-survey-results/.

Lowenthal, L. (1961). *Literature, popular culture, and society*. Pacific Books.

———. (1983). *Literature and mass culture*. Transaction.

Lumenello, S. (2007). The *New York Times Book Review* as cultural gatekeeper. *Colloquy*, 4–5, 20.

Maghbouleh, N. (2017). *The limits of whiteness: Iranian-Americans and the everyday politics of race*. Stanford University Press.

Mahler, J. (2010). James Patterson Inc. *New York Times Magazine*, January 24.

Manguel, A. (2014). *A history of reading*. Penguin.

Mark, N. (1998). Birds of a feather sing together. *Social Forces*, 77(2): 453–485.

———. (2003). Culture and competition: Homophily and distancing explanations for cultural niches. *American Sociological Review*, 68(3): 319–345.

Martin, B. (2013). *Difficult men: Behind the scenes of a creative revolution: From* The Sopranos *and* The Wire *to* Mad Men *and* Breaking Bad. Penguin.

Martin, J. L. (2003). What is field theory? *American Journal of Sociology*, 109(1): 1–49.

Martin, J. L., Slez, A., and Borkenhagen, C. (2016). Some provisional techniques for quantifying the degree of field effect in social data. *Socius: Sociological Research for a Dynamic World*, 2: 2378023116635653.

Maslin, J. (2004). A spunky heroine, and an officer's improbable rise. *New York Times*, November 4.

McDonnell, T. E. (2010). Cultural objects as objects: Materiality, urban space, and the interpretation of AIDS campaigns in Accra, Ghana. *American Journal of Sociology*, 115(6): 1800–1852.

McDowell, E. (1984). Doris Lessing says she used pen name to show new writers' difficulties. *New York Times*, September 23.

McGurl, M. (2009). *The program era*. Harvard University Press.

Mears, A. (2011). *Pricing beauty: The making of a fashion model*. University of California Press.

Menger, P. M. (2006). Profiles of the unfinished: Rodin's work and the varieties of incompleteness. In H. S. Becker, R. R. Faulkner, and B. Kirshenblatt-Gimblett (Eds.), *Art from start to finish: Jazz, painting, writing, and other improvisations*. University of Chicago Press: 31–68.

Menger, P. M. (2014). *The economics of creativity*. Harvard University Press.

Merton, R. K. (1968). The Matthew effect in science. *Science*, 159(3810): 56–63.

Miller, L. J. (2009). Selling the product. In D. P. Nord, J. S. Rubin, and M. Schudson (Eds.), *A history of the book in America, volume 5: The enduring book: Print culture in postwar America*. University of North Carolina Press: 91–106.

Milliot, J. (2016). Catapult, counterpoint merge. *Publishers Weekly*, September 1.

Moeran, B. (2003). Celebrities and the name economy. *Research in Economic Anthropology*, 22: 299–324.

Moeran, B., and Pedersen, J. S. (Eds.). (2011). *Negotiating values in the creative industries: Fairs, festivals and competitive events*. Cambridge University Press.

Mohr, J. W. (1994). Soldiers, mothers, tramps and others: Discourse roles in the 1907 New York City Charity Directory. *Poetics*, 22: 327–357.

———. (1998). Measuring meaning structures. *Annual Review of Sociology*, 24: 235–370.

———. (2013). Bourdieu's relational method in theory and in practice: From fields and capitals to networks and institutions (and back again). In F. Dépelteau and C. Powell (Eds.), *Applying Relational Sociology*. Palgrave Macmillan: 101–135.

Mohr, J. W., and Duquenne, V. (1997). The duality of culture and practice: Poverty relief in New York City, 1888–1917. *Theory and Society*, 26(2–3): 305–356.

Mozes, S. (2010). James Frey's fiction factory. *New York Magazine*, November 12.

National Endowment for the Arts. (2009). Reading on the rise. https://www.arts.gov/sites/default/files/ReadingonRise.pdf.

———. (2011). Artists and arts workers in the United States. NEA Research Note 105. https://www.arts.gov/sites/default/files/105.pdf.

Negro, G., Koçak, Ö., and Hsu, G. (2010). Research on categories in the sociology of organizations. *Research in the Sociology of Organizations*, 31: 3–35.

Negus, K. (2013). *Music genres and corporate cultures*. Routledge.

Nosowitz, D. (2015). A penny for your books. *New York Times*, October 26.

Nystrom, P. H. (1928). *Economics of fashion*. Ronald Press.

Oshinsky, D. (2007). No thanks, Mr. Nabokov. *New York Times*, September 9.

Parker, I. (2002). Showboat. *New Yorker*, April 8.

Parsons, T., and White, W. (1960). Commentary I. The mass media and the structure of American society. *Journal of Social Issues*, 16(3): 67–77.

Peterson, R. A. (1976). The production of culture: A prolegomenon. In R. A. Peterson (Ed.), *The production of culture*. Sage: 7–22.

———. (1977). Where the two cultures meet: Popular culture. *Journal of Popular Culture*, 11(2): 385–400.

———. (1979). Revitalizing the culture concept. *Annual Review of Sociology*, 5: 137–166.

———. (1990). Why 1955? Explaining the advent of rock music. *Popular Music*, 9(1): 97–116.

———. (1994). Cultural studies through the production perspective: Progress and prospects. In D. Crane (Ed.), *The sociology of culture: Emerging theoretical perspectives*. Blackwell: 163–190.

———. (2000). Two ways culture is produced. *Poetics*, 28(2): 225–233.

Peterson, R. A., and Anand, N. (2004). The production of culture perspective. *Annual Review of Sociology*, 30: 311–334.

Peterson, R. A., and Berger, D. G. (1975). Cycles in symbol production: The case of popular music. *American Sociological Review*, 40(2): 158–173.

Peterson, R. A., and Kern, R. M. (1996). Changing highbrow taste: From snob to omnivore. *American Sociological Review*, 61(5): 900–907.

Podolny, J. M. (2001). Networks as the pipes and prisms of the market. *American Journal of Sociology*, 107(1): 33–60.

Powell, W. W. (1985). *Getting into print: The decision-making process in scholarly publishing*. University of Chicago Press.

Purdum, T. (2015). How James Patterson became the ultimate storyteller. *Vanity Fair*, January.

Puzo, M. (1972). *The godfather papers & other confessions*. Putnam.

Radway, J. (1984). *Reading the romance: Women, patriarchy, and popular culture*. University of North Carolina Press.

————. (1997). *A feeling for books: The Book-of-the-Month Club, literary taste, and middle-class desire.* University of North Carolina Press.

Rawlings, C. M. (2001). "Making names": The cutting edge renewal of African art in New York City, 1985–1996. *Poetics,* 29(1): 25–54.

Reay, D. (2000). A useful extension of Bourdieu's conceptual framework? Emotional capital as a way of understanding mothers' involvement in their children's education? *Sociological Review,* 48(4): 568–585.

Reynolds, P. R. (1966). The literary agent: His function, life, and power. *Saturday Review,* October 8, 113–114.

Rich, M. (2009). End of *Kirkus Reviews* brings anguish and relief. *New York Times,* December 11.

Rivera, L. A. (2012). Hiring as cultural matching: The case of elite professional service firms. *American Sociological Review,* 77(6): 999–1022.

————. (2015). Go with your gut: Emotion and evaluation in job interviews. *American Journal of Sociology,* 120(5): 1339–1389.

Rosen, S. (1981). The economics of superstars. *American Economic Review,* 71(5): 845–858.

Rosenberg, B., and White, D. M. (1957). *Mass culture: The popular arts in America.* Free Press.

Rossman, G. (2012). *Climbing the charts: What radio airplay tells us about the diffusion of innovation.* Princeton University Press.

————. (2014). Obfuscatory relational work and disreputable exchange. *Sociological Theory,* 32(1): 43–63.

Rossman, G., and Schilke, O. (2014). Close, but no cigar: The bimodal rewards to prize-seeking. *American Sociological Review,* 79(1): 86–108.

Rubio, F. D., and Silva, E. B. (2013). Materials in the field: Object-trajectories and object-positions in the field of contemporary art. *Cultural Sociology,* 7(2): 161–178.

Sale, F. (1993). Editing fiction as an act of love. In G. Gross (Ed.), *Editors on editing: What writers need to know about what editors do.* Grove Press: 267–279.

Salganik, M. J. (2006). Variance estimation, design effects, and sample size calculations for respondent-driven sampling. *Journal of Urban Health,* 83(1): 98–112.

Salganik, M. J., Dodds, P. S., and Watts, D. J. (2006). Experimental study of inequality and unpredictability in an artificial cultural market. *Science,* 311(5762): 854–856.

Salganik, M. J., and Heckathorn, D. D. (2004). Sampling and estimation in hidden populations using respondent-driven sampling. *Sociological Methodology,* 34(1): 193–240.

Salganik, M. J., and Watts, D. J. (2008). Leading the herd astray: An experimental study of self-fulfilling prophecies in an artificial cultural market. *Social Psychology Quarterly,* 71(4): 338–355.

Salkin, A. (2013). *From scratch: Inside the Food Network.* G.P. Putnam Sons.

Sallaz, J. J. (2012). Politics of organizational adornment lessons from Las Vegas and beyond. *American Sociological Review*, 77(1): 99–119.

Schudson, M. (1989). How culture works. *Theory and Society*, 18(2): 153–180.

Schuster, M. L. (1993). An open letter to a would-be editor. In G. Gross (Ed.), *Editors on editing: What writers need to know about what editors do*. Grove Press: 22–28.

Semonche, J. E. (2007). *Censoring sex: A historical journey through American media*. Rowman & Littlefield.

Shales, T., and Miller, J. A. (2008). *Live from New York: An uncensored history of Saturday Night Live*. Back Bay Books.

Shank, J. (2012). Literary agent Jason Ashlock: Big book publishers not innovating fast enough. *Media Shift*, September 20. http://mediashift.org/2012/09/literary-agent-jason-ashlock-big-book-publishers-not-innovating-fast-enough264/.

Shively, J. (1992). Cowboys and Indians: Perceptions of western films among American Indians and Anglos. *American Sociological Review*, 57(6): 725–734.

Shrum, W. (1991). Critics and publics: Cultural mediation in highbrow and popular performing arts. *American Journal of Sociology*, 97(2): 347–375.

Siddique, H. (2013). JK Rowling publishes crime novel under false name. *Guardian*, July 14.

Siegel, L. (2004). The age of Ettlinger. *New York Times*, November 14.

Spillman, L. (2012). *Solidarity in strategy: Making business meaningful in American trade associations*. University of Chicago Press.

Stebbins, R. A. (1968). A theory of the jazz community. *Sociological Quarterly*, 9(3): 318–331.

Steinberg, R. J., and Figart, D. M. (1999). Emotional labor since the managed heart. *Annals of the American Academy of Political and Social Science*, 561(1): 8–26.

Stinchcombe, A. L. (1959). Bureaucratic and craft administration of production: A comparative study. *Administrative Science Quarterly*, 4(2): 168–187.

Stolls, A. (2008). The NEA literature fellowships turn forty: An introduction. In D. Ball (Ed.), *NEA literature fellowships: 40 years of supporting American writers*. National Endowment for the Arts: 5–6.

Stone, B. (2013). *The everything store: Jeff Bezos and the age of Amazon*. Random House.

Striphas, T. (2009). *The late age of print: Everyday book culture from consumerism to control*. Columbia University Press.

Sullivan, M. (2015). For reviewers, how close is too close? *New York Times*, May 16.

Swanson, C. (2016). It takes 16 people working full time to publish all of James Patterson's Books. *Publishers Weekly*, March 18.

Swartz, D. (1997). *Power and culture: The sociology of Pierre Bourdieu*. University of Chicago Press.

Taylor, N. (2009). Fables of the reconstruction. *The Rumpus*, September 30. http://therumpus.net/2009/09/fables-of-the-reconstruction/.

Thompson, J. B. (2010). *Merchants of culture: The publishing business in the twenty-first century*. Polity.

Thornton, P. H. (2004). *Markets from culture: Institutional logics and organizational decisions in higher education publishing*. Stanford University Press.

Trachtenberg, J. A. (2010). Why ebooks aren't scary. *Wall Street Journal*, October 29.

Trollope, A. (1883). *An Autobiography, in Two Volumes*. Blackwood.

Tuchman, G., and Fortin, N. E. (1984). Fame and misfortune: Edging women out of the great literary tradition. *American Journal of Sociology*, 90(1): 72–96.

Vaisey, S., and Lizardo, O. (2010). Can cultural worldviews influence network composition? *Social Forces*, 88(4): 1595–1618.

Van Rees, C. J. (1987). How reviewers reach consensus on the value of literary works. *Poetics*, 16(3): 275–294.

Van Rees, K., and Dorleijn, G. J. (2001). The eighteenth-century literary field in Western Europe: The interdependence of material and symbolic production and consumption. *Poetics*, 28(5): 331–348.

Verboord, M. (2010). The legitimacy of book critics in the age of the Internet and omnivorousness: Expert critics, Internet critics and peer critics in Flanders and the Netherlands. *European Sociological Review*, 26(6): 623–637.

Wade, J. O. (1993). Doing good—and doing it right: The ethical and moral dimensions of editing. In G. Gross (Ed.), *Editors on editing: What writers need to know about what editors do*. Grove Press: 73–82.

Waldman, A. (2003). How four magazines you've probably never read help determine what books you buy. *Slate*. http://www.slate.com/articles/arts/culture box/2003/09/book_report.html.

Walker, S. (1993). Editing for a small press. In G. Gross (Ed.), *Editors on editing: What writers need to know about what editors do*. Grove Press: 260–266.

Warde, A. (2015). The sociology of consumption: Its recent development. *Annual Review of Sociology*, 41: 117–134.

Weinberg, D. B. (2014). Author survey: Indie authors and others prefer traditional publishing . . . slightly. *Digital Book World*, January 9. http://www.digital bookworld.com/2014/2014-author-survey-indie-authors-and-others-prefer -traditional-publishing-slightly/.

———. (2013). The self-publishing debate: A social scientist separates fact from fiction (part 3 of 3). *Digital Book World*, December 4. http://www.digitalbook world.com/2013/self-publishing-debate-part3/.

Wherry, F. F. (2014). Analyzing the culture of markets. *Theory and Society*, 43(3–4): 421–436.

White, H. C. (1992). *Identity and control: A structural theory of social action*. Princeton University Press.

White, H. C., and White, C. A. (1965). *Canvases and careers: Institutional change in the French painting world*. University of Chicago Press.

Woll, T. (2002). *Publishing for profit: Bottom-line management for book publishers*. Chicago Review Press.

Zelizer, V. A. (2010). *Economic lives: How culture shapes the economy*. Princeton University Press.

Zerubavel, E. (2009). *Social mindscapes: An invitation to cognitive sociology*. Harvard University Press.

Zuckerman, E. W. (1999). The categorical imperative: Securities analysts and the illegitimacy discount. *American Journal of Sociology*, 104(5): 1398–1438.

INDEX

PSCS PRINCETON STUDIES IN
CULTURAL SOCIOLOGY
Paul J. DiMaggio, Michèle Lamont,
Robert J. Wuthnow, and Viviana A. Zelizer,
Series Editors

Bearing Witness: Readers, Writers, and the Novel in Nigeria by Wendy Griswold

Gifted Tongues: High School Debate and Adolescent Culture by Gary Alan Fine

Offside: Soccer and American Exceptionalism by Andrei S. Markovits and Steven L. Hellerman

Reinventing Justice: The American Drug Court Movement by James L. Nolan, Jr.

Kingdom of Children: Culture and Controversy in the Homeschooling Movement by Mitchell L. Stevens

Blessed Events: Religion and Home Birth in America by Pamela E. Klassen

Negotiating Identities: States and Immigrants in France and Germany by Riva Kastoryano, translated by Barbara Harshav

Contentious Curricula: Afrocentrism and Creationism in American Public Schools by Amy J. Binder

Community: Pursuing the Dream, Living the Reality by Suzanne Keller

The Minds of Marginalized Black Men: Making Sense of Mobility, Opportunity, and Future Life Chances by Alford A. Young, Jr.

Framing Europe: Attitudes to European Integration in Germany, Spain, and the United Kingdom by Juan Díez Medrano

Interaction Ritual Chains by Randall Collins

On Justification: Economies of Worth by Luc Boltanski and Laurent Thévenot, translated by Catherine Porter

Talking Prices: Symbolic Meanings of Prices on the Market for Contemporary Art by Olav Velthuis

Elusive Togetherness: Church Groups Trying to Bridge America's Divisions by Paul Lichterman

Religion and Family in a Changing Society by Penny Edgell

Hollywood Highbrow: From Entertainment to Art by Shyon Baumann

Partisan Publics: Communication and Contention across Brazilian Youth Activist Networks by Ann Mische

Disrupting Science: Social Movements, American Scientists, and the Politics of the Military, 1945–1975 by Kelly Moore

Weaving Self-Evidence: A Sociology of Logic by Claude Rosental, translated by Catherine Porter

The Taylorized Beauty of the Mechanical: Scientific Management and the Rise of Modernist Architecture by Mauro F. Guillén

Impossible Engineering: Technology and Territoriality on the Canal du Midi by Chandra Mukerji